PADEREWSKI

BY
ROM LANDAU

" Il est un génie qui joue aussi du piano "
—SAINT-SAËNS.

LONDON
IVOR NICHOLSON AND WATSON, Ltd.
44 ESSEX STREET
STRAND, W.C.2
MCMXXXIV

FIRST EDITION . . . *January* 1934

Printed in Great Britain by
Hazell, Watson & Viney, Ltd., London and Aylesbury.

TO
W. B. H.

FOREWORD

EXCEPT for the author's personal interpretation of Paderewski's character and of various happenings in his life, every definite fact derives either from documentary evidence or from personal accounts of direct witnesses. Personal revelations of Paderewski himself and of his friends and collaborators form the main basis of the book ; the majority of the facts have never been published before. Material of such a personal character could not be collected quickly ; it took the author over four years to gather it, while the whole year 1933 was devoted to its checking and the writing of this book.

Further particulars as to the documentary material existing in various publications and to the making of this biography will be found in the chapter " Conversations at Riond Bosson," page 244, and in the bibliography at the end of the book. For obvious reasons these facts had to be left in their actual places ; to state them in this preface would have necessitated a superfluous repetition later.

ROM LANDAU.

LONDON,
December 1933.

CONTENTS

		PAGE
Introduction		11

PART ONE: THE MUSICIAN

CHAPTER	I.	The Boy from Podolia .	15
CHAPTER	II.	The Virtuoso . . .	28
CHAPTER	III.	London	38
CHAPTER	IV.	Musical Methods . .	52
CHAPTER	V.	The Conquest of America	72
CHAPTER	VI.	The Master of the House	84

PART TWO: THE STATESMAN

CHAPTER	I.	The Thirteenth Point .	103
CHAPTER	II.	H.M.S. *Concord* . .	121
CHAPTER	III.	The Man at the Belvedere	129
CHAPTER	IV.	The Peace Conference, 1919	143
CHAPTER	V.	Prime Minister of Poland .	167

PART THREE: A GREAT MAN

CHAPTER	I.	Rebirth of the Piano .	187
CHAPTER	II.	Anger of the Gods . .	205
CHAPTER	III.	Immortality . . .	214
CHAPTER	IV.	The Tragedy of Greatness	232
POSTSCRIPT.		Conversations at Riond Bosson . . .	244
Bibliography			273
Index.			288

LIST OF ILLUSTRATIONS

Paderewski, 1930 . . . . . . *Frontispiece*

FACING PAGE

Paderewski, at the time of his debut as a virtuoso   34

Paderewski, from the painting by Princess Louise .   46

Paderewski and Saint-Saëns, 1912   .   .   .   62

Paderewski, 1890 : two pencil drawings by Violet
     Duchess of Rutland   72

The van with Paderewski's pianos in London .   .   98

Marshal Pilsudski   132

Paderewski, from the bust by Sir Alfred Gilbert   . 152

Paderewski and Mussolini   188

Paderewski and Mme Helena   .   .   . 206

Paderewski at the piano, 1925   .   .   . 216

Riond Bosson   232

Paderewski's hands   258

INTRODUCTION

EVEN in the Europe of the late nineteenth century a magnificent head of hair and a pair of hypnotic hands were not enough to conquer the world. Victories were no longer to be won by velvet suits and lace collars, in which child prodigies had swayed many of the audiences of Europe and America. The value of genius had reached the bottom of the market. Paganini had shown Europe everything that a clever pair of hands can do, while his sinister appearance had created a vogue for picturesque looks. Music-loving society was spoiled. There were still people living who remembered the emotion created by a slender Pole with a delicate chest and a name that some spelled Szopen and others Chopin. What could have been more fascinating than the musical ecstasies of the Hungarian Abbé Liszt, whose white large hands seemed to bewitch the women sitting at his feet in the drawing-rooms of Paris, Budapest or Vienna? Anton Rubinstein's barbaric grandeur had left thrilling memories of the sweep and power of Russian music. The public had been doped by Liszt and Rubinstein, and it needed more dope, if anything in stronger doses. Hysteria produced by a virtuoso was no longer the exception ; almost it was the rule.

There were quite a number of pianists of outstanding talent trying to impress the public of Europe and of America. There was the mature and intellectual Hans von Bülow, young Wladimir Pachmann, enchanting the masses with his playing of Chopin ; Moritz Rosenthal was just beginning to animate audiences and pianists themselves with his exuberant power, causing Rubinstein to exclaim, " I never knew what technique was until I heard Rosenthal ! " ; D'Albert had just begun his conquest of the musically intelligent, and Busoni was determined to conquer the elect. A whole army of coloratura sopranos, of tenors and of baritones had raised the public's expectations. The suns of Jenny Lind and Malibran, of Patti, Lucca, Sembrich and the de Reszkes were rising or had risen high in the musical firmament. It was not easy for a virtuoso to make himself heard in such an atmosphere of past recollections, present achievements and high hopes for the future.

There may have been times that were more serious in their love of music and when there were more composers living of the highest rank ; but there can hardly have been an epoch richer than the last quarter of the nineteenth century in first-rate virtuosi. The virtuoso represented the real spirit of the time, translating into audible form the creator's primary conception. If men were perfect, then indeed they would not require the virtuoso to interpret for them. It is much easier to understand a Beethoven Sonata played on a Steinway piano than to read it in the form of a paper score ; it is easier to appreciate a play acted on a stage than to enjoy reading it. The last decades of the century revelled in the concrete expression of the arts more than the days which preceded them. Scientific inventions, the impressionism of the painter and the realism of the novelist glorified the concrete expression of the world's creative conceptions. Naturally enough, this process gave rise to a desire to improve those expressions, and it in its turn became responsible for the mania for specialization. To be able to do one particular thing, no matter how trivial it was, superlatively well was all that mattered. To play the Minute Waltz by Chopin faster than anyone else was something worth living for. The virtuoso was the specialist par excellence.

Nevertheless, the many first-rate musicians did not only produce sensationalism amongst audiences : they also gave birth to a more subtle sense of musical enjoyment which prevented the real music-lover from being bluffed by cheap effects.

Such was the state of the musical world when Paderewski set foot upon its threshold.

PART ONE

THE MUSICIAN

CHAPTER ONE

THE BOY FROM PODOLIA

I

WHEN in the autumn of 1860 Ignace Jan Paderewski was born in Podolia, the south-eastern part of Poland, the Warsaw Conference, a brilliant monarchical High Mass—celebrated more ostentatiously than effectively by the Russian emperor Alexander II, Francis Joseph of Austria and Wilhelm I of Prussia, the future German emperor—was taking place in the country's capital. The three rulers assembled in Warsaw to gather from one another advice as to how to govern effectively their more dangerous subjects as the Venetians, the Bohemians, the Magyars or the Poles. They arrived in Warsaw in great splendour, accompanied by many princes with impressively hyphenated names and ministers with limited power. Though no Polish lady would accept an invitation to the glittering ball given by Prince Gortschakoff, the Russian Viceroy of Poland, the monarchs started with the "Polonaise" and danced till the early hours. They even inspired "Mr. Punch" to write in a lengthy poem :

> "But anyhow these Eagles three alighted
> Upon the spot, where on a great occasion
> They had rent Poland's carcase—bound and bleeding—
> Into three parts, for their Imperial feeding."

It is very tempting to look for a hidden meaning in this international gathering. It took place in the capital of a country mutilated by the forefathers of the three monarchs at the time when the man was being born who in later years signed, together with the leading statesmen of the world, a peace treaty which legalized Poland's independence (achieved partly through his own efforts) and at a time when the countries of the three " proud Eagles " were themselves " bound and bleeding." History is sometimes fond of striking ironies that are full of deep, though hidden, significance, and are the true passion of every curious student of the past. There are more of such fascinating associations in the life of Paderewski, and, as we shall discover, strange connections between various dates will play a certain part in his life.

However, the tunes of the " Polonaise " danced at the Warsaw Conference had hardly been forgotten when a more exciting event took place, an event which was to affect directly the life of Ignace Paderewski : the last bloody insurrection of Poland against Russia in 1863. The whole life of the Polish people was spent under the shadow of that sterile outburst of national indignation. The country was swept by political trials and deportations, imprisonments and executions.

The inheritance of a national drama, acted and suffered practically in every Polish family, reigned in Ignace Paderewski's family even before his birth on November 6th. His grandfather, Professor Nowicki of the University at Wilna, had been sent to Siberia by the Russian authorities for having thought too loudly how beautiful it would be if Poland could once again regain her independence. To little Paderewski, even before he was able to read or to write it, the word " freedom " had a deep and most reverent meaning.

Little Ignas—as he was called as a boy—and his slightly older sister Antonina were brought up without a mother. The mother's short history has the sadness of so many personal histories in Poland at the time. She was born in Siberia, where both her parents were serving their sentence of exile. She must have been intelligent, and would have undoubtedly exercised a good influence on her two children. But she

died a few months after her son's birth. Her husband,
Jan Paderewski, was the steward of the property of a landowner, Iwanowski, in Podolia, the farthest south-eastern
corner of Poland. He was the descendant of a family who
had always been stewards or gentlemen farmers. Although
they were hardly richer than prosperous peasants nor
differed from them in their circumstances, they possessed
their crest, they prided themselves on their old and noble
traditions, and their general intellectual level was much
higher than that of the peasantry. Jan Paderewski was
not directly involved in the insurrection of 1863, yet it was
found out that he had kept arms and uniforms for the in-
surgents, and he was duly arrested. He was sent from one
trial to another, one prison to another. As no clear com-
plicity could be proved, he was released after a year of
cross-examination and imprisonment. The two children
had spent the year with an aunt. After their father's final
release the whole family settled down in Volhynia, where
M. Paderewski became steward to another landowner.

Little Ignas, a boy with a pale complexion, a suggestion
of mischief about the mouth, with red hair and with legs
slightly too short for his strong body, was a lively child who
adored all forms of practical jokes, and who in later days at
school was well known for his high spirits. The one thing
he did not particularly care for was work. He was very
fond of music. There was an old-fashioned piano at home,
and both he and his sister had taken piano lessons since their
earliest years. Their teacher, M. Runowski, was a pupil of
the Conservatoire at Vienna. There still exists a photograph which shows us little Ignas surrounded by the three
people among whom he spent his childhood : beside his
little sister there is the father and M. Runowski. Music-
teaching in Volhynia cannot have been a lucrative job.
M. Runowski's suit is shabby, his shoes are dusty, his general
appearance unkempt. Quite different is the moustachio-ed
and benevolent father, with his Sunday suit, shiny shoes and
a wave of curly hair. The year in Russian prisons must

2

have been long forgotten, and little Ignas would naturally cling affectionately to his sturdy father, from whom he inherited his cheerful mind. Little Antonina is more restrained, looking with a calm loftiness straight into the camera. M. Runowski is the only one whose eyes turn away to escape the inquisitive lens, as though he were not feeling at ease in this family picture, in which the spirit of bourgeois comfort is playing such a visible rôle. It is rather M. Runowski, with the deep shadows under his eyes and with the thin greyish hair and beard of Dostoievsky, sitting rigidly in a carved chair, who might have been driven through the prisons of the Okhrana.

Little Ignas cared as little for preparing his music lessons and for playing scales as he did for the ordinary school work or the French lessons with a French governess. He did not mind settling down at the piano and playing what fancy led him to play. But climbing trees and misbehaving with a good grace were his real passion. Even so, it was soon discovered that his love of music and his talent for it were above the average. After M. Runowski had gone, the piano lessons were continued with a M. Sowinski, and eventually, when the boy was approaching his twelfth year, the father decided that his son could no longer enrich his knowledge of music in the forsaken estate in Volhynia, and that he should be taken to the capital. He himself would convey the boy to Warsaw.

II

There are two kinds of pianists : those who are entirely wrapped up in their playing and can hear themselves only from within, and those who are at once both artist and audience. The first are to themselves, while playing, the centre of the universe, the second are at one with it. Little Ignas may have felt himself the centre of the universe, as most young artists do, but at the same time he was too much interested in the reactions of that universe to that particular centre and in the universe itself to become introspective.

The world around was full of the most extraordinary phenomena. Of course, his own thoughts and feelings were vast enough to fill all his days and nights. But outside there were things equally moving—tones, for instance. What mysterious things they were, full of variety, of joy. You used the same piano, the same key, the same finger, and yet each time the tone was completely different. You struck a note, and it came like an answer that, for all its clearness, could mean a thousand different things. Although at first it was like a bubble when it bursts, it seemed to grow stronger for a while and gradually fade away and become more distant. Eventually you were able to hear the individual vibrations. The boy noticed that it was the vibrations that mattered, and that there were within him inner vibrations too, of pity, or joy, or impatience, though the vibrations produced by the piano were more real. One could drink them, as though they were drops of wine. Long after the wine has run down the throat, the taste lingers, titillating the awakened palate. The boy became a fascinated listener to the tones produced by his own playing, as though he were sitting somewhere in the room, listening to another pianist.

He could not play the piano unless he knew exactly how his playing affected the world outside. He could not help drawing the world into whatever he did. He would sit at the piano, an old but sumptuously carved instrument, on a chair slightly too high, and would strike individual notes or play a chord, a passage or a trill over and over again. His long trousers with their broad black braid suggested a schoolboy from a Russian school where uniforms with long trousers were worn ; but the pale face was childish, although it grew keen and intense when he listened to the vibrations pulsating through the room.

III

When, in 1872, M. Jan Paderewski brought his boy of twelve to Warsaw to begin his musical education at the

Conservatoire, the town could boast several good teachers, whose business it would be to initiate the young gentleman from Volhynia into the mysteries of music. His first piano teacher was Sliwinski ; later came Rudolf Strobl and Janotha. The theoretical part of his musical education was in the hands of Roguski. Young Paderewski did not show any particular promise, and some of his masters did not think much of his talent. His active and cheerful mind did not always enjoy poring over the theory of harmony or practising scales. Fortunately, however, he had friends who made life more pleasant, in particular, the family of Mr. Edward Kerntopf, a well-known piano manufacturer. Mr. Kerntopf liked the keen, intelligent boy. No doubt his two daughters fell in love with him. They might well do so, having a father who was rich, who lived in well-furnished apartments, and who enjoyed large meals at regular intervals, while the young artist was poor, a good talker, the owner of a very attractive pale face, a romantic head of hair and extremely expressive eyes. What mattered most was that Mr. Kerntopf took the boy to concerts and to the opera, and that through him the young artist from Podolia received that practical, all-round musical education which is so important in later life and which many musicians have lacked. Once they have decided on their career, they are often too much absorbed in the mysteries of their instrument and the joys of their talent to remember that there have been musicians before them, and that their particular instrument is not the only one that man invented. But Ignace had to learn about other instruments than his own, particularly the trombone, which he played in the school band. Before he was sixteen he already began to be bored with the daily routine of the Conservatoire, and so he decided to conquer Russia. Young men have often had ambition to conquer some country or other. Russia lay nearest, and was quite big enough for a lad of sixteen. Besides, there was his young friend, the violinist Ignace Cielewicz, who had agreed to collaborate

in the conquest.   The campaign lasted almost a year.
The young men went from one provincial town, from one
miserable hall, to another, and from one wretched out-of-
tune piano to the next.   Often they did not possess enough
money to buy themselves a meal, but a twelve-months'
tour with so scant a reward was excellent training for two
ambitious young virtuosi.   No parent, no teacher, could
have taught them so much as that one year's tour or could
have made them see their faults so clearly.   Their dis-
illusioned return from their Russian tour necessitated very
serious work, which eventually resulted in one or two small
concerts on a modest and more reasonable basis.   After
two more years Paderewski passed his final examinations
so well that he was immediately offered the post of piano
teacher at the same Conservatoire.   Financially it was a
poor offer, but it was better than nothing.

Now that the professional half of his mature life was
assured, the more personal half had to be fulfilled.   He
decided to marry.   He fell in love with a very young pupil
at the Conservatoire, Antonina Korsak.   But as he himself
was only twenty the youthfulness of his bride was no obstacle.
It mattered, however, when at the end of the year, satis-
factory as far as love and romance were concerned, but
economically extremely hard and bitter, his young wife died
in child-birth.   This was the first real tragedy of his life.
To be a widower at twenty-one and burdened, moreover,
with a baby boy, was indeed a hard beginning.   The
cheerful boy awakened to find himself a man.   He had no
more illusions about the lightning conquest of a continent,
but he was not the man to brood over his misery till it was
too late to act.   He wanted to compose, to write wonderful
Polish music, to become a second Chopin.   Teaching young
boys and girls how to play Clementi and Czerny and the
easier sonatinas by Scarlatti does not, however, clear the
way to composition nor to all the musical knowledge that
was stored up in the world and that he was burning to
possess.

IV

In 1881 Paderewski was granted a year's leave from his duties as piano teacher at the Conservatoire at Warsaw, and he decided to go on with his studies. Very popular among Polish musicians in those days was Professor Friedrich Kiel of Berlin, his speciality being composition and the theory of counterpoint. Paderewski worked under him for a full year, trying to accumulate the theoretical knowledge that was indispensable to his ambitions as a composer. After a year he returned to the Conservatoire at Warsaw. But he had sufficient judgment to perceive his own limitations. He felt that the technical basis was not yet wide enough for all those potentialities which he felt to be within his range. Besides, a musical education at that time was not considered finished until every path of practical and theoretical knowledge had been thoroughly explored. In the autumn of 1883 he finally abandoned his profession as teacher at the Conservatoire, and decided to pursue his studies farther. He went back to Berlin, where a great musical epoch was beginning. The ambitious new capital of a united Reich had quickly become an important musical centre. The national tendency towards music discovered a number of new and stimulating influences. The increasing success of Wagner's compositions put musical matters in Germany into the forefront of general interest ; it affected the masses through the wide appeal of those " Massen-Opern " ; it affected the purely national spirit in literary and semi-mystical aspects ; it won over the nation's élite not only by its purely musical, but also by its philosophical characteristics, and by its intellectual battle with Nietzsche. If anything, this success was intensified by the death of Wagner himself, more particularly as a number of his disciples were very much alive, carrying the message to new mystical heights. Although Hans Richter, Bülow, Anton Seidl, Mottl and Muck wore the dignified black apparel of the conductor, their spirit was garbed in

the cassock of a priest converting the world to a new
religion. Nevertheless, Wagner's success was only one of
the elements of Germany's increasing importance in musical
matters.

The rapid growth of Berlin and of Prussia brought money
and prosperity to the German capital. Berlin was no
longer the capital of that province of Brandenburg which
Frederick the Great had found so objectionable that he
preferred to live in the more civilized French atmosphere
of secluded Potsdam, but a rapidly growing city, ambitious
and full of new theatres, new academies and new concert
halls. Berlin became a serious rival of both Munich and
Vienna ; great musicians and teachers came to live on the
banks of the Spree as they once did on those of the Danube
and the Iser.

Paderewski's keenness was naturally much attracted by
the general musical activities of Berlin. He went there
for a second time to a special master and with a definite
purpose. This time it was, above all, instrumentation that
interested him. He began to work under a pupil of Kiel,
Heinrich Urban, and at the end of the year his theoretical
education was more or less completed. As he was very poor,
his future was as yet very uncertain. In order to earn
money as a teacher, which seemed the only possible way
of making a living, he decided to devote himself more to
the sheerly technical side of his art. He went to Vienna,
where, surrounded by an army of pupils from all over the
world, Leschetizky, the most famous of piano teachers, lived
and taught. His wife, Essipoff, who had once been as
famous a pianist as her husband, lived and taught with him.
For six months Paderewski joined the crowd of Leschetizky's
pupils. As his meagre financial means were at the end of
that time exhausted, he accepted an attractive offer from
Strassburg, and became Professor of Counterpoint and
Piano at the Conservatoire there.

During his year at Strassburg he spent his holidays in the
house of Helena Modjeska (Modrzejewska), the celebrated

Polish actress, who was considered one of the greatest artists in English tragedy. After some years in Poland, she acted more and more in America, where she eventually settled. She was both beautiful and intellectually acute, and Paderewski considered her his most notable friend. During these holidays, both Modjeska and her husband were impressed by his music and his personality. Modjeska had enough artistic instinct and experience to appreciate her compatriot's remarkable gifts ; she knew the peculiarly Polish heritage in her own art, and she was able to perceive it in his ; but she also had sufficient knowledge of Western culture to see its elements in Paderewski. It seemed certain that he would be able to create in himself a particularly successful blend of the Polish and the non-Polish. In 1876 Modjeska described the young artist of twenty-six as " a man of wide culture, of witty, sometimes biting tongue, a man wide awake to all matters of personal interest who knew and understood the world . . . " Paderewski must indeed have impressed Poland's finest actress : one of the supreme actresses of the world. Her appreciation of his personality strengthened his own faith in himself. It was more to him than just the opinion of a wise friend. The words of an intelligent woman meant to him at least as much as those of an intelligent man. Paderewski believed in women, and there was no superiority, no cynicism, in his attitude towards them. He could make women under-stand everything. A woman's trivial emotions, that other men scarce bothered to cast aside with even a be-littling smile, he could appreciate with all the seriousness that they demanded. He treated women with that inborn chivalry, arousing a sense of thrilling expectation which they particularly treasure in a man. Modjeska's belief in him made him take the most vital decision of his life, to start a career, which until now had hardly dared to venture from the kingdom of dreams, to face the light of reality. He decided to become a pianist. Most pianists of the time took that decision at the age of about five. To be born a prodigy was the rule rather than the exception. To start on a pianist's career at the age of twenty-six was a risky thing to do.   Paderewski did it.

v

When in 1886 Paderewski arrived in Vienna to become the pupil of Theodor Leschetizky, it was not only because the aged Polish musician, after abandoning his career as a pianist, had become the most renowned teacher of his time, but also because no one else would have suited him better. Paderewski's pronounced individualism rendered him antagonistic to any teacher who attempted to impose a method upon him. Practically every music teacher of the time prided himself on having invented a method superior to any other. Whereas one would prescribe a tense and rigid position for the fingers, another would postulate loose, floppy fingers ; one believed in the hand falling from the wrist on to the piano like a dead weight ; another would insist upon his pupil's attacking the keyboard not from the wrist, but from the elbow ; according to one method the fingers must be raised stiffly, decisively and accurately like the legs of Prussian grenadiers ; according to another they must glide over the keys in smooth unbroken sequence. Such professors guaranteed with their particular device the undisputed mastery of the pianoforte. Leschetizky had no method ; he did not subject his pupils to rules governing their arms, their wrists, their hands, their fingers ; the one thing he insisted upon was work, work, and more work. Paderewski's life till now had been nothing but work : lessons given and taken, piano playing for his livelihood and for his personal satisfaction, interpretative work of various kinds and composition. He did not believe in angels, descending from their heavenly bliss, taking possession of an ambitious young man from Poland and leading him straight into the realms of immortality, but rather in twelve hours' serious practising a day. The individual talents had at first to be treated like crude clay. Neither did Leschetizky believe in ready-made geniuses. Henry Lahee describes his teaching as a " method of common sense."

The result of Leschetizky's methodless method was : " hardness and a perverse brilliancy." Leschetizky's insistence upon technical brilliancy saved Paderewski from cheapening the emotional qualities that lay in his playing.

His teacher's confidence in Paderewski was a great help to him. When he first appeared at a small concert in Vienna a critic remarked that " the young man did not seem to promise much," to which Leschetizky replied : " My dear sir, you will have to get used to hearing that young man's name." Paderewski was sensitive and had a strong belief in himself ; a teacher who strengthened that belief was an ideal master for him.

The brilliant clarity, which some critics called hardness, and which none of Leschetizky's pupils developed to a higher degree than Paderewski, was due to a great extent to the importance laid by the old teacher on the absolute efficiency of each individual finger : Annette Hullah, one of his pupils, tells us, in her book about him, that he " lays special stress on . . . the development of strength and sensitiveness in the finger tips ; clear distinction between the many varieties of touch." This efficiency produced beautifully transparent trills, and staccatos as clear as glass. From Leschetizky Paderewski also learned his patient devotion to detail ; every bar, every note, had to be practised over and over again, with constant correction of fingering, pedal, touch and accentuation. Leschetizky worked rather on a synthetic than an analytic basis ; he would take a composition not to subdivide it into individual parts, but to build it up bit by bit, in all its minutest detail, till ultimately he had achieved the finished work. His principle was : " One page each day learned in this way will give you a trunkful of music for your repertoire by the end of the year." During his time spent with Leschetizky, Paderewski also learned another side of piano playing that was essential to an artist whose ambition was to extend the range of the pianoforte, namely the proper use of the pedal. Special stress was laid on the necessity for perfect mastery of the pedal. In later years this was to be one of the most outstanding features of Paderewski's playing.

Nevertheless, Paderewski altered in later years most of the technical foundations laid by Leschetizky, evolving a technique and a method of work of his own.

CHAPTER TWO

THE VIRTUOSO

I

IN the world in which Paderewski decided to become a piano virtuoso art migrated from churches and palaces to museums and drawing-rooms. The concert-hall, with its professional seriousness, its lack of witty chatter, royal pomp or ecclesiastical dignity, was hardly better than a museum. Bach and Haydn and Mozart and Chopin were all given their little labels with dates and explanations in a catalogue called the programme, and there were row upon row of cheerless gas-lamps and depressing black coats. There were still quartets, arias, cantatas and all the other delightful music that required a candle-lit, slightly frivolous rococo room, or a church that prided itself more on its organist and its sopranos than on its priest ; but on the whole, the larger the hall, the more complete the separation between the artist and the audience, and the more pitilessly distracting the lights, the better the true spirit of the period was expressed. Liszt wrote piano pieces that really should have been played by a big orchestra, and Rubinstein treated the piano as though it were an orchestra, often wishing that he could have played on ten pianos instead of one. They were not so much pianists as conductors of their hands.

It was no longer necessary to have received a personal invitation to Prince Lobkowitz's supper party in order to hear the latest compositions of Herr Ludwig van Beethoven. The box-office was the magic gateway into paradise. There were beginning to be too many people in the world, and after having been a traditional aristocratic observance, music had of necessity to develop into a popular one. The virtuoso had become a middle-class institution, and such an institution requires more than talent only : more than ever before, the virtuoso had to be a personality. Women would swoon voluptuously when cascades of notes gushed forth from under the hands of Liszt or Rubinstein. They might have shown more resistance if Liszt and Rubinstein had had less exciting appearances and less imposing personalities. It was hardly a coincidence that the great pianists at the beginning of the century were Beethoven and Chopin, pianists by virtue of circumstance and composers by virtue of genius ; and at the end Liszt and Rubinstein, composers of circumstance and pianists of genius.

Paderewski's appearance in that world was not a coincidence. His blend of aristocratic refinement and power over the masses was certainly what the time required.

II

Was there not some significance in the fact that Paderewski started his successful career in Vienna, and not in Warsaw, Berlin or Petersburg ? Leschetizky's presence in Vienna was not the only favourable omen. Paderewski was not the sort of artist who is so indifferent to his surroundings that he achieves his greatest efficiency under any conditions. He was not like Beethoven, like Verlaine or Van Gogh. Twenty years spent in the dreariness of one uninspiring room would not be the same thing as the variety of a milieu that in itself had some attraction. He had known poverty, and incessant daily work was his natural habit. But there were intervals, when company and a congenial background became a necessity. He was very conscious of the thousand and one things that made up the life around him ; the streets through which he walked, the buildings he saw, the people he met, the meals he ate, all those things mattered. If the houses on his daily walks had been shabby and dull,

if his meals had been badly cooked, if stimulation had not
been forthcoming from his friends, these circumstances
might have affected the start of a brilliant career. Vienna,
however, provided the conditions that he needed. It was
a city of great musical understanding ; but it had also all
the dash and brilliance of social life that the last decades
of the nineteenth century were able to provide so lavishly.
Paderewski did not frequent the imposing palaces around
the Schwarzenbergplatz ; Imperial parties, the vanity of
glittering jewels and waltzing uniforms, were not for his
entertainment. But he perceived them, he felt their intoxicating rhythm behind the baroque façades and the windows
with their damask curtains. And there were concerts
every night, brilliant opera, singers and musicians from all
over the world, anxious to please a highly critical public
and hoping for good notices in the Vienna press.

To Paderewski Vienna represented even more. As yet
politics played no part in his life ; he had no time for them.
But there was always a strong national consciousness in
him. Poles without a deep national consciousness hardly
existed, and Paderewski was no exception, but rather a
particularly eminent example. Of all the big countries
surrounding his homeland none offered the Poles a more
pleasant, even if somewhat deceptive atmosphere than
Austria. Living in Petersburg, one would have been
perpetually conscious of the sufferings and injustices that
had been inflicted upon one's country by Russia. There
was in Berlin the absence of racial and personal sympathy
which Paderewski had been able to forget by his constant
preoccupation with his work. In Austria the Poles were
treated better than in Russia or in Germany, in Galicia
they possessed some form of local home rule, and were
not citizens of a second or third order. The refined
courtesy of the Viennese people would naturally appeal
more to a sensitive Pole than the more savage grandeur of
Russian culture. In Vienna national consciousness was
more at ease ; the general atmosphere was sympathetic

to success. In the autumn of 1887 Paderewski appeared
for the first time before a large Viennese audience. It
was not his own recital, but that of the famous singer Lucca.
Pauline Lucca was only thirty-six and at the height of her
fame. Born in Vienna, the daughter of a German mother
and a Jewish father from Venice, she was adored by the
town. The name of the young pianist who had to fill in
the time while the *prima donna* was resting between her
various numbers was probably not noticed by more than
a handful of people. Nevertheless, the Lucca concert
became a Paderewski triumph ; the morning after this
first appearance his name was known to all the musical
people of Vienna, and there were a great many of them.

III

The gateway to the Western world seemed open, to
Paris, the great ambition and the dream of every Pole.

Annette Essipoff, Leschetizky's wife, went to Paris to
arrange concerts for her husband's most promising pupil.
She was regarded in Paris as the greatest woman pianist of
the age, and the owners of the Salle Erard, the most distinguished concert-hall in town, were willing to let the
unknown virtuoso play in their hall. Mme Essipoff had
innumerable friends in Paris who would certainly help her
in her endeavour to launch the young Pole. She notified
many of them of his forthcoming concert in Paris, and
when Saturday, March 3rd, 1888, arrived, the Salle Erard
in the Rue du Mail was packed. Thanks to newspaper
reports Paderewski's appearance was no longer unknown to
his audience. His looks represented very nearly the ideal of
beauty of that time. Romantic picturesqueness was popular.
Men whose looks faintly suggested those of beautiful women
were then more acclaimed than the favoured ones of years
to come who resembled nothing so much as handsome
Latin hairdressers, or later still, the professional athletes,
with their immaculate shoulders and their boyish faces.

In the overheated atmosphere of the hall the crowd
waits with curiosity. The women are particularly excited.
Here they all are, the great musical hostesses of Paris ;
celebrity next to celebrity. The Cretan princess Bassarava
Brancovan, dark-eyed, mysterious-looking and glamorous,
is seated in the front row with her niece Princess Bibesco.
Legend has it that since her husband's death Princess
Brancovan hardly ever leaves her exclusive home in the
Avenue Hoche—but to-night is one of the rare occasions.
There is also her Russian cousin Princess Gortschakoff,
famous for her musical (and archæological) enthusiasm
almost as much as for her superb " hôtel " in the Rue de
Varenne. Was it not during the rule of Prince Gortschakoff,
the Russian Viceroy of Poland, that Ignace Paderewski was
born in 1860 ? The Polish Countess Potocka is there with
one or two of the other great ladies for whom life without
music would be as unbearable as without luxury : the
Marquise de Saint Paul and Madame Trelat. There are
also both conductors Colonne and Lamoureux, whose concerts are the most popular events in the musical life of Paris.

Is he really as romantic-looking as some paper reported
the other day ? Unfortunately, half the gas-lamps are
not lit, and the light is dim and vague. Someone, who
seems to know all the professional secrets, says that the
young Pole insists upon a half-lit hall, that he cannot concentrate properly unless there is twilight around him.
How absurd ! Did anybody ever hear of such a pose ?
someone asks. The general curiosity becomes keener.
Suddenly a strange figure walks across the platform towards
the piano, like an exotic bird, with a roseate crest. His
flaming crown of hair is of that rarest of colours, a blend
of gold and red. The sensitive women in the front
rows are not startled by a violent red ; they feel the
sting of æsthetic enjoyment. All the beauty that flows
from under his fingers seems to have been foretold by the

rich glow of his hair. Indeed, Monsieur Paderewski corre-
sponds to the romantic ideal which they formed of a
pianist from a far country with a picturesque past and with
Chopin as its most famous son. One gets accustomed to
the dim light ; one can even distinguish his features.
Occasionally he looks down into the audience. The eyes
may be a bit too far apart ; perhaps they are even too
narrow. Once he smiles. In that moment one can hardly
see his eyes, and he reminds one of a satyr. But he becomes
exquisitely human when one looks at his fine mouth, which
has nothing of the satyr about it. It has a touch of sensuous
dreaminess in its well-defined lips, which is heightened by
the softness of the moustache above them. There is a
slight thickness in the nose, but it is well shaped. So
indeed is the whole of the face. Does not its sensitive outline
suggest a drawing by Ingres ? And then there is that
strange pallor of the skin, which gives the impression of
highly civilized beauty. It is accentuated by the whiteness
of the strong neck, which is not disfigured by a high collar.
That impression of light that he suggests begins at the
pale forehead ; it continues in the white bow of his tie,
the long white waistcoat. The press illustrations show
that he wore a long white waistcoat even for ordinary wear.

Most of the listeners have never heard music that excited
them so much. The older ones are reminded of Liszt and
Rubinstein ; the young ones are looking in vain for some
standards of comparison. At certain moments the piano
sounds like an orchestra and the notes seem to come from
different places of the hall ; or it is as though the Pole
played not on one but on several pianos simultaneously.
So terrifying are the chords that are ringing through the
hall that one imagines the walls are shaking. Occasionally
one can see quite clearly that he hits the keyboard not
with a finger but with the whole fist. After a while, however,
the piano begins to sing and a human voice seems to rise
from it. Indeed, there is more in the young man than
merely picturesqueness.

3

During the interval both Colonne and Lamoureux rush to the artists' room, equally eager to secure the young Pole for their concerts. There and then Paderewski signs a contract with Lamoureux to play at his famous orchestral concerts.

After the interval the audience becomes more and more enthusiastic. There is no longer any doubt as to the new pianist's success. At the end of the concert he is given a tremendous ovation. All the lights are turned on. He bows and bows again with an incomparable grace.

Next morning the newspapers are full of his success. He plays again at the Salle Erard on March 26th. He immediately receives an invitation to play at one of the *Conservatoire* concerts which are the most distinguished events of musical life in Paris. His reputation is made. The newspapers are full of him. " *Le lion de Paris.*" That name is known by everybody. He plays for the Countess de Montesquiou, the Marquise de St. Paul, the Princess Bibesco and the Princess Brancovan. They will take care of him ; he must meet the right people. He is invited to the houses of the Napoleonic aristocracy, but also by people bearing names that were the crowning glories of the *Ancien Régime*. Gounod, grand old man of French music, expresses his admiration openly, thus giving the lead to musical Paris. Saint-Saëns, at the height of his fame, exclaims enthusiastically : " *Il est un génie qui joue aussi du piano.*" The *bon mot* becomes famous. Success, success, success ! He goes to parties, he works fourteen hours a day, he smiles, he impresses dignified gentlemen, he fascinates the smartest women of a smart society. After one of his recitals a famous hostess rushes to him exclaiming ecstatically : " *Maître, c'etait sublime, maintenant que je vous ai entendu vous pouvez mourir.*" He is enchanted with Paris as Paris is with him. Of course he will remain here. It is so much more beautiful, so much more stimulating than anywhere else. He takes a flat on the ground floor of No. 96 Avenue Victor Hugo, not far from the Etoile. Paris is at his feet.

PADEREWSKI
At the time of his debut as a virtuoso

V

Now it is no longer difficult to conquer the continent of Europe. Even Germany's provincial capitals, with their high musical standards, have to admit the superiority of the Polish pianist. " *Fabelhaft !* " they exclaim. The critic in the *Leipziger Zeitung* writes : " Not since Liszt has a pianist been received as Herr Paderewski was last night." The *Tageblatt* writes : " The public did not applaud, it raved . . . " Ferdinand Pfohl in Hamburg says : " It was like a Nikisch concert, the same exultation, the same enthusiasm. His Chopin playing fairly electrified his audience. . . . Enthusiasm bordering on intoxication . . . " And in Munich the critic admits that the public " acted as if crazy with joy."

Paris and the Continent, however, were not enough for a virtuoso. America lay across the ocean. But the bridge to America was England. Across a narrow strip of water beckoned that strange island, and the greatest city of the world : London.

Paderewski looked conspicuous. Newspaper cartoonists and jesters in the street delighted in him. The little felt hat which he wore on the very top of his exuberant hair only accentuated its singular appearance, and many anecdotes of the day showed how extraordinary he must have looked to the man in the street. One night after a recital in Berlin he called a cab to take him home. Rather loudly the driver asked where he should go ; but before Paderewski had time to answer, a voice from the crowd on the pavement shouted : " To the barber's." Paderewski was sensitive about his appearance. He disliked those cheap jokes and anecdotes. He well knew, too, that his audiences expected him to look as he did. His wife was certainly right when, in later years, asked by a too inquisitive interviewer in America why her husband did not cut his hair short and make himself less conspicuous, she answered : " It would make no difference. Besides, the

public would be disappointed if his hair were short." The
appearance of a virtuoso counted for a good deal. Nothing
in Paderewski's appearance was left to chance. He was
not smart, but he was always extremely tidy ; he looked
artistic but not Bohemian ; there was a seeming careless-
ness about him, but no disorder ; his shirts were made of
fine Japanese silk, and the black cloth of his long coats
was soft and of the best quality. His whole appearance,
as practically everything in his life, was the result of a
particular habit of mind, which is best described as unity
of purpose.

Only a rigid self-discipline could have produced that
habit. Although from his earliest days there were always
a good many interests in his life—people, conversation,
books, things in general—although he was always able to
jump from one subject to another, identifying himself with
each one, he could concentrate entirely on one particular
thing. If he knew what he wanted, everything else would
be sacrificed to it for the time being, and he would not
allow himself to be distracted. It was not only the piano
that required constant effort. The same attention was
given to everything that mattered in a life which was for
him one great unity. It was not enough to have an artistic
disposition and hands that were more facile than those of
other pianists. There are many small details on the
virtuoso's road to success that are of vital significance.
To the mass of listeners the virtuoso is not just the possessor
of outstanding talent : he is the fusion of a number of
different elements of which his art is only one. His name,
his private life, his appearance, his clothes, everything
matters. Paderewski's clothes were not chosen by accident.
At first this may have been so ; as soon, however, as he
realized the striking effect of luminosity, which was produced by his white ties, light waistcoats and low collars,
that particular impression had to be maintained once and
for all. It kept alive the picture which the crowd had
formed of the artist. The visual memory of the public is

hardly less important than the musical one ; the name
" Paderewski " had to evoke not only the nostalgia of
Chopin's Nocturnes and the thundering magnificence of
Liszt, but also the vision of a strange creature of white and
gold. At first many newspapers accused him of seeking
sensationalism in his appearance, which only showed how
little they understood the virtuoso. No matter how wonderful his art may be, to his audience he remains the visible
bridge that leads from his art to the shrine that the audience
has formed around his name.

The romanticism of Paderewski's playing corresponded to
the picturesqueness of his hair ; the elegance of his
arpeggios and his scales was not surprising in one who
moved with such grace ; the gentleness of his touch
went well with the courteousness which his audiences
admired so much from the moment he appeared on the
platform. Inasmuch as those artistic qualities were the
outcome of hard work, so were also the corresponding
details of his personal appearance. His graceful manner,
his elastic walk across the platform, may have been natural ;
but he tried consciously and in front of a mirror to make
them more perfect. Nothing was left to chance—from his
hair to the smiling bow with which he thanked his audiences.
Movements of the body during his playing, too, were controlled. The emotion of his playing might have excused
him, had he rocked back and forth on his seat as he flung
his hands upon the keyboard, or swayed from side to side
the while his hands stormed in impressive passages up and
down the piano. Yet nothing of the kind happened, the
body remaining almost motionless on the stool. Discipline
had mastered it. Paderewski never forgot his audiences
who came, after having bought expensive tickets, full of
expectation ; only a fool thinks lightly of his audience.
Theatrical effects played an important part at the end of the
nineteenth century, and Paderewski decided that he could
leave no room for accident or chance.

CHAPTER THREE

LONDON

I

IN London, meanwhile, the stage for Paderewski's appearance was set. Here he would cause neither shock nor surprise. The Pole who could impress his audiences as a great virtuoso and also as an exquisite personality would conquer the romantic souls as well as the æsthetic, without having any fear of being taken for a quick-fingered charlatan in a magnificent wig. The fervour with which certain sections of musical London were fighting for the recognition of Wagner had brought about a more vital attitude towards music. That part of society which revelled in a wealth to which the reign of Queen Victoria had opened the gilded gates preferred the effects of a brilliant virtuoso to the artisan conceptions of William Morris or the new architectural gospel of Ruskin. The " Souls " were responsible for the fact that Æstheticism was becoming a reality, and the social and the artistic worlds were beginning to mix. In Paris Manet and Degas have certainly meant more to Montmartre than to the Faubourg St. Honoré ; but in London the acknowledged artist strove hard to enter society's magic circle. London's painters had helped to prepare the proper atmosphere for the new pianist's success. Did not the laboriously drawn faces of Rossetti's youths and Burne-Jones's knight-errants suggest Paderewski's finely chiselled profile, with its crown of red-gold hair ? The very moment Burne-Jones set eyes on the young pianist, he saw the likeness between the guest from Poland and his own knights.

And the women of London would patronize him. When such women as were guided by the Duchess of Devonshire, Lady Londonderry or Lady Ripon took up a new artist, his success in London was assured. The influence of these women over London's musical life was not to be disregarded, and to strive after their patronage was not snobbery. Often the most serious artistic ambitions could not be realized without the sanction of society. Did not the future Marchioness of Ripon, the beautiful Lady de Grey, revive Opera in London? Not all hostesses succeeded in doing as much as she did, but it sufficed that there were one or two in whose houses even the most fastidious artist would be glad to appear. Melba, who never sang in private houses except once a year in the house of Alfred de Rothschild, and then only for a great deal of money, sang at Lady de Grey's house at Coombe for nothing. The same could be said of Jean de Reszke, of Ternina. But there they would be heard by the Princess of Wales, and thus they would become the fashion among those hostesses, whose dearest hopes were set on an invitation to Coombe. This meant that Covent Garden, where everyone could hear them, became fashionable once more, and that which had ceased to be a musical institution of any importance would once more become a leading Opera House. It mattered little whether a Lady de Grey or another great hostess were genuinely musical or not. What mattered was that her own interest created conditions without which serious musical activities were impossible. It mattered also whether the reverberations of a virtuoso's success became loud enough to reach even Her Majesty's attention. It was not snobbery that made musicians anxious to play at Windsor or at Marlborough House. The spirit of the time made it essential that a musician's activities should find scope in a milieu that conformed to the general trend of social life. Paderewski's general attitude met these English conditions half-way.

II

Paderewski's first appearance in London had been advertised rather loudly from Paris, and when he arrived in the British capital he was by no means unknown. His success in Paris had been both a genuine artistic success and a *succès de sensation* in which the boulevard newspapers, Paderewski's hair and the frenzy of the ladies had played equally important parts. The Paris correspondent of the *Daily Telegraph* called him "The Lion of Paris." In the streets appeared row upon row of big posters with the words "Paderewski the Lion of the Paris Season." London was rather suspicious of lions, especially if they were not Empire-bred; but London's suspicions grew to a feeling of uneasiness when the Paris correspondents talked about the "wonderful aureole of golden hair." The days of press glorification of the physical assets of film stars had not yet dawned upon Fleet Street. Paderewski himself felt instinctively how harmful the sensational press reports must have been, and he was feeling particularly nervous when he appeared at the St. James's Hall on the 9th of May, 1890.

It was one of those spring days when after a month of summer-like conditions, with glorious daffodils and tulips flowering in the parks, London is suddenly recalled to rainstorms and winds. The hall was empty; the box-office reported receipts to the poor extent of £10. Paderewski had not been able to overcome his stage fright before the concert; he felt nervous throughout the performance. The audience felt, however, the outstanding quality of the performer and the applause was more enthusiastic than usual. After the concert a strange little man came into the artists' room, introduced himself as Frank Schuster and asked Paderewski enthusiastically to supper. They went together into a lovely Queen Anne house overlooking St. James's Park, and a lifelong friendship was the outcome of this first evening in unknown London. The press on the whole was cool, in many cases even antagonistic. Joseph Bennett, the *Daily Telegraph's* musical critic, disliked much in Paderewski's playing, but he realized the possibilities of the future. He wrote : " Plainly we do not like Mr. Paderewski as an exponent of physical force. The result of his labours may be marvellous, but it is not music." And : " It was the march of an abnormally active mammoth about the keyboard, while the wondering observer expected the pianoforte to break down at any moment." But he also wrote : " There is another Mr. Paderewski . . . he is gentle and pleasant, refined and poetic to a degree which makes him altogether charming." The *Standard* critic testified : " The performer was more anxious to astonish than to charm. . . . His physical powers . . . were exercised in a manner which resulted in much noise, but little music . . ." An Irish musical critic of the *World* seemed to have felt that the newcomer's red nimbus was challenging the effectiveness of his own ginger-coloured hair and beard, and so he used the words after Paderewski's second concert : " Sensational, empty, vulgar and violent." But eventually the red-haired Irishman, George Bernard Shaw, was conquered by the new pianist, as the third recital evoked the words : " . . . dignified, intelligent, almost sympathetic . . ." Some of the critics were enthusiastic from the beginning. The *Globe's* expert, who thought Paderewski was second only to Rubinstein, wrote : " His mastery is complete, his touch so exquisite, in the art of singing on the pianoforte, that he can only be compared with Thalberg . . ." And the *Saturday Review* called him " One of the most remarkable artists who have been heard of late years."

Paderewski's impresario, Daniel Meyer, tried to extract from the press notices sufficient favourable material to print a pamphlet for the provinces ; for he feared for the success of Paderewski's provincial tour. But Paderewski disliked the idea of amending the truth, and he agreed to publication only if all the press opinions were included. The provinces felt a traditional scepticism towards London's artistic judgment, and the unfavourable tone of the London press had automatically made them sympathetic. The provincial tour was a success both with the press and with the public. In London, as a matter of fact, only the critics were cautious or antagonistic in their judgment, while the public came under the spell of Paderewski's music and personality even during his first visit. The third concert in London was splendidly attended, and the delight of his audience, particularly of the women, went so far as to create a new fashion in musical life. After Paderewski had finished playing, enthusiastic ladies rushed to the platform, surrounded Paderewski, plucked flowers from their dresses and held them up to him or threw them over the heads of those in front. From now on it became a fashion for audiences to storm the platform at the end of a concert and to surround the artist like an animal in its cage, while he gave them encore after encore with the sweat pouring off his forehead. Nevertheless, his first English tour brought Paderewski in only £280. In the following year, however, his English visit created a sensation even before it was begun, and the tour in the provinces was booked up weeks beforehand. Although some of the critics were still cautious, London and the country acclaimed Paderewski as the greatest pianist they had ever known. No success could be compared to his triumphal progress from recital to recital ; the crowds for his concerts began to queue up two and three days before the doors of the St. James's Hall were opened ; when he entered a drawing-room or a theatre people would stand on their chairs, as eager to catch a glimpse of him as though he were Lily Langtry. Before he was thirty-five London was conquered as never before by any virtuoso.

III

Not only society and the big crowds, but also the connoisseurs were enchanted. Paderewski realized in London more than in any other previous place what it meant to be a success. Vienna and Paris and the musical centres of Germany were very wonderful, but London gave one a feeling of real power, a security that in other places would probably have proved an illusion. At first the public had not been easy to impress ; the crowds in Vienna and Paris had been easier. Now, however, that the London audience had opened their heart to him, their sentiments seemed as stable and reliable as the whole trend of life in the British capital. To know that London was at one's feet gave one a feeling of tremendous superiority and power. It was almost frightening.

Paderewski was making friends ; famous people wanted to meet him ; the leading painters of the land asked him to sit for them. Alfred Gilbert made a bust of him. The beautiful Duchess of Rutland sketched him several times. Burne-Jones had asked to be introduced to him in order to draw him, and after a sketch or two he made a profile portrait that certainly could compete in delicacy of design with Ingres, and in emotional subtlety with almost any Italian drawing of the fifteenth or sixteenth century.

The day after Burne-Jones made this drawing, he wrote to his friend Lady Horner :

" There's a beautiful fellow in London named Paderewski and I want to have a face like him, and look like him and can't . . . there's trouble. He looks so like Swinburne looked at twenty that I could cry over past things, and the pretty ways of him . . . courteous little tricks . . . and low bows and a hand that clings in shaking hands, and doesn't want to go . . . and a face like Sir Galahad, and the Archangel Gabriel . . . very like Swinburne's only in better drawing, and little turns and looks, so like that it makes me jump. I asked to draw from him and yesterday he came in the morning and Henschel brought him and played on the organ and sang whilst I drew . . . which is good for the emotions but bad for the drawing . . . and knowing people say he is a great master in his art . . . which might well be for he looks glorious. I praised Allah for

making him . . . how nice it must be to look as fine as
one is inside."

After Burne-Jones came Laurence Alma Tadema, one of
England's most successful painters of the day. He asked
Paderewski to sit for a large portrait. These sittings seemed
symbolical of the spirit of the time and of the exalted
enthusiasm which Paderewski evoked among England's
artists and . . . women. Beauty had in those days a very
definite meaning. It did not stand for abstract relationship
between certain shapes and colours, or qualities of pictorial
texture that only a trained and experienced eye could
detect, and it did not postulate a very specialized
professional knowledge. There may have been more
social snobbery among successful artists than in more
recent years, but inverted professional snobbery was as yet
unknown. For artists like Alma Tadema a young and
well-proportioned woman with perfect features was beautiful. His criterion of beauty was based on the classical
standards, derived from ancient statues and antique frescoes
in the museums. Roses were beautiful and the play of the
sunlight on them ; water, blue and clear in a marble bath,
was beautiful, and so was the graceful pose of a graceful
youth. Art was for Alma Tadema, as for most of the English
artists, not a formula of abstraction or of creative translation,
but a life-like representation of all those things that were
considered lovely. Even daily life, out of which such art
was to come, had to have its standards of beauty. The
luxurious surroundings sought by so many artists were not
ends in themselves, but means of beautifying life, which
seemed essential to a painter's art. Alma Tadema built
himself a house in St. John's Wood, in which every detail
had been carefully thought out and designed by himself.
The house had to recreate the atmosphere of ancient Rome ;
colour schemes, shapes and ornaments were designed accordingly, and it mattered little that the ladies who moved amongst
the Roman furniture wore high-heeled shoes and any number
of petticoats, instead of tunics, sandals and flowing garments.

The artist tried to escape the horrors of rapid industrializa-
tion of life by building himself a house modelled on a
Spanish castle, a Roman patio or a Gothic cathedral,
the outer shells of which were mostly red-brick walls of
uniform houses in Chelsea or St. John's Wood. What
mattered was, that within those walls the artist was able to
lead his own life in an imagined atmosphere and in pursuit
of those ideals of beauty which meant so much to him.

Roman frescoes on the walls and Roman furniture in
front of them were not enough if the emotions did not
harmonize with the surroundings. Love of good literature or
of serious music, and noble sentiments were as necessary as
the beauty of the painted picture ; hospitality did not mean
that one was bored with one's own company and therefore
invited a guest to amuse one during a meal ; it sprang from
a desire to share with others the comeliness of one's home
and the pleasures of the table.

IV

Alma Tadema's life was representative of the life of a
successful R.A. of the day. He originally came from
Friesland and he did not speak English until he was thirty-
four, yet he was typical of the late Victorian painter who
had been knighted and whose pictures were " on the line "
at the Academy. If so successful a man, at the height of
his fame, expressed a keen desire to paint the portrait of a
young pianist, this could almost be considered a tribute
from contemporary English art. Painting a portrait was
in those days a much more serious affair than it is now.
When Queen Victoria's daughter, Princess Louise Duchess
of Argyll, a great friend of the Alma Tademas, and herself
a very talented artist, heard of the projected portrait,
she asked to be allowed to paint the Polish pianist also.
So did Alma Tadema's wife, and his older daughter Anna,
both painters themselves.

The time was June, 1891. The vast studio, with its

costly Roman furniture made of beautiful woods, looked more like an impressive stage setting than a studio ; but no Victorian painter could have conceived a more significant picture than that of this studio, with its blend of social elegance and artistic purpose, with Paderewski posed in the middle of the room in a large ornate chair, sitting very upright with his hands slightly outstretched as though touching the keyboard. His hands were not long and slender like Chopin's " pianist's hands," but masculine, though small, with rather short fingers and very short fingernails. They were well, almost delicately shaped, and their paleness emphasized their sensitive appearance. Sometimes they would forget their posed inertness and would practise some particularly difficult trill of the fourth and fifth fingers or they would try out an arpeggio on the arm of the chair. Around Paderewski stood the four artists at their easels : to his left Anna, a girl in the early twenties, drawing the sitter's profile ; next to her her mother, whose heavy hair with its red-gold tint seemed almost to reflect the hair of the model. With her grey-green eyes and her picturesque appearance, she seemed the incarnation of a Victorian painter's ideal. In front of Paderewski stood Alma Tadema himself, bearded, neat and quiet, much too absorbed in his work to utter a word ; on Paderewski's right was the Princess Louise, tall and stately, with her keen blue eyes, and a crown of rich hair. Patient in their midst sat Paderewski, from time to time exchanging a word with the painter's younger daughter, Laurence, who sat in the middle of the circle, busy with her sewing and trying to save the sitter from utter boredom. Into the monotonous sound of brushes on canvas their words would fall like drops of water on sand. Everyone was conscious of the importance of the occasion ; the whole house seemed to radiate it ; none of the servants ever dared to enter the room and no guests were admitted while the sittings were taking place. If a very urgent message or guest arrived, one of the maids would gently strike a little Burmese gong in

PADEREWSKI (1891)
From the painting by Princess Louise Duchess of Argyll

the Atrium, which was divided by a curtain from the studio itself ; otherwise no interruption was allowed till the louder sound of a larger gong would reverberate through the whole house. That was the first signal for lunch. Paderewski leaped from his chair ; the ladies withdrew to prepare for the meal and Alma Tadema himself went down to the cellar to get out the wine : in an existence which was meant to be a harmonious whole, even the choice of wine was not without importance. Half an hour after the first, a second gong announced that lunch was ready. Meanwhile Paderewski and his host wandered up and down the garden, trying to outvie each other in epigram. Both believed in the seriousness of work, work was to be done, not talked about, and so neither talked shop. Each had a strong sense of humour and there was usually a duel of wits, which often lasted throughout the meal. Occasionally Paderewski would attempt a joke in English, although as yet he hardly knew the language. They conversed for the most part in French, which everyone spoke fluently. Work was resumed soon after lunch, and the sitting came to an end when the Princess's carriage was announced.

After six long sittings the portraits were ready.

v

Hand in hand with his artistic and social went Paderewski's financial success. A concert in London rarely brought in less than £1,000. *Punch* published a drawing showing Paderewski sitting at the piano and surrounded by policemen. The title of the drawing was " Police Protection for Pianists ! ! " ; underneath were the words : " Made necessary by the antics of the Padded-Roomski devotees at St. James's Hall, who rush at, try to embrace, and deck with roses a certain master whenever he appears." The smartest hostesses tried a year in advance to get Paderewski for one private concert at their houses. When he was invited to a dinner-party, the other guests would speculate beforehand as to whether he would play after dinner or not. If he did play, his hostess could consider herself the most envied woman in town.

Most of London's great houses had opened their doors. Devonshire House and Grosvenor House, Londonderry House and even Marlborough House were no longer merely names to him. One day in June, 1891, a letter on white note-paper, surmounted by a crown and the words Windsor Castle in blue print, signed by Sir Walter Parratt, the Queen's Master of Music, arrived. Paderewski was requested to play before Queen Victoria. The Queen-Empress, living at Windsor or at Balmoral behind a wall of dignity, royal seclusion and an over-emphasized widow-hood, no longer took part in the artistic or the social life of her people, but to play for her was a great honour, made the more significant by the Queen's musical knowledge and taste, which were both genuine and not without distinction.

Paderewski left London in the evening, going by train to Windsor. When he arrived at the Castle it was after nine o'clock and the Master of the Household was awaiting him. He was led through half-lit passages and high rooms to a large drawing-room with green panelled walls, containing occasional tables bearing many photographs and souvenirs. A piano stood in a corner of the room, near a window. At nine forty-five, five minutes before the appointed time, a door was opened and the Queen walked in, leaning heavily on a stick. She looked exactly as Paderewski had pictured her : clad in black, short, stout, with heavy eyelids. But her dignity was more compelling than he had anticipated, and her shortness had a grandeur in keeping with a much taller person. The simplicity of her dress strengthened this picture of a Queen who was half-legend, half-symbol, yet nothing so much as a woman. The Queen was accompanied only by her youngest daughter Princess Beatrice and one or two ladies and gentlemen in attendance. She nodded appreciatively or applauded after each piece, and when the programme was finished, she asked Paderewski to go on. " Yes, some more Chopin, and some Schumann too, but above all some Mendelssohn, please, some of his old songs." When Paderewski had finished playing Mendelssohn, the Queen thanked him in a voice in which even the royal self-discipline could not master entirely the undertone of emotion. And she began to tell Paderewski about the days when Mendelssohn used to come to the Castle to give the Queen music lessons and about the nervousness, nay, the fright, which the Queen always felt before a lesson. It had been more than half a century ago. Later in the evening, when the Queen retired to her rooms, she opened her Diary and wrote : " 2 July, Windsor Castle. Went to the green drawing room and heard Monsieur Paderewski play on the piano. He does so quite marvellousely, such power and such tender feeling. I really think he is quite equal to Rubinstein. He is young, about 28, very pale, with a sort of aureole of red hair standing out."

When Paderewski played for the Queen some years later, the Queen no longer walked in leaning on her stick, but she was wheeled into the green room in a bath chair. She received Paderewski like an old acquaintance whom she was anxious to introduce to as many members of her family as were present at the moment at Windsor or in London. There were her three daughters, the Princesses Christian, Beatrice and Louise, the Princess of Wales, Prince Batten-berg, several other relations and most of the ladies and gentlemen of the royal household. Paderewski had to play a great number of encores, and when the introduction and the small talk had eventually finished, and he was allowed to kiss the old Sovereign's hand to take leave of her, the Queen said that she would send him her photograph. Soon afterwards a large photograph arrived, signed and dated in a firm hand. A few months later the Queen died. The Prince of Wales succeeded his mother on the throne of England and the beautiful Danish Princess became Queen. Paderewski had played for Queen Alexandra long before

4

Queen Victoria's death. He had met the Princess of
Wales at the house of Lady Randolph Churchill, whom
he had known in Paris. Lady Randolph Churchill had
asked him to play at her house, and it was at one of those
musical parties that he was presented to the future Queen.
His hostess had told him beforehand : " Although Her
Royal Highness is rather deaf, yet she is able to hear and
to enjoy music." The Princess of Wales seemed enchanted
with Paderewski and with his playing and she frequently
asked him to play for her at Marlborough House.

Nevertheless, Paderewski would not allow his life to become
just a brilliantly lit stage accompanied by the usual routine
of success, and personal friends and interest meant as much
to him as they did ten years ago. He did not lose his sense
of values, and he retained his appreciation of things beyond
the concert platform. To play for some old friends without
a fee was still to Paderewski a greater pleasure than a
packed concert hall. Particularly in London were there
such friends. Now and again there was an evening party
given by one of his most devoted friends, Lady Barrington,
whose husband was Private Secretary to Lord Salisbury.
In their Victorian house in Cadogan Place there were no
powdered footmen ; the music-room was built out over the
courtyard, and only some two dozen friends would be
invited ; dinner was good, but not ostentatious, and so were
the names of the guests. They dined together and Paderewski knew them all. He was not playing to a crowd, but
to individuals. The same happened at Alma Tadema's,
in whose Roman studio, with its perfect acoustics, he loved
playing to a particularly cultured and artistic group of
friends. It was the same at a few other houses : that of
his oldest London friend, Frank Schuster, or of Mrs. S. H.
Beddington at 21, Hyde Park Square. Mrs. Beddington
was one of the few among Paderewski's friends who had
heard him at his first recital in London in 1890, having
been taken to the St. James's Hall by Teresa Carreño, the
celebrated Venezuelan pianist. She was a pupil of Lesche-

tizky and was considered one of the best amateur pianists in London. In her house Paderewski met once or twice the aged composer, Charles Salaman, an uncle of the hostess and a friend of Mendelssohn, with whom he used to play in earlier days. Paderewski also played for Mr. and Mrs. Egerton Castle. And there were many women who had become his friends without having ever been social lions ; Lady Lewis and the exquisite Duchess of Rutland, who liked to draw him while he was sitting at the piano, and in later years, Lady Stuart-Wortley and Lady Cory, into whose house in Belgrave Square he would come occasionally in an afternoon to give his hostess an " unofficial " piano lesson.

His contact with individuals was not lost, as so often happens to successful virtuosi, and his piano did not isolate him from the world of every day.

The friends who helped in preserving his life from a state of enchanted loneliness were everywhere, in London, in Paris, in Vienna, even in Poland.

CHAPTER FOUR

MUSICAL METHODS

I

WHEN asked one day how he had achieved his tremendous success, Paderewski answered : " My success is due one per cent. to talent, nine per cent. to luck and ninety per cent. to work. Work, work, work is the main secret of success." Only on such a basis of work could his individual attempts make history in piano playing.

It was not by accident that on the only occasion when Paderewski agreed to write down some of his musical theories, he chose for his subject : *Tempo Rubato*, the tempo "stolen" by the virtuoso. Individualism was part of his general attitude towards life. The romanticism which he represented sprang from the same roots as his craving for spiritual and personal independence. He who believed in the power of men, and in the individual, did not willingly submit to the orthodox view, which blindly accepted all laws drawn up, by, and for others. But the will to independence was by no means revolutionary. It aimed at enriching the older laws with new substance, which the new-found individuality of the artist should illumine. The liberties taken by such artists as Rubinstein, Paderewski, and the violinist Isaye, were in accordance with the high opinion that by now Man had formed of himself ; the scientific conquest of the world had made him feel master of the world. He believed that his power over life was stronger than ever before, and that therefore it was practically his duty to exercise it over previous creations of nature or of his fellow men. For a pianist like Paderewski, the composer was not merely his score, but his feelings, his ambitions, his life, the world in which he moved. Such knowledge is a very important element in the storehouse of subconscious experience ; it influenced Paderewski's playing, who goes even farther than that. He does not conceive the piano as an independent unit, standing in a void and separated from the outside world by the magic circle of its own laws, but as an expression of life in general. Piano-playing must not separate the successful pianist from the rhythm of ordinary life and his human contacts must find their analogy in the " physical " contacts of his instrument with the outside world. In his few pages on *Tempo Rubato*, written in 1910 for " Success in Music," the work of the American musical critic, Henry T. Finck, Paderewski says : " The tempo depends on physiological and physical conditions. It is influenced by interior or exterior temperature, by surroundings, instruments, acoustics. It reflects life, organic human life, with all its attributes."

It is the child of a scientific century that speaks. Paderewski does not live in the clouds, but has both feet firmly planted on the earth. Even when absorbed in his music he does not forget the temperature of the room about him, its size and shape and other material circumstances. There is not one world of music and another of everyday life ; they are one ; and to talk of the " tempo " of one is to express the vibrations of the other. Speaking of musical rhythm, he concludes : " Rhythm is life."

But inasmuch as this general " scientific " attitude was a logical expression of the age, so was the personal will for independence. Modern man is master of fire, water, acoustics, master of the wood and the metals that become parts of musical instruments. The artist is equally master of the rhythm and tones of a composition. The composer builds the road, but does not ride on it. That is the interpreter's part. And so Paderewski feels entitled to say : " There is no absolute rhythm." He wants the musical interpretation to be made to live through his own emotions, and not through laws that are supposed to be infallible. "To be emotional in musical interpretation, yet obedient to the initial tempo," he says, "and to the metronome, means about as much as being sentimental in engineering." And later: "The tempo as a general indication of character in a composition is undoubtedly of great importance, but a composer's imagination and an interpreter's emotion are not bound to be the humble slaves of either metronome or tempo." He then makes a definite statement in which he shows clearly how much the independence of the virtuoso means to him: "Beethoven could not always be precise. Why? Because there are in musical expression certain things which are vague and consequently cannot be defined; because they vary according to individuals, voices, or instruments; because a musical composition, printed or written, is, after all a form, a mould : the performer infuses life into it, and whatever the strength of that life may be, he must be given a reasonable amount of liberty, he must be endowed with some discretional power. In our modern meaning discretional power is *tempo rubato*." When, in conclusion, Paderewski mentions Chopin, it becomes quite clear that he is defending, or rather explaining himself: "It would be unthinkable to play Chopin without *tempo rubato*." Orthodox critics had attacked Paderewski over and over again for his extensive use of *tempo rubato*, thus showing that they not only misunderstood him, but also the composers whose works he played. Paderewski used *tempo rubato* only with those composers whose own egotism obviously required such a method. He remained "classical" when he played Haydn, Handel, Bach or the lesser harpsichord composers, saying that : "*Tempo rubato* . . . ought to be used in the works of Chopin, Schubert, Schumann ("Papillons," "Carnival"), Brahms, Liszt, Grieg. . . ."

When Mr. Bernard Shaw as musical critic of the *World* wrote in 1890 of Paderewski's playing, that : "He is always

sure of his notes ; but the licence of his *tempo rubato* goes
beyond all reasonable limits," he was not the only one
to attack Paderewski on that score. To-day that attitude
seems less comprehensible. Authoritative knowledge of
musical history has shown that most of the composers
mentioned by Paderewski were guilty of using *tempo
rubato* " beyond all reasonable limits." None used it more
than Chopin ; but the press long continued to attack
Paderewski's rendering of Chopin's works. Did not Berlioz
say about Chopin that he " chafed at the bridle of the
measure " and that " he could not play in strict time " ?
And one of the greatest authorities on Chopin, Liszt, wrote
in his " Life of Chopin " : " This manner of execution . . .
was first indicated by the words, *Tempo Rubato*, affixed
to his works : a tempo broken, agitated, interrupted. . . .
This direction is no longer to be found in his later pro-
ductions : he was persuaded that if the player understood
them he would divine this regular irregularity. All his
compositions ought to be played with this accentuated and
measured swaying and rocking. . . ."

Only a man with a deep conviction of his own possibilities
could become such an ardent defender of *tempo rubato* as
Paderewski, who knew that he could not be judged by
the orthodox standards applicable to the average " brilliant
pianist." His talent required the independence that only
tempo rubato could offer the tempo " stolen " by the
interpreter from the directions of the composer. To
Paderewski *tempo rubato* stood for the superiority of the
man who knows that he is master. Had he not had the
emotional and the technical aptitude to show quite clearly
that his ideas about *tempo rubato* were right, they must
have sounded false ; but his Schumann, his Liszt, his
Chopin, even his Beethoven were the most persuasive
illustrations of what he meant by the advantage of *tempo
rubato*.

Tempo rubato, however, was only one instance of
his musical method. Another was his use of the pedal.

Even before he became Leschetizky's pupil in Vienna, he had tried to widen the scope of the pedal. The goal was for him not the correct, classical playing of the piano, but the music, no matter by what means the perfect rendering was obtained. Had it been possible to enrich his pianistic effects by a method of playing with his teeth or his toes, Paderewski would certainly have made use of it. But the pedal sufficed, and he would practise command of it for hours. The sureness of his " foot-work," the subtlety of his touch on the pedal, and its power of expression were second only to his similar qualities on the keyboard. Finck, in a minute description of Paderewski's pedalling, says : " So perfect is his pedalling that he never by any accident blurs his harmonies and passages, while at the same time he produces tone-colours never before dreamt of in a pianoforte. By rapid successive pressure of the pedal he succeeds in giving the piano a new power, that of changing the quality of the tone after it has been struck. . . . He has a way of his own for producing orchestral effects which depends on the skilful use of the pedals instead of on muscular gradations of forte and piano."

Of course there were critics, who considered that such a use of the pedal was wrong, unfair, like cheating at cards. For them the pedal itself was almost a fraud, and they agreed with the remark of Moscheles, Liszt's famous pupil, who once said : " A good pianist uses the pedals as little as possible. Too frequent use leads to abuse. Moreover, why should he try to produce an effect with his feet instead of his hands ? " Why indeed, except if he wants to tie himself down to the limited " classical " way of musical representation, in which the piano, instead of being the means to an end, becomes an end in itself?

II

Paderewski's pedalling was one example of his pianistic independence. He had built up such a solid technical foundation that he considered himself at liberty to express, in his playing, his very personal feelings about Chopin or Beethoven. He was able to co-ordinate his own feelings with the particular mood of a composition, identifying himself completely with it. The single-mindedness, which dictated every action throughout his life, was also responsible for his musical discipline ; it was, in fact, just the gift of concentration, through which he was able to obliterate every emotion, every interpretation but the one he desired. Thus, certain states of mind or emotions could be placed in definite frames of mental discipline for just as long as required by the study of that particular mood. Yet all Paderewski's emotional gifts and artistic talents would have been of little value if he had not given them the right form. Mental self-discipline would have become dryness ; passion would have turned into noise ; his lyrical rendering would have been degrading into sentimentality, if they had not been used to a definite purpose. And this he did by sheer hard work. For years he practised for ten and twelve hours a day, and when he was preparing a new repertoire he would work as much as sixteen hours a day. Compositions which he knew by heart he practised as though he had never played them before. Yet he hardly ever prepared a whole composition in its entirety. What he studied and prepared laboriously were the individual fragments of a composition. He considered that playing from memory was indispensable, even for beginners, and that no effect could be obtained on the platform unless it had been most carefully prepared and worked out. In his playing there would be an un- expected ritardando, sudden pauses, certain fresh accentua- tions, an unfamiliar dreaminess, a surprising humorous emphasis on a last note, new elements, which made his Schumann or Chopin remarkable and stimulating. Yet not one of these effects was unrehearsed. There must be no sudden moods on the platform : their place was the studio. Long before the audience heard these effects their apparently accidental character would have been carefully studied and investigated. Innovations were only permissible if there was logic behind them, and logic can only be conveyed to an audience of five thousand people if the form is perfect. Paderewski's process of training was only in part mechanical, although endless hours were spent at the piano. The constant activity of his brain made mental training a necessity. Practically every musician or writer is so deeply absorbed in his work that even in moments of relaxation it will not let him rest. Sleepless nights in which difficult scales, unpolished trills, and passages apparently unplayable, pursue each other in wild sequence and exaggerated importance, are the nightmare accompaniment to the virtuoso's profession. Paderewski suffered from them as much as anyone, but by mental discipline he did not allow himself to drift into the customary state of nocturnal torture and exhaustion, but instead began a definite routine of rigorous training. He would run over in his mind the entire programme of the forthcoming concert ; he would go over bar after bar ; certain notes, certain passages would have to be repeated, thought about more carefully, corrected, and gradually each composition would disclose itself. This concentration on a composition, with the mind released from any preoccupation with the hands, brought about a most successful identification of the artist with the music, and became one with his breathing, with his every nerve and fibre.

In the daytime Paderewski would also practise thus, without using the piano. But on the whole he knew only too well how essential it was to escape in the hours of leisure from the haunting visions of his music. Ordinary physical exercise did not give him the necessary relaxation ; walking or swimming did not prevent his thoughts from revolving around a difficult passage. He found mental release in billiards and patience, which he could play for hours on end, both requiring absolute concentration. In his own words they gave him either exercise or " mental rest." His physical strength and his robust health made strenuous exercise unnecessary. The muscles of his arms were like those of an athlete ; his fingers, although not long, were strong. His only concession to physical exercise was a short space given up each morning to rather strenuous gymnastics ; an occasional swim, an occasional ride on horseback, that was all. After his exhausting hours of work at the piano, solitary relaxation could hardly appeal to him ; he needed people, conversation and the atmosphere of human companionship.

III

It was always the human factor that decided Paderewski's approach to different composers. Although he gave his undivided attention to the musical content of a composition, disapproving of a literary line of approach, his interest was so universal that, consciously or unconsciously, the human element had to be there. The " Appassionata " or the " Waldstein " Sonata would be inseparably linked with Ludwig van Beethoven as a man ; in the background was Vienna and such names as Lobkowitz or Guicciardi ; elegant drawing-rooms, the Prater, and, above all, the tragedy of a great mind. At the centre of things stood Beethoven, the man of flesh and blood, directing the pianist's hands.

Paderewski rarely played works by composers who were not in some way in sympathy with his own character. Once he said to an interviewer, " I am firmly of the belief that the pianist, in order to produce the finest and most delicate effects, must . . . identify himself absolutely with his work. . . . Yet "—and this seems to explain his rendering of Beethoven—" he must put his own personality resolutely, triumphantly into his interpretation of the composer's idea."

These words do not imply the purely musical individuality of the pianist. Paderewski's national consciousness came even before his musical sensibility or rather it nourished it. Therefore a composer's mood that did not find a natural counterpart in Paderewski could only be assimilated through this national consciousness. Feelings of a romantic, lyrical or heroic kind were of his nature : they did not require such assimilation.

Beethoven's impulsiveness, his emotional passion, his heroism lay beyond purely German and intellectual qualities ; they were the elements in his music that Paderewski played best. Speaking of them, Finck remarked : " He plays this music with a poetic freedom which Beethoven would have been the first to applaud." And later he says : " Like Liszt and Rubinstein, Paderewski dares to linger fondly over a beautiful melody, and to storm wildly . . . even to pound . . . just as Beethoven himself did, according to the testimony of his friends." Liszt's pupil, Mason, even went so far as to accept unreservedly the intellectual qualities of Paderewski's Beethoven : " His conception of Beethoven combines the emotional with the intellectual in admirable poise and proportion." Undoubtedly, it was the emotional structure of Beethoven's genius that Paderewski found easiest to recreate. It was not by chance that one of the things that made him famous was his rendering of the " Moonlight " and the " Appassionata " Sonatas.

But often he would encounter in Beethoven moods that lay outside his own nature, purely Germanic, intellectual qualities, which, though by no means circumscribed, did not come so naturally to Paderewski. They were best absorbed by " national translation." The Polish avenue of approach was for Paderewski the most direct and most vital. When such translation was possible, then he was able to play the composition even if its basic idea was subconsciously not congenial to him. Beethoven's individual sufferings transformed themselves under Paderewski's hands and became the sufferings of Poland. Not that such a process of transformation was undertaken consciously. That would have been an obvious cheapening of Beethoven and in contradiction to Paderewski's general musical attitude. Rather was it an automatic process, more perceptible to the listener than to the performer himself. It was there to open wider the doors of his sensitiveness so that the composition might flow more freely. The final product, as heard by the audience, possessed so few traces of this transfiguration that only the most discerning ear was able to detect it. This perhaps explains why Paderewski's Beethoven was more discussed than his playing of any other composer was, and why so many critics who accepted him wholeheartedly, would hesitate when confronted with his Beethoven. Edward Baughan, a great admirer of Paderewski, wrote in his little volume on Paderewski : " His Beethoven is unequal. Sometimes, if in the mood, he will give you a performance of one of the later sonatas which cannot be surpassed . . . ; at other times his readings are rather small and not sufficiently architectural."

With Chopin no translation was needed. Liszt was so congenial to him, that he could play him as though he, himself, had written the compositions. The harpsichord composers, even Mozart, had worked largely on the basis of a purely artistic conception and in a cultural tradition that was much akin to earlier Polish traditions, and it was not difficult for Paderewski to play them without any inner process of acclimatization. His self-control and mental discipline removed the difficulties of Bach. Mason, in fact, thought that he was one of the greatest, if not the greatest, Bach exponent of his time : " As Moscheles played Bach half a century ago and Rubinstein played him later on, so does Paderewski play him now, . . . with an added grace and colour which put these great contrapuntal creations in the most charming frames. It is the great, deep musical playing combined with the calm, quiet repose and great breadth of style. Paderewski has an advantage over Rubinstein, however, in that he is always master of his resources and possesses power of complete self-control. . . ." A romantic similarity connected Paderewski with Weber, Schumann, Mendelssohn and Grieg.

But Beethoven was a different matter. Paderewski was passionately attracted to Beethoven. There was probably no composer whom he studied with greater zeal. But Beethoven remained a problem.

IV

Liszt embodied that which Paderewski himself stood for—brilliant achievement in a world that loved both the virtuoso and the creator. Both Liszt and Paderewski appreciated the high place that life had given them ; yet neither of them lost the faculty of making individual human contacts. Both were in harmony with a world that filled the largest concert-halls to hear the dazzling effects of a virtuoso, but could also be moved by Liszt's religious compositions, by Parsival and Siegfried's funeral march. Liszt did not necessitate opening intellectual doors to which Paderewski's nature lacked the key ; it was piano playing par excellence : elegant and serious, strong and sensitive, godly and profane, grand and lyrical. Paderewski's Liszt poured from under his fingers like a native stream. Even the religious side of Liszt did not present any particular difficulties. Paderewski may not have shared the religious exaltation of Liszt, but he felt sympathy for the expression of any religious feeling ; and he had that æsthetic curiosity, which could devote itself to a religious drama, less for religion than for the drama's sake. In Liszt, even in his most ecstatic religious moments, there remained the artist, who could preserve the legend without being burned by his faith.

It was natural that Paderewski should play Liszt better than any other pianist played him. They aimed at the same goal. Mason, who learned under Liszt, wrote : " It seems strange that the best Liszt performer of to-day should be Paderewski, who was not a pupil of Liszt and never even heard him play." The resemblance, however, was closer than that between teacher and pupil. In the works of Liszt, more than in those of Beethoven or even of

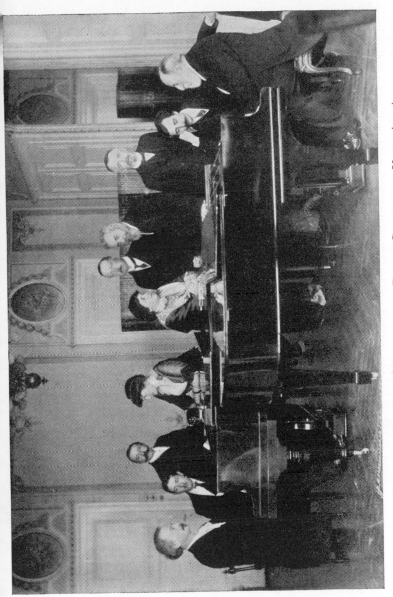

PADEREWSKI AND SAINT-SAËNS PLAYING A DOUBLE CONCERTO AT VEVEY (1912)

Behind the pianos Mrs. Schelling and Mme Paderewska ; next to Saint-Saëns the American composer Ernest Schelling

62]

Chopin, Paderewski was able to exercise all his gifts as a
pianist ; here the piano could become an orchestra ; here it
could use an almost unlimited range of colour. Liszt wrote
a book about the " Gypsies and their music " ; both in his
composition and in his playing he tried to produce effects
that were common to gypsy music. A proper rendering of
Liszt required all the arts and tricks of pedalling, of impressive ritardandos, of almost affrighting crescendos of which
Paderewski was the supreme master and in many cases the
inventor. Even antagonistic critics, who felt compelled to
mistrust an artist with such power over the masses, came
under Paderewski's spell when he played Liszt. His
intelligence and sensibility helped him to penetrate the mere
technical brilliance of Liszt, and even when the musical form
seemed meaningless, he was able to give it a content. This
impressed the critics and made such men as Alexander
MacArthur, who was Rubinstein's biographer, testify :
" Paderewski made one forget the display of technique, and
he put meaning in his passage work."

Liszt himself stressed most of the elements that constituted
Paderewski's talent, and like him he, too, used to take
technique for granted. He played all the outstanding
scales or arpeggios for his pupils, showed them the most
surprising fingering and pedallings, all those astonishing
" tempi rubati " which made Chopin write one day :
" Liszt is at this moment playing my studies and transports
me out of my proper sense. I should like to rob him of his
way of rendering my own études."

Many critics used similar words about the way in which
Paderewski played Liszt. Both were opposed to classical
or orthodox playing ; both were individualists, who kept
their own musical ideas alive without letting them be swept
aside by foreign influence ; both possessed a highly developed
sense of their own value. And both possessed the means to
convey this to their listeners.

V

Paderewski's attitude to Chopin was distinctly different from his attitude to other composers. It was the least musical and the most personal one ; which seems paradoxical, although it only expresses the force of the human relationship between pianist and composer. It was due to the depth and vitality of this personal contact that Paderewski played Chopin better than he played any other composer, and that he came to be considered as the greatest exponent of Chopin. Mason wrote of Paderewski's Chopin : " Neither Pachmann nor Godowsky plays Chopin as a poet would play, and Chopin with all his absolute musical fastidiousness was a poet. Busoni's Chopin playing can alone be compared to Paderewski's, for Busoni had a poet's imagination. But Paderewski had more emotional fibre." Baughan, too, preferred Paderewski's Chopin, saying : " Neither Busoni nor Pachmann can play the great Scherzo in C sharp minor as Paderewski plays it." And Finck was reminded by his Chopin of " Æolian harps, whose harmonies seem to rise and fall with the gentle breezes," and of "magic tone colours and mystic sounds that come up from the invisible Wagnerian orchestra at Bayreuth."

The patriotism that flowed naturally and without effort in Chopin's works, was for Paderewski a conscious reality, with which he identified himself both in emotion and intellect. He not only felt, but understood Chopin's every note. Chopin represented for Paderewski the soil, the very soul of Poland. When on October 23rd, 1910, he opened the Chopin Centenary Festival in Lemberg, he put his Chopin creed into words. He spoke little about music, but much about Poland, summing up with a purely national statement : " No man, however great, can be above his nation, or beyond his nation. He is seed of her seed, a portion of her, blossom of her bearing, fruit of her ripening. . . . We know too that he " (Chopin) " was great with our greatness, strong with our strength, beautiful with our beauty. . . . The whole of our collective soul is in him made manifest."

This Polish inheritance, which found its most perfect musical expression in Paderewski's rendering of Chopin, showed itself also in other ways, more fundamentally, more philosophically. Music is a state of soul, as form is a state of consciousness, colour lying half-way between the two. Amorphous shapes of music were more congenial to the spirit of Poland than sensuous qualities of colour or definite statements of form. That spirit lived in the sounds of Poland itself, dreamy and not too intense in colour, not too definite in shape : next to poetry, music was Poland's chief mode of expression. Paderewski possessed that national sense of music ; he also possessed the poetic imagination, and the dramatic sense, which is often the heritage of a nation that is rather theatrical, self-centred and sensitive. The heroic vein in him was the natural tradition of a people who could forget the misery of the present in exaltation over the heroism of the past.

These gifts, however, were only the raw material that had through a definite, systematic effort to be translated into a work of art. Paderewski's sense of the need for continuous and patient work was not a national characteristic, rather the reverse. While emotionally he surrendered himself to the spirit of Poland, intellectually he was often in open revolt against it ; he acknowledged the negative elements of his national inheritance by deliberately converting them into positive ones. Had these negative national elements not been in him, he would not have bothered about them. By the process of organized work, as he learned it in the West, he replaced his racial shortcomings and contrived to lift native qualities which were the soul of Chopin's music into the highest art.

VI

When one day Paderewski was asked to honour a lady's autograph book with a contribution, he wrote : " *La Patrie*

5

avant tout ; l'art ensuite.'' It was not an epigram ; it was his fundamental belief, reduced to its simplest formula. The desire to compose was one of his deepest emotions ; but " *la Patrie* " reigned supreme. National feelings were so closely interwoven with personal ones that the latter would mostly take the shape of the former in trying to find musical expression. When Paderewski was twenty-five years old, there was a Paderewski concert in Warsaw, at which only his own compositions were played. The dominant feature of the concert was its national character.

Polish composition of the nineteenth century was naturally overshadowed by Chopin, and it was hardly possible to compose anything without in some measure imitating Poland's greatest composer. The idea of the nation as a free and independent unity was the foremost idea of all creative efforts, whether artistic or intellectual. The poems of Mickiewicz, Slowacki, Krasinski, Wyspianski, may in their breadth embrace the deepest human problems, but their roots and their colour are national. The national idea had often been the undoing of Poland, but in the nineteenth century it was undoubtedly the centre of creative inspiration. As Chopin himself lived almost entirely in these national elements, it was natural that his music should hold all that was characteristic of the Polish spirit. Other composers found refuge in the same folk-lore and similar emotional structures, and it was therefore hardly possible to avoid those elements which Chopin had crystallized more perfectly than anyone else. The only other composer who found the individual note and created in " Halka " an opera of national character, though not without international importance, was Moniuszko. Composers like Zelenski, Noskowski and Zarzycki hardly counted outside Poland.

In Paderewski's creative efforts the national element was predominant from the first. The desolation of the Polish plains and fields, the chivalrous gaiety of Polish feasts and dances, the melancholy of a people longing for freedom, the whole rhythm of a nation that liked to express its feelings in music—all these guided his hand as it wrote down the notes on paper. Composing came naturally to Paderewski. When he was only seven and could hardly manage the keyboard, he composed his first set of dances, Polish dances of course. And romantic dances too—the romantic streak in him was as much a national inheritance as his sense of music. At the age of twenty-two, when his compositions first appeared in print, he had already composed a vast quantity of music, mostly for the piano.

One feature was characteristic of all those piano pieces— an unmistakable sensitiveness to Melos. These early compositions hardly seemed the work of a man who was to become the greatest piano virtuoso of his time ; they are not piano music so much as songs sung not by a human voice, but by the piano. As a composer Paderewski had not yet discovered the possibilities of the piano. One must not forget that his decision to become a pianist was taken comparatively late in life, long after his musical taste had been formed. As in his playing, so it was in his earlier compositions : the piano had to express the composer's emotions, no matter whether it had to play or to sing. Soon he came to compose more and more for the human voice, and of these the most notable were his settings to poems by the Polish poets Asnyk (op. 7), and Mickiewicz (op. 18).

Paderewski's interest and preoccupation with instruments augmented his desire to compose for instruments and voices, the logical outcome of which was of course the composition of an opera. On May 29th, 1901, a brilliant audience attended the first performance of Paderewski's first opera " Manru," in the Royal Opera House in Dresden. The musical world had been on tiptoe with expectation ; all the leading musical critics in Germany were on the spot ; Polish, French and even American newspapers sent their special correspondents. E. Schuch conducted and the principal singers were Scheidemantel, Anthes and Anna Krull. Paderewski himself witnessed his first operatic success. Ten days later, on June 8th, he was able to repeat the experience at a performance at

the Opera House in Lwow ; again in the winter months in
the United States, where " Manru " was first produced at
the Metropolitan in New York, with Sembrich-Kochanska
in the leading rôle, and still again in the following months in
Philadelphia, Boston, Chicago and other American towns.
If Paderewski had not yet realized his position in the musical
world, the anxiety with which the leading opera houses
tried to secure " Manru " must have made it clear to him.
The libretto was written under Paderewski's supervision by
Alfred Nossig in German.   The subject was taken from a
popular Polish novel by Kraszewski, "The Cabin behind the
Village."   The opera had a character, partly national,
partly gypsy, which suited the romantic and symbolical
subject.   But the musical character of this dramatic love
story between the peasant girl Ulana and the gypsy leader
Manru was based on Richard Wagner.   The press was
sympathetic, but in the words of Baughan, " some of the
critics were reminded of Bizet ;   others noted a strong
likeness to Wagner."   There was, in fact, so much trite
drawing of analogies amongst the critics that Paderewski
felt compelled to state in an interview his attitude towards
operatic composition in general.   He said : " In music
absolute originality does not exist, it is the temperament of
the composer that makes his work.   In method one cannot
help but follow those who have gone before.   When a great
genius like Wagner introduces a method that will give better
expression to an idea, it is not only a sin not to follow it,
but it is a duty to follow it. . . . A piece of music must be
built like a house or a church.   You would not accuse an
architect of being a copyist if he put windows in a house,
would you . . . ? "
    But if there was a natural and unconscious assimilation of
foreign elements in Paderewski's composing, there was also a
talent which could consciously adopt and recreate an alien
spirit as well as an alien form.   That natural talent, coupled
with his quick intelligence, enabled him to create music which
lay outside his national sphere and which expressed the

Western side of his mentality. That gift was responsible for a number of compositions which were conceived in the spirit of a foreign and a distant epoch : they were Gavottes and Sarabandes, Minuets and minor classical compositions, in which Paderewski was interested mainly from the point of view of counterpoint. They expressed the spirit and the style of their day no less convincingly than did his fiery Cracoviennes and Mazurkas. The grace of the harpsichord composers and the epoch they represented appealed to Paderewski's fastidiousness as their delicacy did to his sense of order.

VII

As his technical maturity increased, instrumental compositions developed in the place of simple melodies, and their national character became even more apparent than before. The national character had never been expressed except in vague forms. As a student in Warsaw Paderewski decided to make a thorough study of those elements in Polish music that he considered most significant : the folk-lore of the songs and the dances of the Gorals, the mountain-dwellers of the Tatra. He got into touch with their most famous musician, Bartek Obrochta, a simple countryman, who from tradition through constant preoccupation knew all the ancient local folk-music. This contact with Obrochta was of greatest value to Paderewski ; it took him away from the musical drawing-room nationalism and the artificial interpretations of folk-music as known by other composers, and made clear to him the pure symbolism of the Polish musical spirit. He decided to recreate the old tunes. He made accurate piano transcriptions of them, which appeared under the title of " The Tatra Album " (op. 12). Without changing the tunes, he cast them into definite instrumental shape. In later years, however, he consciously developed not only the melodic atmosphere, but motive and execution out of Polish ideas. There was a piano concerto in A minor, op. 17, dedicated to Leschetizky and played by Paderewski in London during his first English concert tour, " strongly pervaded by the characteristics of Polish national music with its proud, chivalrous and dreamy accents " (C. A. Barry). The A minor violin Sonata (op. 13) was based on classical lines and showed a strong melodic predominance. In Opus 18, " *Fantaisie Polonaise sur des thèmes originaux pour piano et orchestre,*" national elements were the leading motive. In later years Sir Edward Elgar, a great admirer and friend of Paderewski, used in his own Symphonic Prelude " Polonia " various motives taken from the " Fantaisie Polonaise." Musically more important was the later piano Sonata (op. 21), of dramatic conception and ending with a new kind of double fugue having the effect of a fugue for four voices. Smaller pieces now appeared between his bigger compositions, pieces that were full of charm and had an appeal that made some of them the most popular compositions of the time, and which were played by innumerable pianists, orchestras and bands.

After " Manru " his most important work was the Symphony in B minor, begun in 1903, but not finished until four years later, which is, perhaps, the most vital and personal of Paderewski's compositions. It is a grandiose representation of a sustained inner struggle, in which the feelings of the individual expand to truly national dimensions. In the Finale there is a " Song of the Legions," the Polish Legions, for which Paderewski used as motive the Polish national anthem, " Jeszcze Polska nie zginela." With its great sincerity and solemnity this symphony made a deep impression at the Conservatoire in Paris, and one of the leading musical writers of France, Jules Combarieu, wrote : " One feels in the symphony the trembling that comes from shocks actually experienced. A work like this symphony, the creation of a true artist, is the altar on which the artist sacrifices himself." The symphony was played in America, in London under Richter, in Paris under Messager, and eventually in Poland for the celebrations of Chopin's centenary, when Henryk Opienski, one of the composer's most devoted friends and Poland's leading musical writer, conducted it before an enthusiastic audience.

Throughout his compositions Paderewski did not content himself with occasionally stressing the Polish characteristics and letting the national undercurrent run its own course. Composition had to serve a definite purpose, apart from the purely musical one, the glorification of Poland. Once again the outside world had to be drawn in. Only this time its name was Poland, and its fundamental purpose was not purely artistic.

CHAPTER FIVE

THE CONQUEST OF AMERICA

I

IN 1887 the firm of Steinway was on the lookout for a new pianist, who, by playing effectively enough, would stem the disquieting success in America of one or two American piano firms. In Europe Paderewski played on Erard pianos. When the head of Steinway's Paris Office heard the young Pole at the Salle Erard he immediately saw his opportunity : Paderewski was becoming a *succès de sensation* in Paris ; there was in him all the promise of a great future as a pianist, and there was his very striking appearance. He was the right man for Steinway's. They signed the contract : Paderewski was to play in the States on nothing but Steinway pianos.

The news of his successes in Paris and in London soon travelled across the Atlantic. New York awaited him as keenly as London had a year before. On November 17th, 1891, he was to appear for the first time before the American public. " One man " recitals were so far unknown in the States. " The recital idea was still in its infancy, the great virtuosi . . . like Rubinstein and Bülow, having other artists associated with them to give the interest of variety to their entertainments " (Krehbiehl). Nevertheless, New York already possessed her own musical standards and a very musical public. Most of the famous virtuosi from Europe came over to the States, and there was great keenness in musical matters. The growing popularity of the Metropolitan Opera, and, some years earlier, of Italian Opera at the Academy of Music, showed America's musical

PADEREWSKI (1890)

From pencil drawings by Violet Duchess of Rutland

72]

interest as much as fierce musical quarrels did, in which some of the most distinguished conductors of the day, Theodore Thomas, Leopold Damrosch and Anton Seidl, were involved. New York was the true home of Patti and Lilli Lehmann, of Materna, Nicolini, Campanini, Sembrich-Kochanska, Emma Eames, and their outstanding successes kept musical interest alive. Just as London had been suspicious of the enthusiastic reports from Paris, so was New York of the criticisms from England. But Paderewski was by now already a famous man.

II

Yet even fame did not prevent him from suffering agonies of stage fright, as though he had been merely a beginner. He knew it all—in New York it would be the same as it always was, whether in London or Paris or Leipzig—supreme joy and utter agony. His customary will power was eclipsed on days when he had to give a concert. The trouble began in the morning as soon as he opened his eyes, realizing that he would have to play. He would get up very late to kill at least a part of the day. He might practise, but it would be useless with the thought of a new platform and a new audience before his excited senses. He would hardly be able to eat his breakfast, he would have no lunch, his natural sensitiveness would almost become physical pain. Only by the greatest self-control could he keep his temper ; the slightest sound got on his nerves.

He arrived purposely early in the artists' room of the Madison Square Garden Hall. This would give him time to compose himself. But it was no good ; as the minutes dragged on, his fright increased. At last a bell rang, the ordeal was drawing to an end. The moment had arrived for bathing his fingers, and a small basin with hot water was brought in. He used always to bathe his fingers in hot water before going on to the platform. He put his fingers into the water, exercising them in it for a minute or two, to revive them and to give them greater suppleness. He had often to travel with his own spirit-lamp and basin, as in many of the smaller towns one could not get hot water in the artists' room. While he was drying his fingers, the bell rang again. A voice said : " Mr. Padrousky, it's time." A little door in front of him was pushed open. It seemed madness to go on to the platform in such a state. He did not think he could walk, yet his legs carried him on. There was even the slight swing in his body and that springing feeling which walking across the platform always gave him. Suddenly he saw the crowd, hundreds of faces. He had loathed everybody's face all through the long day, but now he liked them ; they made him feel awake. The crowd was almost as much an instrument as the piano, as the wood and the metal of which it was made. He now realized that it was not the crowd that terrified him, but something unspeakable, a demon within him, a demon that seemed everywhere, even in the friendly crowd, in the black piano, in the music of Couperin and Schumann and the other composers whom he had to play. The crowd below the platform had real faces and real ears with which to hear, and he would make them listen to his music. He had almost reached the piano and a smile came into his face. Had he not trained himself by hard work never to betray what was going on inside him ? The audience began to applaud. The frozen sensation suddenly started to thaw before a wave of pleasant warmth. Thank God they had applauded, otherwise he would have hardly been able to face them. At last his hands felt the resistance of the cool ivory. They fell on the keyboard, as though to revenge themselves for all the terror of the last twelve hours, a terror that must be drowned finally in the shattering chords with which he took possession of the black Steinway. Each new chord gave him a feeling of freedom and strength. The spell was broken.

The audience did not grasp the meaning of those deafen-

ing chords that seemed to shake the familiar walls of the
hall into shapes unknown. But they were more impulsive,
perhaps more childish and more primitive, than were
Paderewski's European audiences. They responded to the
new pianist after his very first piece, and their enthusiasm
grew with each fresh item.

III

The critics next morning were more cautious, and many
press notices were most antagonistic. However, after he
had played several times with the orchestra under Walter
Damrosch, and after he had given a number of recitals,
all within a few months, the Madison Square Garden Hall
proved too small, and Paderewski could pride himself in
being the first virtuoso to give a recital in the vast newly-
built Carnegie Hall, which held almost three thousand
people.

The custom of women rushing to the platform and
surrounding him, inaugurated in London, was also adopted
in New York. He was forced to give concert after concert,
and each successive hall proved too small. In New York
alone he played on eighteen occasions ; altogether he gave
one hundred and seventeen recitals during his first American
tour of six months' duration. Once the musical public
seemed to have satisfied its first hunger, the whole population was anxious to go to his concerts. Music may have
meant little to them, but they were much impressed, when
after his American tours they read that Paderewski's first
American visit had brought him in $95,000, his second
$160,000 and his third $248,000. A man who, all by
himself and with his two hands alone was able to earn more
than a quarter of a million dollars in less than six months
must be different from anyone else, and one would have
to see and hear him. They queued up, they waited, they
bought the most expensive tickets they had ever indulged in,
they filled the immense halls ; and then they did what they

had never dreamed of doing : they listened, patient and enraptured, to Beethoven, they shed tears over Chopin, they became delirious with excitement over the Liszt Rhapsodies. Was it surprising that it was said that Paderewski must have some sort of magnetism whereby he could plunge common-place, unmusical Americans so deeply into the voluptuous-ness of music ? Even Rubinstein had never been offered more than $2,500 for one recital. After Paderewski's third American tour there was not a town or a ranch or a farm between New Orleans and Seattle, San Pedro and Boston, where the name and the face of the Polish pianist were not known. " In Texas whole schools marched many miles to hear him, and such was the interest aroused by his personality that crowds frequently waited at railway stations, merely to see the train pass, in hopes of catching a glimpse of his remarkable countenance. Sometimes crowds would line the streets from his hotel to the concert hall and make it impossible for him to get past." (Baughan.)

IV

Before the century was over Paderewski was to the Ameri-can mind the virtuoso incarnate, as the novelists depicted and the masses imagined him. He seemed to meet the require-ments of his age more perfectly than any other musician. In Vienna his musical success was strengthened by his general artistic elegance ; in Paris, by his intellectual and social brilliance ; in London, by his personal charm and his picturesque beauty. In America it was his very success that appealed to the public imagination : success and the expression of success, which made the most convincing criterion. As much as the dazzling figures of his receipts, the stories of his strenuous yet brilliant life appealed to the American public. He incarnated for them those elements of fame which a later age was to crystallize into cinemato-graphic form. In his case, and for the first time, the daily life of a famous man became of absorbing interest to the masses. They wanted to know how he spent his mornings, what he ate for lunch, and how many hours he slept. And here it was : exciting, luxurious, enviable, like the life of the hero in the films as yet to come. In the United States Paderewski travelled in his own railway coach. His life was very strenuous. Sometimes he had to play night after night; it was essential not to waste any time. In his coach he had his piano, on which he practised for hours while the train thundered across the American continent ; he could get food that suited him, which in hotels would have been difficult to obtain ; exhausted, he could come straight from a concert to his railway carriage, there to enjoy the meal of his day—a large supper at eleven o'clock after the concert. There he had his cook and such comforts as were essential, but which to the crowds were a thrilling expression of an extraordinary, successful life.

His name was popular enough to make Paderewski Candies and Paderewski Soap pay irrespective of their quality. Children were given for Christmas toys representing a little man with a black frock coat, a white bow tie and a huge head of flame-coloured hair, sitting at a piano ; when a screw was turned the little man's hands rushed up and down the keyboard and his head shook violently. Long before beauty or fame could be effectively commercialized in the form of press advertisements for cosmetics, cigarettes or lady's stockings, Paderewski was not spared the sight of his own name on posters or in newspapers to vouch for the superiority of various goods. The most striking of such advertisements was undoubtedly the following :

PADEREWSKI IS THE KING OF PIANISTS
BUT
FINKELSTEINS IS THE EMPEROR OF DRY GOODS.

The American climax was reached when, on March 8th, 1902, Paderewski filled on the same afternoon the two biggest halls in New York, the Carnegie Hall and the

Metropolitan Opera House. He gave a recital at the Carnegie Hall, and at the Metropolitan his Opera "Manru" was given. The critic of the *Evening Post* wrote proudly : " The gross receipts of the two houses cannot have fallen far short of 20,000 dollars. This was something new under the sun." Indeed it was. Success mounted upon success. In London Robert Newman paid him £1,000 for an orchestral concert at the Queen's Hall, undoubtedly the highest figure hitherto received by any pianist for two or three pieces played with an orchestra. He made tours in most of the European countries ; he visited regularly America, and then Australia.

Paderewski went to Russia, and he played in Poland. His rare visits to Poland always caused him especial excitement. The strenuous life, which his constant success demanded, did not leave much time for Poland. He tried to force a stronger intimacy with his native country ; he bought first one and then another country estate in it ; but he had no time to stay there. The estates were not looked after properly by his agents and consistently lost money for him. So he sold them. He would have to try other methods of getting into intimate touch with Poland.

v

While Paderewski's individual methods helped to build up his musical success, it was due to certain traits in his character that he made friends wherever he went and that he was almost as much beloved as he was famous. His most striking characteristic was his charm, the essentially feminine element in a man whose character seemed a perfect blend of masculine and feminine elements. It was natural and unaffected. He was charming in the way that a woman may be beautiful or graceful. Next to his sensibility, his charm was undoubtedly the foremost of his feminine, but not effeminate, characteristics. It was mainly this that gave him such an influence over men, over

serious men of repute, whether in politics, business, the
army, the arts or diplomacy. It was the " woman " in
Paderewski which attracted them.

Besides his feminine element of charm there was also a
strong masculine element also responsible for his power
of making friends among men : his rectitude. Almost
always the spotlights were focused on Paderewski's activities ; each step was witnessed by a crowd. There were
no plans or achievements effected in secret studios or silent
laboratories, and there was never any reason to avoid the
straight and open way. Twelve or more hours of work a
day assured the success that others might have achieved
in less direct ways. The frankness of his attitude, his
unhesitating and firm manner in all his activities, clearly
revealed his inborn integrity. Men liked that ; and they
liked the result of this uprightness : his talent for friendship
and his unwavering loyalty. A very obvious expression of
that talent was his generosity, which was an inheritance
from his ancestors. There was always a good deal of
generosity east of the Vistula, known to the Western world
mainly under its Russian name of " shirokaya natura "
(broad, wide nature). Although the generosity of the
Polish nobleman or well-to-do peasant did not compete
in magnitude and savage splendour with its Russian
counterpart, it was big enough to be considered in a
more Western world as extravagance. One specific trait
of that national heritage was hospitality : there would
be guests at dinner, at lunch, in the afternoon. Long
meals, rich food and plenty to drink were old traditions of
good Polish living, and Paderewski loved each and all of
them, though hospitality was only one minor instance of
his generosity. He did not subscribe to charities that,
directly or indirectly, implied self-advertisement ; there had
to be a personal element, and charity of the cheque-book
alone was therefore unknown to him. However, when it
was a case of need which required also personal advice
and interest, there was no end to the pains he took. Fellow-

countrymen, old music-teachers, artists who had lost their
employment or who were anxious to continue their studies,
the most distant relations, Poles who had suffered injustice
in the Russian or Prussian parts of Poland, former school-
friends—all these and many others rarely appealed to
Paderewski without obtaining help—but it was only much
later that the great dimensions of his charitable work made
his generosity known to the outside world. His attitude
on the concert platform was also typical of his generosity.
He treated his audience, no matter where, with a gracious
kindness which was the most delightful form of gratitude.
Even when at the height of his fame, and when receiving—
according to an industrious American critic who worked
out the figures—almost $1,000 for each piece he played at
a concert, he would give encore after encore, sometimes
remaining at the piano for an hour after the actual programme
was over. Twelve encores were by no means exceptional,
and the crowds adored him for that.

VI

But finally, nothing helped him so much to popularity
in any circle as his specific social gifts. Society was the
permanent frame of his life, and wise statesmen and
witty women meant more to him than musicians discussing
their individual technique, their royalties and their con-
tracts. It was not unimportant to possess graces which
would show up well in such a frame : his talent for conversation and his exquisite manners were the chief of these.
Conversation was in some way music to him : duets,
chamber-music, occasionally a solo. He did not mind how
many instruments were played, so long as the musician did
not insist on performing only Bach, and would join in with
Debussy or Liszt or even dance music. The quality of the
instruments was equally important. Intelligence of conversation must be coupled with a proper delivery and a
sympathetic voice. Paderewski was extremely sensitive to

the quality of a voice, and often, after having met some
important person, he would complain that he had hardly
been able to carry on the conversation because the other
person's voice had affected him so adversely. His own
voice had no special quality of timbre or individuality,
but it was quiet and melodious, and his pronunciation was
very distinct. Sometimes in pronouncing the sibilant there
would be a hardly detectable lisp which only heightened
the picturesque attraction of his speech. A child of his
epoch, in some ways even of a past epoch, conversation
was for him an art, both socially and intellectually. It
need not be a means to an end ; sometimes it sufficed that
it should be an end in itself. So it came to pass that it was
not a particularly intellectual type of conversation that
Paderewski most enjoyed. He could discuss without
precipitating a deadlock by too definite a defence of his
own argument ; he did not talk unless he knew his subject,
yet he did not try to impress with his knowledge ; he liked
changing the subject, leaping to new side-tracks that seemed
promising, or that might provide the opportunity for an
epigram. His sense of humour had something akin to that
of the English, but it had also the precision of French wit. He
had a natural love for playing upon words. There is a story
told by Cuthbert Hadden, illustrating effectively Paderewski's
love for puns. One night in London Paderewski arrived
rather late at a house where he was to play. He overheard
his hostess asking one of the guests, a famous polo player and
an amateur pianist, to play until the arrival of Paderewski.
Paderewski withdrew, and did not make his entry into the
drawing-room until his " understudy " had finished playing.
He then approached the young man and congratulated him
on his performance ; but the polo player answered modestly:
" It is very kind of you to congratulate me, but nobody is
more painfully aware of the fact how great the difference
is between us." To which Paderewski replied smilingly :
" Oh, the difference is not so very great after all. You
are a dear soul who plays polo, while I am a poor Pole

6

who plays solo." His knowledge was extensive even as a young man. He was not a scholar, but he possessed the faculty of accumulating knowledge from wheresoever it came, and a wonderful memory helped him to retain facts, figures and names. In the course of conversation, in a newspaper article, in a book, on a poster or in a theatre anything that seemed of interest would be stored away in some pigeon-hole of his memory. At some future time it would be produced, embellished by apt association and a brilliant delivery. His vast store of learning was the envy, not only of professional speakers, writers and politicians, but also of artists. When the American critic Finck was speaking about Paderewski's erudition, the pianist Reisenauer, jealous of Paderewski's success, interrupted him with the words : " Yes, he knows everything, except music." People were almost as eager to converse with him as to listen to his playing. Friends particularly enjoyed his company, as he never failed to leave them with a feeling of pleasure and optimism. He hated gloomy faces ; he hated a pessimistic attitude. People in whom failure did not automatically evoke a determination to win a new success were worthless for him ; people who did not possess sufficient self-restraint to hide their sorrows from the outer world were not acceptable company. Paderewski's own mentality was too active and too nervous to allow him to brood over a failure, and as he had trained himself so well to conceal all forms of inner depression, he inevitably expected a similar attitude in other people. The man who could make a good joke, who took defeat cheerfully, who enjoyed good food and good drink, was sure to make friends with Paderewski.

Even as men delighted in his charm and his brilliant intellect, so women adored the flattery of his manner. The best traditions of ancient social life in Poland seemed re-incarnated in him. Indeed, he had the art of making a Queen remember that she was a woman, and of making every woman forget that she was not a Queen. He was sensitive to feminine beauty, and the feminine element was a necessity to him, less in the form of intimate relationships, than as a constant atmosphere in which he liked to move.

In the course of years in a career like his susceptibility to flattery could not be avoided. It fitted into the whole bright scheme of things. He did not care to hear adverse opinions about himself or about his art. As the years went on, ever fewer of his friends dared to make a critical remark ; they adored him, but they also feared him. His friendship and his loyalty meant a great deal not only in themselves but also in their potentiality. Paderewski believed that no one knew him as well as he did himself ; no one knew his methods as well as he, and therefore no one had the right to criticize. To him criticism was not a form of friendship or loyalty.

CHAPTER SIX

THE MASTER OF THE HOUSE

I

EVEN now, as the acknowledged great virtuoso, whose musical artistry seemed in logical agreement with the general æsthetic tenor of his life, Paderewski still remained in his heart a true descendant of the Polish country nobility. Brilliant drawing-rooms with admiring women and appreciative men, concert-halls with ecstatic crowds, luxurious hotels with gilded chandeliers were all very well, and he certainly enjoyed them. Nevertheless, the peasant wants his land, he wants a portion of the soil, with trees or vegetables that belong to him; he is not satisfied with impersonal property invested in the vaults of vast banks in London or New York, but desires property that can be enjoyed with eyes and hands. Paderewski too must have begun to feel like this. It was easier to sleep each night in a different bed, each with its imitation Louis XV curtains, if one knew that somewhere there was a bed that no one else had slept in before one's arrival or would sleep in after one had gone. But Paderewski was not a sentimentalist, and he had a very shrewd knowledge of his own tastes. He had seen the most attractive side of *le grand monde*, and he had enjoyed the luxuries of modern society, without surrendering to them. He would not have wished to give them up, even when he stepped into the kingdom of the Polish peasant. He would not have wished to follow the example of the literary sentimentalists, who expected to find the powers of the earth and the sun by moving amongst the flowers of a picturesque but uncomfortable Elizabethan cottage.

He wanted his own land, but he also wanted the luxurious comforts that he had learned to appreciate during the last ten years ; and he wished to repay the many debts of hospitality that he had incurred in all these successful years. The Polish peasant in him was not the peasant of striving avarice, but the squire with the most noble ancient traditions, with the open hand and the grand inviting gesture of the " *szlachcic* " (nobleman). In some of Chopin's Polonaises he used to play the stately step and the grand manner of that peasant who had become a nobleman.

He had not yet had enough time to become a collector and connoisseur. He could be enthusiastic over a Chinese vase or a Florentine Madonna, but he would never lose himself in them, forgetting the room in which they stood, the thousand other things in life, which might be equally delightful. His house should not be a collector's paradise : it must be rich and hospitable, it must have flowers and fine ornaments, but at the same time good beds ; a lovely view on to a lake or mountains, but also good food and excellent wines.

The wish for a home of his own was, however, of less importance than the desire for a place in which his son Alfred would be comfortable. Alfred was keen and intelligent, but he could not walk, and had to be wheeled about in a bath chair. A large garden, at once peaceful and interesting, must be the main consideration.

II

For a number of years Paderewski had been to Amphion, on the Lake of Geneva. One of his most intimate friends was the instigation of the visits : the Princess Brancovan, one of those women who attracted him by their artistic sensibility and their physical beauty. He loved women who were musical without being priggish, elegant without being flashy, carrying distinction without haughtiness. The beauty of Princess Brancovan was striking, almost exotic :

" *Elle ressemblait sans nul défaut aux gracieuses Vénus des musées d'Athènes, de Florence, de Naples, de Sicile.*" Her ancestors came from the island of Crete : her father, a noble Cretan, was in the Turkish diplomatic service and represented the Sultan at the Court of St. James's. She herself was born in Constantinople, whence she came to London. She never could forget in her later life that as a girl she had been allowed to sit once on Queen Victoria's knees. She lived in London until she married Prince Brancovan, one of those Rumanian aristocrats, whose school was St. Cyr, who found their spiritual home in Corneille, Racine and Molière, and their physical home anywhere between the Black Sea and the Sussex Downs, between the *Rive Gauche* and Vienna. Prince Brancovan and his wife divided their existence between Paris and Amphion, where they had a beautiful estate. The borders of the Lake of Geneva formed the fashionable background of a life of wealth and social culture. There were many elegant estates and delightful villas built by some of the finest French or Swiss architects of the eighteenth and early nineteenth centuries ; there were also historical old châteaux with a romantic past and a luxurious present. The life of cultured leisure that at a later period and in more obvious and less æsthetic form was led by European society on the French Riviera centred in those days round the charming Lake of Geneva. At Pregny lived the Baroness de Rothschild, whose glittering yacht, *Gittana*, seemed to embody all the luxurious comfort of the late Victorian days. At Prangins lived the French sugar king, M. Say, in a house that was famous for its past and was to become notorious in the future : it had belonged to Prince Jérôme Napoléon, Napoléon the Third's cousin and rival, whom a frivolous world called *Plonplon* ; and some thirty-five years later it was to become the home in exile of the last Habsburgs, Charles and Zita, and the starting-point of Emperor Charles's fatal flight to Hungary. Monsieur Say's magnificent yacht was as impressive as any of the plutocratic toys that were gliding across the green waters of the lake, and the receptions at his residence were as brilliant as those in any of the houses along the shore, houses in which art was an accompaniment to their daily lives. Many writers and composers and painters also lived round the lake, and the artistic life was not less active than the social.

The Princess Brancovan was passionately devoted to music, in which she found especial consolation after the death of her husband. Paderewski came to Amphion during the early years of her widowhood. He was introduced to her by Leschetizky's wife, Annette Essipoff. There began a deep and devoted friendship. Paderewski soon became one of the most intimate friends of the family, and used to stay with them for months on end. His first appearance at Amphion was thus described in later years by Anna, the daughter of the house : " *Ainsi vint chez nous, un jour d'avril vers quatre heures, baigné des rayons du plein soleil alors qu'il montait dignement les quelques marches, éclairées par un blanc vitrail, qui menaient au salon de peluche bleue, Ignace Paderewski. . . Je vis une sorte d'archange aux cheveux roux, aux yeux bleus, purs, durs, examinateurs et défiants, tournés vers l'âme.*"

The Princess possessed a yacht *L'Ariane* ; often in the evening they would sail out : Paderewski, his hostess and her two daughters, sometimes only one, Anna, who wrote so beautifully about him. She was a passionate yet self-controlled girl with jet-black hair, thick eye lashes surrounding brilliant dark eyes, the determined chin of the Duchess of Mantua in the Adoration by Rubens, and an exquisitely chiselled nose. Often after Paderewski had finished playing, she would begin to talk in beautifully rounded sentences and words, full and rich like the whole of her sensuous personality. Paderewski loved the sound of the voice that inspired him ; he appreciated the beauty of her words ; he loved the ennobling influence of Anna's youthful company, although at the time he could not know that she was one day to become one of France's most exquisite poets, the Comtesse de Noailles.

He was given a room of his own, *solitaire de la tourelle,* where he practised for hours every day. In Amphion his music was treated with an almost religious reverence ; it deeply affected both the hostess and her children. " *La musique chantait par ses mains avec quelque chose de parfaitement proche du divin, répandant avec une pensive abondance les larmes de Niobé, le sang des héros invisibles. Elle accordait à la nostalgie, à l'exil, aux sublimes souhaits, à tout ce qui est errant et mendiant dans l'espace un toit auguste et charitable.*" But it was not only the pianist who was appreciated at Amphion : Paderewski the man was as much admired, and his personality inspired every member of the family. Anna de Noailles wrote some forty years later that Paderewski simply saved her soul, the soul of an exalted and precocious child. " *Ce n'est pas seulement la guérison d'une vie blessée par le regret filial et l'ennui songeur que je devais à Ignace Paderewski, c'était une réintégration de toutes mes forces d'espérance . . . Cet enchanteur puissant, sérieux, possédait la noble faculté de ne rien dédaigner . . . C'est par son respect pour un monde auquel je n'étais pas habituée, que Paderewski me sauvait.*"

Paderewski felt that his spiritual home was here. The countryside was lovely. The thought occurred to him also how ideal it would be for Alfred to have a suitable place somewhere near.

Alfred had for years been living with Paderewski's great friends the Gorskis. Gorski was a Polish violinist of some distinction. He was married to Helena de Rosen, the daughter of a nobleman from the Baltic and of a Greek mother. Mme Helena's dark Eastern beauty was much admired not only in Poland but also in London and Paris and the other cities which she visited with Gorski on his concert tours. Mme Gorska had known Paderewski since his youth ; they were great friends and she had a profound admiration for Alfred's father. Paderewski's strenuous life, spent between trains, hotel apartments and concert-halls, was out of the question for his invalid son. The Gorskis brought him up with their own son, who was about

Alfred's age. In the summer Paderewski liked them to take a house in the country where the boy would be happy and where friends could occasionally come to stay. Generally it was left to Mme Gorska[1] to find a suitable place. One day in 1897 the Princess Brancovan told Paderewski and the Gorskis that there was a large property to let, Riond Bosson, across the lake from Amphion. Mme Gorska went to see it. There was a large room on the ground floor from which Alfred could be wheeled in his bath chair straight on to the terrace, and from which he could easily be carried to his pony carriage. Mme Gorska took the house and they spent the next summer there. In 1899 Paderewski was in particular need of a quiet place, where he could work undisturbed : he was trying to finish his first opera, which he had been composing for the past two years ; but when the summer came to an end, the opera was still unfinished. Paderewski tried to obtain an extension of the lease, but the owners insisted upon his either leaving or buying the place. Paderewski could not possibly leave the house in the midst of his work. Almost against his will fate had chosen a home for him which, with all its possible drawbacks, was to fulfil his deeper ambitions for a home.

III

Riond Bosson lay only a mile or so outside the charming old town of Morges, near Lausanne. The garden sloped down towards a big open space like a village green, and beyond it lay the Lake of Geneva, the Alps and Mont Blanc. The place had been built by Fouché's widow, the Duchess of Otranto, in 1823 ; a famous French garden architect had designed the garden. After her death it became the property of her relative the Count de Marois. Marois left it to his nephew the Count D'Estournelles, who in 1883 built a large house in the style of the period, elaborate, and without any consciousness or unity of style. There

---

[1] The feminine ending in Polish names with " ski " and " cki " is " a " ; e.g. Paderewski's wife is Mme Paderewska.

were balconies with balustrades of wood such as were seen
on Swiss peasant cottages ; a terrace suggesting a French
château, and columns that were half-way between a strange
Renaissance form and the first discoveries of " *Art Nouveau*."
With all that, its general appearance suggested the kind of
chinoiserie that had been fashionable in France for some
years. In 1883 the house had a certain curious beauty
and originality, and it was sumptuous and comfortable.
The gardens were lovely. Near by stood charming old
houses in the best traditions of Swiss country architecture
of the eighteenth century. The nearest village, with its
central church, was Tolochenaz. It was an old Swiss name,
but it sounded exotic, while the name Riond Bosson had
a certain distinction.

Soon before its acquisition the marriage of the Gorskis
was annulled. Towards the end of May, 1899, Paderewski
married Mme Helena in the Cathedral in Warsaw.

IV

From the moment Mme Helena fell in love with
Paderewski, it was not only her future husband whom she
worshipped in him, but also the outstanding artist. Although
intellectually he was her superior, she was able to substitute
an accurate instinct for what she lacked in culture and
musical education. Coupled with her great love for him,
this was to prove a tremendous power. Things she did not
know she seemed to acquire by a process of emotional
assimilation. He represented to her everything that an
heroic genius might mean to one who was not only an
adoring wife but also a sensitive woman. It is doubtful
whether she really cared for music ; but as music was the
perfect medium for the expression of her husband's feelings,
she tried to understand it in order to find him in it. It
was perhaps a strange mixture—romantic adoration and
a strong instinct in an otherwise matter-of-fact woman—
but they became the guiding principles of her married life
with Ignace. She accepted joyfully the rôles of wife and

helpmate. She helped him most efficiently in all the thousand little details of a life preoccupied with art ; she protected him from people ; she saw to it that he always had the right conditions for work, for leisure and for enjoyment ; she stimulated him to ceaseless work ; she prevented him from spending too much money and re- strained people from taking advantage of his generosity. In financial matters she kept a cool head and controlled Paderewski's enthusiasms. One day a deputation of Polish students arrived at their hotel in Dresden and asked him to contribute to an important charity for Polish students. Paderewski was full of enthusiasm, and when the students thanked him, he answered : " It is I who should thank you for having come to me, thus showing me that you trust me and that you know that I shall not disappoint the youth of Poland." When he got up and went to his desk to make out the cheque it was Mme Helena who named the sum which she considered adequate to the occasion.

Even more important than her assistance in the petty difficulties of an artist's existence was the less tangible psychological help which she was able to afford. Paderewski was very highly strung, and his work and his eminent position increased that natural tendency. Behind his mental energy there was his artistic disposition, and his romantic point of view, neither of which could thrive in a banal domesticity. The counterbalance of serious realism was provided by many long hours of hard work, which were the sobering element of his day. Mme Helena must have known instinctively that it would be wrong to put their personal relations on a basis of prosaic sobriety. She herself was very emotional, and it would not have been easy to submit to such a condition. She felt that she must fan the fire that was within him and that she must reflect his own fervour. This must hold especially of that most important aspect of his life : his concerts. Before his appearance on the platform his nervous tension reached its height, and Mme Helena did not attempt to calm him, but she would

work herself up to a similar state of excitement. They
would sit together in the artists' room, and embrace and
kiss and embrace again, as though he were condemned to
death. When he was just about to leave the room, in a
state of complete exaltation, she would seize his hand, and
put it to her lips without uttering a word. This was done
with a look of drama on her face, almost of terror, and
Paderewski was now in that state of hyper-sensitiveness
which seemed necessary to his playing. Even if her anxiety
was not as great as his, she would still suffer his agonies,
for she knew how much he needed such unmistakable
expressions of sympathy. Although she would do everything to show him how deeply she was stirred by his anxieties,
she was also clever enough to stifle her own exaltation when
this seemed necessary. No annoyance was ever allowed
to upset Paderewski before a concert ; no troublesome
people, nor letter, nor news. Right up to the moment
when he had to leave home for the concert-hall, Mme
Helena would show him a cheerful countenance. Gloomy
faces he always hated. Before a concert such faces or bad
news would cause him actual physical discomfort. After
a concert Mme Helena's instinctive knowledge of the
behaviour required was as effective as before it. From the
very beginning of their married life she had put him on a
pedestal, dazzling in its elevation, and did everything to
make him believe that he deserved that pedestal. This
was probably necessary for the self-assurance which a
virtuoso needs above everything else. When he returned
from the platform into the artists' room, there she was,
waiting for him. Before he had time for a moment's rest,
she would take his hands, raise them to her lips and kiss
them, at first reverently, as though they were the hands of
a saint, then with increasing passion.

Every detail of the life of Niuncio, as she used to call him,
had a deep significance for Mme Helena. Few things,
however, mattered more than his hair. She " believed "
in it with fervour, as though convinced that something of his

art would be lost if anyone else touched his hair. In the morning, on getting up, Paderewski would wait until she was ready to do his hair ; and in later years, even when they did not share the same bedroom, he would wait until she came into his room to attend to her self-imposed duty. She did it lovingly, carefully, with the hands of an expert ; and in the evening, before going to bed, she would come and do his hair again. She herself washed it ; she would not even allow anyone else to cut it ; trimming it herself, and carefully collecting the cut hair, which was never thrown away.

Apart from Niuncio there was only one interest in her life. Music interested her only in connection with him ; the arts, literature, politics mattered little to her ; but she had a passion for animals and birds, particularly hens. At Riond Bosson, with its lovely big garden, she could make this passion her chief hobby. She started a poultry farm, and she applied herself to it almost with the same fervent devotion that she gave to her husband. Experts from all over the world were called to Riond Bosson and the most up-to-date chicken-houses were erected. Every morning soon after seven o'clock she would come down to the lower end of the garden and work amongst the chickens. She tried to propagate rare breeds, and she sent her chickens to most of the big shows in Europe. She even decided that there must be a group of expert poultry breeders in Poland, and a number of Polish girls came at her expense to Riond Bosson, where under her tuition they learned the arts of scientific chicken-breeding. She spent thousands of francs every year on her chickens. Not even in her days of poverty with her first husband Gorski, had she had any real conception of economy. Paderewski himself, quite incapable of looking after money, and in love with his wife, allowed her to spend as much as she wanted. Wonderful orchards were planted and a big hot-house built where they would grow fruit out of season. The adjoining fields were made into vineyards, so that they might drink their own wine. Besides her chickens there were always one or two dogs and a couple of parrots. The lack of a child from her beloved Niuncio may have been responsible for her exaggerated devotion to pets and poultry.

v

Ignace Jan Paderewski was the acknowledged king of pianists, and he lived in a fashion which certain people considered to be the authentic way in which kings lived. His friends throughout the world were men and women famous for their beauty, importance or wealth. His hair was one of the sensations of the new century ; his shirts of Japanese silk were of precious texture and his silk hats were specially ordered from Lock's in St. James's street. He travelled from one end of the world to the other with his private secretary, his French tuner and his valet. In America he had always his own railway coach. Wherever he stayed there would be a Steinway or an Erard piano waiting for him in his room at the hotels ; kings, nabobs, prime ministers and artists begged him to accept their invitations. He had an estate in Switzerland which had belonged to a duchess and which the journalists called his château, a ranch in Paso-Robles in California, properties in Poland and in South America, and the reputation of being the most generous man alive. On the feast of his patron Saint, St. Ignace, his friends came from all over the world to Riond Bosson to celebrate the occasion and the man. The festivities were planned like those for a king's birthday. Guests arrived, deputations called all day long. In the evening two hundred people would sit down to dinner, which was served at the long tables in the illuminated garden, and which lasted for three hours. Theatricals, music by the world's leading virtuosi who had come as guests, dances, presents for the guests, the rarest of wines. St. Ignace's feast day was indeed a royal one.

The features that had once suggested an exotic flower

were changing gradually into those of a lordly animal : the great head with its fiery mane, keen eyes, and nostrils that seemed to savour life, gave Paderewski a striking resemblance to a young lion. He still retained the charm of the young man who used to come on to the platform in Vienna or in Paris with the grace of a ballet dancer, but he now had a dignity in which there were both poise and determination. To meet him was no longer like meeting a famous pianist, with whom one would feel it one's duty to discuss Chopin and the latest Debussy : rather one realized instinctively, that whatever the subject, Paderewski knew it and would command the conversation. His attitude became more authoritative. One knew that contradiction would not be appreciated ; one had to accept him without reserve, or else abandon any hope of contact. The sphere in which Paderewski ruled was no longer confined to that of the concert platform.

His dominating position did not, however, cause him to relax his efforts. He knew that geniuses are not born but made. The supreme gift must be there. Quite a few may have it, without knowing, however, how to use it or bring it to perfection. Only a very few are able, at the height of their success, to work with the same devotion as they did in their early days. Paderewski even now worked for more than ten hours a day : he memorised new compositions, and went over the old ones again and again. He introduced Debussy into his repertoire, and also a certain number of compositions by young composers, such as his pupils : the Pole Stojowski or the American Schelling. In 1909, however, continuous concerts and ceaseless exercises strained his left hand. As far back as 1887, when he was preparing a repertoire and working at times up to sixteen hours a day, he strained his right hand, which was never after entirely without pain when used. Sometimes when playing at a concert he went through real agony. Now, for almost a whole year, he was unable to play. This enforced holiday, however, did not mean inactivity. His friends, his all-round interests, his preoccupation with agriculture at Riond Bosson or with pig-breeding, did not leave him much leisure. He had a passion for growing grapes, not only for his own pleasure, but also to show the grape growers of the Canton what could be done with their soil and the existing conditions. One day an English lady, whose chief interest was gardening, and who knew nothing whatever about music, was being taken over Mme Paderewska's chicken-farm. She had not previously known that her hostess was an expert chicken breeder, and so she thanked her in the deepest admiration : " Really, dear Mme Paderewski, you deserve to be as famous as a chicken breeder as your husband is a vine-grower."

In such times as this year of professional leisure, Paderewski was able to read hundreds of books on politics, history, philosophy and literature, for which he had previously not found the time. The nervous tension of his mind rarely allowed him to settle down with a book. As other people read for hours, Paderewski read for minutes, in any place and at any time. Sometimes he spent hours over his toilet, when dressing in the morning ; but between putting on his waistcoat and his tie, he would walk across the room to a table or a chest on which lay a book ; would pick it up, open it casually, and see at a glance whether it was the right page. He had an amazing aptitude for opening a book exactly where he had left off. He would read one or two pages, standing there with his tie hanging over his arm or walking up and down ; he would turn over ten, twenty or a hundred pages, read another page or the index, put the book down, go back to the mirror and tie his tie, and then return to his book and open it again, at the page he meant to read. Once he had gone over a page thoroughly, it remained in his memory as though he had learned it by heart. Often five or ten minutes would suffice for him to find everything that mattered. How he contrived to select just those pages which gave him the main subject-matter or the centre of the plot is a mystery—

but he did it, not once but a thousand times.   And then he would be able to cite all the main points, describe the author's individuality, expose his faults, and quote his best passages.   With his quickness, his power of concentration, and his active imagination, he conquered the world of books. With the same aptitude he might pride himself that he had conquered the world at large.

VI

Paderewski's favourite piano was still the Erard.   Since his first appearance in Paris in 1888 he had played this old French instrument in most countries of Europe.   He liked its crispness and the distinctiveness of its individual notes. He did not use a specially-built instrument, but any ordinary concert grand that happened to appeal to him.   The only peculiarity about his pianos was in the extra stiffness of the felt hammers, so as to produce a harder and crisper tone. Yet there were innumerable stories current about the special pianos that were secretly constructed for him by Erard ; about the fabulous sums of money that Erard's paid Paderewski ;   about the number of pianos that were used up by him and that could not be used any more after he had played on them.   In reality he never received a penny from Erard's ; if he particularly liked a piano he requested it for his tour. For practising he preferred an upright to a grand, explaining that if the desired effects could be produced on the smaller upright, then they could certainly be achieved on a concert-grand.   The concert-grand for the evening performances was also sent by rail from town to town.

On the very day Paderewski arrived in a town, he would go round to his piano-makers to try out the instrument. He was very worried about the piano on which he was to play and as the evening of the concert came nearer his anxiety increased.   Sometimes he would sit in the show-rooms for two or three hours, playing through the next evening's programme or practising scales, and would then

7

get up with an impatient sigh and exclaim : " I cannot possibly play on such an instrument. It will ruin my career." It was one of his favourite expressions. Generally it was the head of the piano firm, M. Blondel in France, Mr. Adlington in England, or the tuner who would have to deal with the problem. They would reassure Paderewski, tighten up the hammers, retune the piano, but at the end of a few hours' hard work it was the same. " It is quite impossible to play on such an instrument. I tell you, it will ruin my career." Both M. Blondel and Mr. Adlington were wise men and they knew that the best thing to do was to keep quiet while the first symptoms of Paderewski's approaching stage fright manifested themselves. After the concert Paderewski would say " Dolmetsch, that was a wonderful instrument. Keep it for the next tour." And M. Dolmetsch would give an appreciative but enigmatic smile. Dolmetsch was the French representative of the family who were making musical history in England and whose name in Switzerland, their country of origin, had been identified with music for generations. Albert Dolmetsch, a kind little man with a well-cared-for moustache and a sensitive pair of eyes, firmly believed that pianos possess souls. He was as much devoted to them as he was to Paderewski, to whom he always referred as " Maître." Dolmetsch was Erard's chief tuner, and he travelled with Paderewski and his pianos throughout the world. He also had to look after the lighting arrangements and he saw to the special chair which Paderewski used on the platform. It could be folded and packed with the luggage. As Paderewski's body was in proportion rather bigger than his legs, he needed a particularly low chair. Dolmetsch was an excellent pianist himself, and whenever Paderewski's piano produced a not quite perfect note it gave M. Dolmetsch acute pain.

Paderewski liked these men who surrounded him in the hours of preparation and whose job it was to see that the technical side of his concert was a success. His agents,

The Van with the Three Pianos for One of Paderewski's Tours in England

his piano makers, his tuners adored him. They remained undisturbed by Paderewski's angry outburst when he was testing the piano. After the storm was past Paderewski treated them as members of his family ; they were given presents, invited to supper, asked to spend their holidays at Riond Bosson. Old Mr. Adlington, whom Paderewski called the " Governor " and who spoke of Paderewski as the " Boss," worshipped him. Privately he and the other members of the Erard family referred to Paderewski as " Paddy."

The piano was not the only thing that taxed Paderewski's patience and nerves, and that gave his agents and tuners some anxious moments. There was also the lighting : Paderewski could never play in a lighted hall. The white, brightly lit keyboard was an agony to him and ruined his concentration ; in fact, any light distracted Paderewski and strained his eyes. A dim light somewhere in the farthest corner of the hall was all that he would allow. Sometimes they spent hours arranging the lighting to his satisfaction. When it was found that technically it was not possible to dispense with some light or other, Paderewski would give the attendant what some friends used to call his leonine look, and with a tragic sigh would say : " That light will ruin my whole career ! "

PART TWO

THE STATESMAN

CHAPTER ONE

THE THIRTEENTH POINT

I

MORE and more did Paderewski feel the need of giving expression to his fondness for Poland. His future as a pianist was assured and that part of his life had long been transmuted from an ideal to a reality. His rich nature, however, did not easily confine itself to one channel, especially as his constant preoccupation with the future of Poland strengthened his political interests. His music was one way of approaching the central problem of his life, Poland ; but it was not the only way. Now that his artistic ambition had been achieved, he might look to more tangible means of serving the cause of Poland. He could become a professional politician or write on behalf of Poland ; which would mean the immediate sacrifice of his artistic career, and the choice of a medium that hitherto had lain outside his nature. Whatever the medium, it must have artistic significance.

No one had a deeper knowledge of the ideal for which he was about to work than Paderewski himself. His study of Chopin had helped him to grasp the finest subtleties of the Polish mind. The step from his artistic past to a new political future by no means implied the negation of those former studies, but rather the reverse. His almost natural approach to political activity presented itself in the form of oratory, for oratory or its social form, conversation, had always been one of Paderewski's passions. He appreciated wit, but he had not lost a certain *naïveté*, which made him enjoy even the simplest of jokes.

Epigram and witty conversation, however, were the poor relations to oratory. Now that oratory seemed the natural medium for his political activities, it had to be raised to an artistic level. Paderewski set out to perfect himself in the right use of words, and studied to enrich his already large vocabulary. Although he knew both French and English well, he began to take English lessons and he spent many hours studying French. It was his ambition to express himself in a foreign language, English or French, with even more beauty and precision than a native might do.

Once the new instrument was found, all he needed was an excuse for its application, and it was natural that art should provide that excuse. But if he were to perform, the issues might be confused, and therefore the artistic excuse must be provided by a different artist and in a medium other than Paderewski's own. He commissioned the young Polish sculptor, Antoni Wiwulski, to create a large monument in bronze to commemorate the Polish victory over the Prussian "Teutonic Order" at Grünwald in 1410, one of the great victories in the history of Poland. He himself would pay for it and present it to Poland as the first tangible manifestation of his feelings towards his country. The subject was chosen deliberately. Paderewski was not a chauvinist ; his love for England, his admiration for France, his intimate connections with America, his friendships in a number of other countries saved him from provincialism. He admired the Germany of Beethoven and Goethe, of the philosophers, of scientific achievement, of musical appreciation, of the romanticism of Eichendorff and Möricke ; he owed a debt of gratitude to his musical teachers in Germany ; he knew long passages from Lessing and Schiller by heart, and he loved quoting them ; he had the greatest admiration for the culture that came from the Rhine, from southern Germany with its characteristic ancient towns and its romantic scenery—but he hated Prussian aggression as he saw it in the rule of the Hohenzollerns, and the argument of the mailed fist revolted him. The terms "justice," "fair play," and

" right above might " had some meaning for him.   In the deeds of the Knights of the Teutonic Order, the " *Kreuz-ritter* " of the fifteenth century, he saw a contemptible menace.

The inauguration of the Grünwald Memorial was considered of great political importance, not only in Poland.   A number of foreign newspapers sent their special correspondents to Cracow, where the ceremony was to take place; thousands of Poles came from all over the world.   Standing at the foot of the unveiled monument, Paderewski delivered his speech.   After he had finished the enthusiasm of the crowd was enormous.   Besides beauty of form there was in his speech that clarity and persuasiveness which is the mark of the orator, and that deep ring of sincerity to which no audience is insensible.

Paderewski had spoken on Polish subjects on several previous occasions, his most important speech having been delivered as far back as 1898 at the Town Hall in Warsaw ; but the Grünwald speech put him for the first time on the political platform in full view of the whole world.   He now realized that he could use his powers of oratory in the same way as he used the piano.   When in October, 1910, during the Chopin celebrations in Lwow, he made another speech, it was again the artist who spoke, not the politician. He did not impress his listeners by argument, but enchanted them by imagery.

II

Before his gift for speaking enabled him to impress an audience it had helped Paderewski to make friends among statesmen and politicians of various countries.   They were fascinated by his conversation, and his keenness on politics created a common ground of understanding.   After a dinner-party the politicians and diplomats present would surround Paderewski in order to discuss political matters with him, or else to glean something from his vast store of historical and political knowledge.   Riond Bosson was

generally the meeting-place of such of his friends as
Arthur Nikisch, Felix Weingartner, Sembrich-Kochanska,
Laurence Alma Tadema, Josef Hofmann and Melba, while
the many cities in which he gave concerts offered him opportunities of meeting those men whose conversation would
turn not on music, but on politics : Aristide Briand, Stephen
Pichon, Asquith, Arthur Balfour and Theodore Roosevelt.
His intimate friendships with many of the leading statesmen
of Europe and America paved the way for future political
activity. The gifts of oratory and conversation were the
tools for such activity ; human contacts provided a very
important, if more impalpable, introduction. Within a few
years Paderewski came to be considered one of the experts
on matters connected with the problems of Poland.

III

When war broke out, Paderewski was at Riond Bosson.
It was particularly fortunate that he lived in Switzerland.
Had he lived in Poland or in any of her neighbouring
countries, his activities would have been greatly curtailed.
Besides neutrality, Switzerland had other favourable
qualifications. She could pride herself on being the traditional refuge for Poles who were endeavouring to fight
for their country's independence. Her ideals of humanitarianism and liberalism made Switzerland a most popular
country with political, religious and even intellectual rebels
and combatants. Most of the great Polish poets, men like
Mickiewicz or Slowacki, whose national ambition was the
basis of their artistic creation, had spent part of their lives
in Switzerland. One of Poland's (and, incidentally,
America's) greatest military and patriotic leaders, Kosciuszko,
lived during the last years of his life in Switzerland, in
Solothurn, where he died in 1817. In the twentieth century
that tradition was still alive. Two Poles who were teaching
as distinguished professors at Swiss Universities were to
become in later years Presidents of the new Polish Republic :

Gabriel Narutowicz and Ignace Moscicki. Henryk Sienkiewicz, Poland's most famous contemporary novelist, author of *Quo Vadis* and winner of the Nobel Prize, lived not far from Riond Bosson, at Vevey. As soon as war broke out, the shores of the Lake of Geneva became the centre of Polish political activities. Lausanne, Vevey and Morges became overnight the headquarters of the various Polish parties. Of the many groups formed in Switzerland and in other countries, the leading one was the National Committee, first in Warsaw, then in Petrograd, eventually in Paris, and headed by Poland's foremost politician, Roman Dmowski. The Committee represented the anti-German, pro-Ally, Western outlook in Polish politics ; it was Conservative, anti-Socialist and nationalist ; it worked only by lawful methods, on a basis of " *Realpolitik* " ; it tried to unite in its hands all Polish activities in the Western world. In 1917 the Committee was recognized as the true organ of the Polish cause. Paderewski was appointed its chief delegate to the United States ; Dmowski was its head ; Erazm Piltz its delegate in France ; Konstanty Skirmunt in Rome and Count Sobanski in London.

Roman Dmowski, leader of the National Democrats, the most important political party in Poland, was one of the few Poles who, even under Russian rule, was given an opening for political activity. His early scientific education as a biologist made him a realist in politics. After a quasi-revolutionary start he came to the conclusion that Poland could find her freedom only in collaboration with Russia and not with Germany or with Austria. He stood as a candidate for the second and third Russian Duma, in which he became the leading Polish parliamentarian. He was intelligent, shrewd, well educated, an excellent linguist and a man of the world. He showed great charm, if he wanted to, which he did mainly when women were present. Unfortunately he was a cynic ; his convictions were purely intellectual ; his reason overshadowed his imagination. He believed that the world was ruled by secret organizations, working in the dark and by international Jewry. He became a violent anti-Semite and antagonized both the Jewish masses and the Jewish intelligentsia. This accounted in the main for the reluctance on the part of Polish Jews to join in any activities aiming at national independence. For many of them Polish independence was linked with Dmowski's hatred of the Jews. As dangerous as his anti-Semitism was Dmowski's tactlessness, which he scarcely troubled to disguise ; but his political experience and his intelligence were so dominating that practically the whole conservative element in Poland submitted to him. He also impressed foreign politicians, Sazonoff in Russia, Balfour in England and Clemenceau in France ; they appreciated his political perspicacity and his lucidity of thought. His looks showed his intellectual qualities, his moral determination and, above all, his outstanding personality, though they also betrayed a lack of personal charm : his chin was strong and massive, his eyes were penetrating but impersonal and without warmth. He was appreciated by many intellectually, emotionally by few.

IV

From the point of view of a sensitive and patriotic individual like Paderewski, the Polish problem was overwhelming. It was the problem of a country of ancient civilisation, with its own rich language, religion, literature, art, with old traditions and customs, with a burning national consciousness, yet without freedom : in fact, without any political existence. The partition of Poland, one of the most dangerous blunders in history, had not yet been rectified. At the same time a generation was rising, to which all other human problems were of secondary importance, dominated as it was by purely national aspirations. The cowardliness of Western European statesmen of the nineteenth century, the selfishness and the family considerations of the crowned heads of Europe, the stupid shortsightedness of the governments under whose rule Poland was allowed to lead her unreal existence, became responsible for one of the most acute political problems of modern Europe. Paderewski was deeply convinced that the moment of Poland's final liberation was near. Exactly a hundred years earlier one of the world's shrewdest diplomats, Talleyrand, had put into prophetic words the same conviction. The sage prediction of Europe's most experienced statesman painted in 1815 the exact situation with which Paderewski was confronted a hundred years later. Talleyrand had written : " By remaining partitioned Poland will not be destroyed for ever. The Poles, although not forming a political entity, will always form a family. They will no longer have a common country, but they will have a common language. They will, therefore, remain united by the strongest and most lasting of all bonds. They will, under foreign domination, reach the age of manhood, and the moment when they reach it will not be far distant from the moment when, having won their freedom, they will all rally round one centre." Such a restoration of Poland could only be achieved if the Allied leaders, when leading the world out of war into victory, could be made conscious of that historical crime of 1795. But if these men were to be sympathetic when the time came for readjustment, they would have to be backed by their own national public opinion, which had to be educated even as they themselves ; the name of Poland, forgotten for so long in the political world, must sound again from chancelleries and from editorial offices ; the world must be made conscious of a brutal crime, for the reparation of which the moment had come. Antagonistic propaganda, directed by enemies with unlimited means, had to be countered. The real nature of Poland had to be shown to the world : not that distorted nature which was the result of more than a hundred years of Russian and Prussian régime, but that which existed before. Such a work of enlightenment would be colossal : propaganda work of the most elaborate and varied description.

V

Paderewski decided to go to the United States to undertake this work. In no other country outside Poland were there so many Poles as in America, almost three millions. No other country could supply so much money to prepare the Polish cause and to relieve the devastated, war-stricken Polish countryside. America itself was of the utmost importance in any Polish propaganda. A voice raised in the neutral United States would more easily be heard in other countries than if it came from behind the frontiers of one of the belligerent nations. The work of Polish propaganda in the States would be a whole-time job. Paderewski realized this and decided temporarily to give up the piano as a career. He was aware that propaganda alone would not suffice, that he would have to be orator, diplomat and statesman, as well as propagandist.

Few men were better fitted for the work in America than Paderewski : his name was more famous in the United States than that of any other foreigner, and many of the country's leading men were his friends. He became the official delegate of the National Committee to the United States. In itself the appointment meant but little : what mattered was Paderewski's individual activity. He made several journeys across the American Continent, delivering speeches at universities, in working men's or women's clubs, in concert-halls and theatres, addressing crowds of ten thousand and groups of a few hundred ; coupling the name of Poland with the future victory of the Allies, in which he had complete confidence. The tickets for his public lectures were generally very expensive, the money being spent on Polish charities. Nevertheless, he never spoke in a hall that was not crowded to overflowing. He would speak for about half an hour stating the case of Poland, and afterwards he would sit down at the piano on the platform and would play Polish music, mainly Chopin. That roused the people's emotions, showing them another aspect of the problem.   Paderewski gave over three hundred of these concerts combined with speeches, and after each one of them the cause of Poland was a little more advanced.   Lord Reading, one of England's soundest judges of oratory, remarked when Paderewski had spoken after him at a large festival in New York in 1918, that the Polish pianist's speech was the finest oratorical achievement he had ever heard.

For the majority of American citizens the name Poland became synonymous with the name Paderewski.   Never before in the history of America was the name of Poland so widely known as it now became through the efforts of Paderewski.   Simultaneously Paderewski was spending his vast fortune on numberless charities.   They were generally connected with Polish sufferings and with political preparation for Polish independence ; but he gave large sums also to a number of foreign charities, mainly connected with the sufferings inflicted by the war upon citizens of the Allied nations.

As in the countries of Europe, many Polish individuals and political bodies in America were at work with the freedom of Poland as their ultimate goal ; but before Paderewski's arrival they were divided among themselves, and it was due entirely to him that they achieved unity.   Describing this situation, Colonel House says : " When Paderewski reached America, the entire situation under his direction was immediately changed.   He gave to the American Poles a single purpose, checking all futile and scattered desires. . . . . Having foreseen before others the part the United States was to play in the great tragedy, Paderewski never lost faith in the ultimate outcome. . . . In what measure the efforts and sagacity of Paderewski were crowned by success may be gauged by the fact that towards the end of 1916 his countrymen in America, without dissent, chose him as their plenipotentiary, conferring upon him power of attorney to act for them and decide all political matters in their name and on their behalf. . . . Paderewski encouraged Polish youth to enter officers' training schools, and presently he brought about the foundation of a Polish organization for the training of officers. Finally, when the United States entered the war, he sounded an eloquent call to arms."

Any of Paderewski's political declarations were reproduced conspicuously in the American press, that always took them for authoritative statements. The German Ambassador in Washington, Count Bernstorff, wrote in a letter to the Chancellor Bethmann-Hollweg, how well informed the American press was about all Polish matters, and that this was due to Paderewski's activities.

More important, however, than all these activities were Paderewski's contacts with one or two American individuals.

VI

In the summer of 1916, a big evening party was in progress at the White House in Washington. Dinner had been over for almost an hour ; the men had joined the ladies, and the guests were assembled in the big drawing-room. Some of the curtains had not been drawn : through the windows one could see the outlines of old trees in the garden. One or two rooms in the distant Government Offices still sent a yellow beam of light into the dark night. It was hot and rather close. The room, with its neo-classical walls and ceiling, had the characteristics of Colonial domesticity and the dignity of Georgian architecture. Most of the heads of the foreign missions in Washington were present with their wives ; so were the members of the Government and some of the more distinguished citizens of Washington and New York. Conversation had ceased, the guests seemed eager for something. The keenness in their faces betrayed an inner excitement. It was not the anxious excitement of the past two years that was brought about by news from the European war zones, but an air of curious expectancy. Someone opened the shiny black grand piano. All eyes were turned towards it. The man at the piano—vigorous-looking with a crown of reddish-silver hair—had also been at dinner. Ignace Paderewski. Someone whispered : " Do you know, he has not touched the piano in a private house for two years ? " The whispered answer flew from one guest to another : " Yes, and he only consented to play to-night because the President begged him to do so."

The silence was almost uncanny ; as though every breath might rob the listeners of some unusual gift. Paderewski played Chopin, nothing but Chopin. Not far from the piano sat a man with a large, pale face, a calm brow and a heavy chin. He was leaning forward slightly, as though trying to absorb the notes that came from the instrument. His kind eyes behind rimless pince-nez were focused on some pattern in the carpet, and he seemed to want to avoid the glances of other people. This was Woodrow Wilson, the host, and President of the United States. He was not particularly musical, but he had the same high opinion of music which he held of any of the nobler expressions of human genius. He sat in silent concentration given up to Chopin's melancholy cascades. It was not by coincidence that Paderewski had chosen Chopin. The breach of his silence did not mean the continuation of his career as a pianist ; the piano was nothing more than the instrument of deliberate patriotic service. More than any words Chopin would be able to reveal to the President the true Polish spirit, in its longings. The Polish character of Chopin's music was emphasized in Paderewski's performance, but no one could tell whether any of these national strains were touching the President's sensibility, or perhaps opening some little door to a deeper understanding of the Polish cause.

After Paderewski had finished playing, President Wilson advanced towards the piano and thanked him with the greatest cordiality. The solemnity of his smile showed that he had not remained untouched by the music. A conversation followed, during which Poland was the only subject. Wilson's keen sense of justice and of the rights of men was deeply shocked by the historic crime committed on the Polish nation. It was the sort of cause that appealed to

8

him : its political aspect was for him less important than the larger moral issue. The idea of the rehabilitation of Poland had acquired the attraction of a moral task. He was not a quick thinker, and certainly not a superficial one ; but once an idea struck him as being of decisive importance, he would hold to it, contemplate it and try to find a solution that would satisfy both his theories of justice and his moral beliefs. One could reasonably expect the seed to grow which Paderewski had planted in that heavy but fertile soil.

VII

This contact with the President of the United States was the most far-reaching event of Paderewski's war years in America. It developed into a friendship of decisive importance, both to Poland and to the future map of Europe. Early in 1916, through the industrialist, Robert Wooley, Paderewski had met President Wilson's most intimate friend and adviser, Colonel Edward Mandell House. House was attracted by Paderewski's charm. The brilliant enthusiastic Pole contrasted so strikingly with the silent matter-of-fact House that the latter enjoyed the acquaintance of Paderewski as something unusual and entertaining. Soon after their first meeting House had introduced Paderewski to President Wilson and his wife. He had been asked to dinner and Mrs. Wilson had been charmed from the very first. It seemed certain that the hostess of the White House and her Polish guest would become friends.

The contact with Colonel House soon developed into a very intimate friendship, and the two men were in constant touch with each other. Frequently House would drop in between tea and dinner to discuss with Paderewski the latest political developments and the situation of the European fronts. In House's own words : they " pored over maps— his maps and mine—of Central and Eastern Europe, and together we traced what we thought should be a homo- geneous Poland. . . . The Poland we outlined during those fervid days proved to be practically the Poland created by the Versailles Conference. . . ."

On November 6th, 1916, the Presidential election was in progress, and Wilson had retired to Shadow Lane, a country estate in New Jersey, to await the results. Early in the morning Paderewski drove out from New York to New Jersey to see the President. Wilson had asked Paderewski to come and see him in order to thank him for his support in the election campaign. Paderewski's influence made practically all the Poles in the States vote for Wilson, and even the partly Republican Catholic clergy among the Poles voted for the Democrat Wilson. As was shown later, the Democrats in three big States won a victory through the votes of the Poles.

On the previous day the Germans had published a manifesto in which they declared the independence of Poland. Outside Germany no one believed in its sincerity. People realized that Germany was trying to win over Poland in order to augment her own troops from the Polish population. Wilson had just been reading a number of European telegrams which reported this German step. For him Paderewski had become the supreme expert on Polish affairs. The President had a sincere admiration for the great pianist who was also such a devoted patriot, and whose generosity, whether for Polish or American causes, seemed to know no limits. He was aware of the vast sums that Paderewski was spending on behalf of war widows, on refugees, on orphans and on many other charities, both in Europe and in the United States. His own humanitarianism was touched by that of his Polish guest.

"What do you think of the German manifesto?" he asked after they had shaken hands. Paderewski told him that he took the manifesto to mean only a German desire for more troops, and that he thought it would result in a State without real freedom, dependent upon Germany. Wilson replied : " I am glad to see that we both absolutely agree about the subject."

The moment had come for Paderewski to show the American President the importance and the acuteness of the Polish problem. When Wilson started to explain his own ideas about the future of Europe and the necessity for a new structure, Paderewski began describing the strivings of Poland for independence and the importance to the world of achieving that freedom. Wilson sat silent, his large hands motionless on the arms of his chair. From time to time he interrupted Paderewski, asking for more details, particularly as to the plan for Poland's access to the sea, which especially interested him. Every now and again he nodded. His mouth remained unmoved in its melancholy, kind expression. It seemed as though he were maturing a plan. None of his guest's words would be forgotten.

This conversation lasted for almost an hour. Paderewski had spoken with ardour and sincerity; it was as if he pleaded for a dear friend, suffering wrongful imprisonment. It was not so much a political conversation between two statesmen, as a personal " credo," and the foundation of a friendship in which political questions became personal and moral.

It was an important day in the life of both men. Wilson's fate was not yet decided. Paderewski realized that Poland's fate was more than ever before in the hands of one man ; but a man who was fast becoming a guiding spirit in the world of politics. As they left the room, Wilson stopped and said, in that slow, grave manner which so often gave to his utterances the weight and solemnity of a nonconformist sermon : " My dear Paderewski, I can tell you that Poland will be resurrected and will exist again. For Poland the miracle of independence will come from the West, as my own victory will come to-day through a miracle from the West."

Paderewski realized that by his " West " Wilson meant the Western States of America in the presidential election ; otherwise the President's meaning was not quite clear. But in their obvious sincerity his words were very moving.

Late that night, telegrams announced that Wilson had been defeated and that the new President of the United

States was to be the Republican, Charles Evans Hughes. Paderewski's conversation with Wilson had stirred and excited Paderewski, and he had spent the whole day in a state of expectation and high tension. Now he remembered only too well Wilson's strange words, in which he coupled the resurrection of Poland with his own electoral victory. When Paderewski finally withdrew to his room, he was seized with an attack of sheer terror, under which he broke down altogether. There had been a prophetic ring in Wilson's words, and now the first part of his prediction was shattered.

At 5 o'clock in the morning more telegrams came through to the effect that the news about the victory of Hughes had been wrong, and that, through the weight of favourable votes from the Western States, Woodrow Wilson was for the second time elected President of the United States.

Now that Wilson's power was established for a further four years, would he remember his promise?

VIII

A few months later, on January 8th, 1917, Colonel House visited Paderewski in his suite at the Gotham Hotel on Fifth Avenue and asked him to prepare as soon as possible a detailed Memorandum on the Polish problem. The President, he said, was preparing a very important international statement and that he himself was leaving in a few days' time for Washington to see him. Paderewski shut himself up and worked for thirty-six hours on end. When House left New York on the 11th, he carried in his pocket the detailed exposé dealing with the necessity for an independent Poland. He returned from Washington several days later, and when Paderewski asked him about his Memorandum, House answered : " On my way to Washington I read your text four or five times. I practically learned the essential passages by heart. In the course of the following few days I constantly mentioned during lunch

and dinner your arguments to the President. On a number
of occasions he declared that he absolutely agreed with them.
To-day the President withdrew to his room. In solitude he
is preparing his message. The bomb will explode in a few
days' time. . . ." On January 22nd, 1917, Wilson, for the
first time in his capacity as President of the United States,
spoke of the future of Poland. It was the first time in a hundred years that a leading statesman had dared to mention
on a public platform the need for a new Poland. " Statesmen everywhere," he said, " are agreed that there should
be a united, independent and autonomous Poland." He
foreshadowed the Fourteen Points of a year later. On
January 8th, 1918, his Fourteen Points were announced to
the world. It was exactly twelve months after Colonel
House had invited Paderewski to prepare his Memorandum
on the problem of Poland. The seed planted less than two
years earlier in the President's mind had grown to full
maturity.

In formulating his thirteenth point, which dealt solely with
the necessity of the new Poland with " a free and secure
access to the sea," the President was actuated by his deep,
almost religious convictions. He was assisted by a special
Commission of Experts, which had been appointed to work
out the details and the precise facts upon which the
President's declaration was to be based. Under Colonel
House a Commission of Enquiry was appointed to enquire
into the problems of Poland. Among its most distinguished
members were Robert Lord, Professor at Harvard University, and Walter Lippmann, America's leading publicist.

Woodrow Wilson, the man whose voice rang louder
through the whole world than that of any other of that
time, had become an ardent advocate of the cause of
Paderewski's great love, Poland.

When the war came to an end, Paderewski decided that
his mission in America was completed, and that his place
was no longer abroad, but in Poland. At the beginning of
December, 1918, he left New York and went to Paris,

where he arrived on the 15th. There he conferred with members of the French Government, but mainly with Dmowski and other members of the National Committee, whose pro-Ally policy was now victorious. Together they drafted a memorandum, in which Poland's proposed attitude during the forthcoming Peace Conference was defined. From Paris Paderewski went to London, to approach the statesmen of Great Britain. Although his visit lasted only a very short time, it was long enough to convince him of the popularity he enjoyed amongst the leading men of the country. They trusted him and welcomed his entry into Polish politics. The first person whom Paderewski went to see in London was the Foreign Secretary, Arthur Balfour. The interview between the two men who had known each other for a number of years took place at the Foreign Office. Balfour had assured Paderewski in 1915 of a future Polish independence and he had reassured him on this point again a few years later when they had met in New York. Now Paderewski asked Balfour for the third time whether he still stood by his earlier promises.

Balfour answered : " Of course I stand by them. We all want an independent Poland. In my personal opinion Poland is at present in both a very lucky and unlucky position. Although in England Poland's independence is most sincerely desired, I don't see how she can be represented at the Peace Conference in which her fate will be decided. You know that His Majesty's Government have not recognized the National Committee as the responsible Polish Government. But neither have we recognized the present Polish Government in Warsaw, and the latest news from Poland is anything but reassuring. Yet Poland must be properly represented at the Peace Conference." Balfour paused for a second or two, and then he said with special warmth and emphasis : " It is your task, Paderewski. I want you to go to Poland to unite the Polish hearts."

Paderewski was impressed by Balfour's words ; he agreed entirely with them and he saw their wisdom. He promised that he would go to Poland as soon as possible, but he would only travel there by way of Danzig and Posen, and this could be done only in a British man-of-war. Balfour seemed surprised at such a request and hesitated with his answer. Eventually he said : " It is almost impossible. You can go to Poland by special train with a British convoy, or in a special motor-car accompanied by armed cars. Of course we can put an aeroplane at your disposal. But a warship is hardly possible." It was not the technical but rather the political aspect which seemed to make it difficult for Balfour to make up his mind. But as this question was of the greatest importance, Paderewski remained insistent.

He waited for twenty-four hours. Then an official from the Foreign Office came to see him. All he said was : " I have to notify you that your wish has been granted. You can start on the twenty-first from Harwich." Paderewski asked : " What is the name of the ship ? " " *Concord.*" Was there a connection between the name of the ship chosen by Balfour and the words in which he had asked Paderewski to go to Poland " to unite the Polish hearts " ?

Being loyal to the National Committee, Paderewski went to Paris to report his London negotiations. The Committee were delighted, and Paderewski returned to London the next day.

CHAPTER TWO

H.M.S. *CONCORD*

I

THE sea was rough, and several times the ship had to reduce speed, manœuvring cautiously on account of the mines which blocked the North Sea. But Paderewski did not feel anxious. In fact, he seldom felt safer than he did on board H.M.S. *Concord*. He was accompanied by Mme Helena and by Major Iwanowski, who had been appointed his military A.D.C. Paderewski had a tiresome chill, contracted, no doubt, in the damp atmosphere of London, and Mme Helena insisted upon his going to bed. She even gave up her own comfortable cabin which Captain Paton, who was in command of the *Concord*, had put at her disposal, and instead of a narrow sofa Paderewski was able to use now a proper bunk. It was high and narrow and he could see from it the violent waves splashing against the thick glass of the port-hole, continually plunging his cabin into grey semi-darkness. London had been as helpful as he had expected. The Allies looked upon him as the guardian of law and order, whose very presence would guarantee the application of Western methods to Polish politics. Once again the Western world offered him its assistance. It was of great importance to Paderewski's personal prestige that he should not arrive home via the barbed wire of the Polish-German frontier, but in a fashion which represented power and victory, and not to Polish minds alone. It might have been dangerous to arrive in Danzig and to travel to Poland through German territory. Yet he preferred approaching Poland on board a British man-of-war. Ship- and train-travelling in general formed an important part of his life. Before every significant event in his life there was a long journey with hazy memories of porters and suit-cases, the smell of smoke, and the monotonous rhythm of a locomotive.

Paderewski felt the vibrations of the ship's engines more distinctly than he remembered feeling them before. They seemed to be quite close to his quarters. H.M.S. *Concord* was not a large ship, but Paderewski felt more secure in her than he had in any of the big liners in which he regularly crossed the Atlantic. Altogether it was wonderful to travel to Poland in this fashion. The very kindness of the people on board had impressed him. Both the captain and his officers had been friendly and sympathetic. To Paderewski's especial delight the captain was a good listener and was apparently interested in the future of Poland. After lunch they would sit round the table, discussing the future of Poland, till the captain was called back on to the bridge. Paderewski also liked the young officers in the ship. One evening they invited him to their wardroom. " Imagine telling the chaps at home that while we were manœuvring between the mines of the North Sea Paderewski played for us," said one of them. There was something fascinating in the idea. It would also be a compliment to ask him to play. Paderewski did not hesitate, but he did not realize the ordeal before him. The fact that his musical silence of the last four years had been broken only on very important occasions faded into insignificance before those excited young faces, full of curiosity and expectation. More important, however, was the pedal of the piano, and the piano itself. The day was in the far-distant past when that piano last felt the tuner's skilful touch. The hands that had played on it in the last few years were good and honest hands, but they had not troubled overmuch about the delicacy of those little felt hammers which connected with the keys. The worst, however, was the pedal. Had not Leschetizky, thirty years earlier, insisted on the supreme importance of

correct pedalling ? Such knowledge becomes a part of
one's very nature, certainly of one's muscles. But even
Paderewski with his strong muscles had to abandon the
struggle, when he realized that the pedal would not respond
because it was broken. When he stood up, while the wardroom cheered and clapped, his arms and one leg ached as
after a fight. But when his hosts, rather self-consciously,
apologized for the instrument, he only laughed, assuring
them that he had often played on inferior pianos.

The whole atmosphere of the ship was propitious. There
were no superfluous gestures, no frivolities, only the logic of
necessity. Paderewski's cabin was small. His cabins on
the large trans-Atlantic liners were much bigger and more
beautiful. Here were no panelled walls, no prettily shaded
lamps. For decoration there were just a few pipes that
ran across the wall towards the ceiling, and the walls were
painted in a strange white colour that was neither grey nor
blue, but both, and which he never remembered having seen
before. There was something inevitable in its cold, matter-
of-fact tone. He felt as never before the ship cleaving
the water : one seemed to be nearer the essentials of the
voyage.

II

Throughout his life Poland was Paderewski's one great
love. Until now she had been his distant love, courted
from afar with sumptuous presents, with speeches and with
music. But only across seas and mountains could he
perceive her. When a friend exclaimed, one lovely summer's day at Riond Bosson : " What a blessed country !
Look how gorgeous the snow-covered Alps are ! " Paderewski answered : " I hate them more and more every day.
Don't they hide Poland from me ? " In the course of years
Poland had become more and more a memory, illumined by
the radiance which glows around things past : she was the
idealized mistress, contemplated with sighs and passion.
But now at last the ordeal of waiting was to end. A

marriage would be celebrated, of which the bells of every church in Poland would peal the consummation.

It is doubtful whether, in his fever of expectation, Paderewski quite realized what his trip to Poland might mean. To pass from distant preparation to active contact was not without its dangers. Up till now his preoccupation with Poland had been mainly artistic ; it had not required daily contacts with prosaic reality. It was not the first time that Paderewski tried to identify himself with Poland. He had hoped to achieve it in his compositions. But Poland was in reality not the instrument on which he played, only the key in which he lived. Poland was not like a human being, like speech, like the piano : all these were instruments to him. To descend from the glittering heights on which hitherto he had lived and worked to the solid worries of everyday existence was a dangerous experiment. Would his union with Poland prove a happy match or a fatal entanglement?

Paderewski foresaw clearly his first tasks in Poland. He would have to unite the various political factions so that a united country could, at the forthcoming Peace Conference, assist in the final legalization of her new-found liberty. It would not be easy, as political individualism and particularism were old traditions in Poland. There would be great differences between the men whom he represented, between the National Committee which combined Nationalism with a Western outlook on the one hand, and the Socialists and former pro-German elements at home on the other. He was conscious of the magnitude of his task, but, in addition to his native optimism, there was his joy, which even the voice of national duty could not drown : it was he, at one time struggling to become a piano teacher, who now, on board a British cruiser, was bringing unification and perhaps ultimate independence to Poland.

III

The *Concord* had to call at Copenhagen to take on board the leader of the first British Mission to Poland. It was not without significance that Great Britain's first envoy to Paderewski's country was to meet him before any other of the Polish leaders at home or abroad. Officially there was no Polish State as yet, and he himself was only Mr. Ignace Paderewski. Yet England's envoy was to be received by him first, even before Pilsudski. That name loomed large, and cast a shadow in the cabin. Paderewski had even been entrusted by the British Foreign Office to hand over the Government's instructions to their envoy.

Colonel Wade was announced. Paderewski was in bed. Madame Helena had not allowed him to get up : he would have enough opportunities to catch chills and to ruin his health. Colonel Wade, who until now had been Military Attaché at Copenhagen, was a man in the forties. With his khaki uniform and his quiet demeanour he seemed to bring with him all that natural simplicity of manner which Paderewski so much admired in the British. Colonel Wade's moustache was trimmed close, and his uniform had that masculine smartness which only English uniforms achieve. It was good to be accompanied by such a man. Paderewski sat up in bed, and held out his hand with a cordial gesture. During the short trip from Copenhagen to Danzig Paderewski felt that he had behind him not only the power of the British navy, but also that of the British army. He was almost sorry to leave H.M.S. *Concord*, when early in the morning of December 25th they arrived at Danzig. To show his gratitude, he took off his gold wrist-watch and presented it to Captain Paton, his host.

IV

It was Christmas Day. There were few people about in Danzig, but innumerable flags, flags on every building, every bridge, every gateway : the red flags of Socialism. The quayside was deserted. A cold mist hung over the empty docks. A few Poles arrived to greet Paderewski. They were very excited, particularly at seeing Paderewski in person. They hid their emotion behind a torrent of enthusiastic greetings and half-finished sentences. It mattered little to Paderewski who they were or what they said. He felt the warmth in their voices and he saw the glow in their eyes.

The railway station was near by. In the early afternoon Paderewski boarded a special train bound for Posen (Poznan). The determination that he had felt while he was on board ship was now enhanced by a feeling of joy. After all, he was not a stranger, coming home merely as a messenger from the West. They received him as one of themselves. The saloon-coach was full. Besides Colonel Wade and the two British naval officers, who were accompanying him on his mission, there were Korfanty, the leading Polish politician in the German region of Poland, and one or two other officers and politicians. Half-way to Posen the train stopped, and a German officer entered the carriage. In Danzig they had only seen uniforms with the red Socialist badges instead of epaulettes or marks of rank ; the shabby-looking soldiers had reminded them of disintegration and the nearness of Bolshevist Russia, not of the most powerful army in the world. But there were no signs of humiliation or defeat in the officer who entered the carriage. He clicked his heels and in a loud voice announced that Paderewski would only be allowed to proceed if the train did not stop anywhere on its way to Warsaw ; it was particularly important that he should agree not to stop in Posen. The Province of Poznania was as yet German territory. Paderewski decided to speak to the officer personally. It was the first German officer on duty he had addressed during the years of war, and probably one of the last of the great army. When he emerged from his compartment the officer saluted ; he seemed impressed by Herr Paderewski. The latter explained that he was travelling with orders from the British Government, that the British envoy, Colonel Wade, was going on a special mission to study conditions in Poland, and that he was to meet other members of the same mission at Posen. It went without saying that they would stop at Posen. The officer clicked his heels, and formally repeated his instructions. Paderewski returned to his seat. With anxious eyes Mme Helena enquired what was happening. " Nothing, darling, we are going to Poland, to a free country." Once again Paderewski was coming to conquer Poland from the West. Poland's Western region, Posen, had to be freed before he entered Warsaw, the heart of the country.

The enthusiasm created by Paderewski's arrival in Posen knew no bounds. A wave of national ardour was released. Thousands of people were at the station to see him ; people's cheeks were wet with tears. On the whole it was the German part of Poland which had the greatest sympathy with the nationalist spirit of the National Committee and of Paderewski. The whole town was en fête, and every house was gay with flags. The German Soldiers' Council feared an outbreak, and allowed the display of any flags that people cared to show, and so there were red flags and a few British and French and American ; there were German flags and thousands of the red and white flags of Poland. But during the night shots were fired and certain groups of German soldiers attacked the Poles. Other German soldiers who had not joined in the occupation of public buildings by the Poles were forced from the streets. But most of the soldiers, though they wore the German " Feldgrau," were Poles by birth, and eventually there was not much resistance. Shots were even fired into Paderewski's room at the Hotel Bazar, but after a few days the disturbance came to an end, leaving the Poles master in Poznan. Paderewski had not tried to bring it about. Merely his presence had done it.

When after a few days in Poznan Paderewski finally departed for Warsaw, he was no longer only the Allies' messenger to Poland. The last few days had shown him to be a national hero. At most of the stations on his route there were delegations to greet him. Usually he would come to the door of his carriage to thank them, while Mme Helena stood in the back of the carriage holding his hat over his head in an endeavour to prevent him from catching cold. He needed all his self-control in the face of such universal enthusiasm, and could not but be deeply moved when he realized the strength of the ties between himself and Poland, and the feelings that he was able to inspire in his people.

They were to arrive in Warsaw in the morning of January 3rd. Paderewski had not been in Warsaw for a good many years. The day was cold but bright. On the fields along the railway track one could still see the relics of war : uprooted trees and houses burned to the ground. Slowly the train rolled into the station of Warsaw. The platform was dark with a sea of people, and even before the train stopped, a tremendous cheer rent the air. When Paderewski appeared in the open doorway of his carriage, the enthusiasm became almost an orgy. There were old men and young men, girls and women, soldiers, and school-boys with coloured caps, and they carried little Polish flags and wore badges with the Polish eagle. Nothing seemed the same : the station and the big square in front of it were transformed. There were still the familiar houses : the big Hotel Polonia, the old-fashioned houses with their hundreds of shops in the Marszalkowska Street, the irregular sky line round the vast square ; there were still the old trees of the Jerozolimska Avenue, bare and black at this time of year—but the whole picture was changed, unreal, as though the whole square had become one tremendous waving banner. There were uniforms of the new army with silver tassels and adorned with deep red, with the historical four-cornered caps of ancient Poland ; and " bekeshas " : fur coats with trimmings, high collars and fur cuffs, such as were worn a hundred years ago. How happy Helenka[1] must be. It was wonderful, wonderful.

. . . .

It would have been more wonderful if another man had not been received with similar enthusiasm when he entered Warsaw a few weeks before. That man was Joseph Pilsudski.

[1] Helenka—diminutive of Helena.

CHAPTER THREE

THE MAN AT THE BELVEDERE

I

JOSEPH PILSUDSKI was the son of an impoverished nobleman whose estate in Lithuanian Poland was called Zulow. The family prided themselves on being descendants of the Lithuanian princes Dorszprung ; until the eighteenth century their name had been Giniatowicz. Pilsudski's father, also Joseph, was a landowner of considerable education but limited means. His son Joseph was born in 1867, four years after Poland's last bloody insurrection of 1863 against Russia. He was brought up in an atmosphere of the most fanatical patriotism : in Zulow patriotism was a more vital and sacred thing than religion or love or indeed anything else in life. From his early school-days he was interested in politics and antagonistic to the Russian rule in Poland. As a boy of twenty he was suspected of having dealings with Russian anarchists, was tried, convicted and sent to Siberia, where he spent five years. These idle years of exile clarified his ideas, and hardened his determination to sacrifice everything for the sake of Polish liberty. But these years of dark prisons, of whispered conversations and secret literature also strengthened his natural leanings towards conspiracy. His power of rhetorical persuasion enabled him to win for his schemes friends and followers. The result of his years in Siberia was a plan of political conspiracy by which the masses in Poland, mainly the workmen, should be awakened and prepared for a fight against Russian tyranny. Soon after his return from Siberia Pilsudski became a leading power in the

9

newly founded Polish Socialist Party, the " P.P.S. " But
his romantic and adventurous spirit could not content
itself merely with party work. He created fighting units,
called *Bojowki*, whose chief object was literally to fight
for funds for the new movement. Russian railway trains
carrying government funds were held up in the true Middle
West manner, attacked and robbed. The loot was dis-
tributed amongst the various centres of the Socialist movement. Members of the party who fell into the hands of
the Russian police and were imprisoned were liberated in
the most courageous fashion. The Bojowki performed all
kinds of unlawful and highly dangerous feats. It was a
romance of physical adventure. But Pilsudski's chief aim
was the enlightenment of the people.

The only possible medium for the accomplishment of
that was a newspaper, that should be circulated from
hand to hand, if necessary illegally. It had to be both
Socialist and Nationalist. The production of *Robotnik* (The
Worker) was as romantic as it was heroic. It had to be
done in secret. Pilsudski was not only chief editor but
also printer and distributor. *Robotnik* was printed on
a small hand-press in Pilsudski's private flat in Lodz,
with the help of his wife. Each night the printing-press
was taken down and concealed in different pieces of furniture ; the printed sheets were cut, piece by piece ; the
completed numbers were smuggled out through guarded
railway stations, from one town to another. For years the
Russian police sought the owners of this very influential
newspaper, but it was not until 1901 that they discovered
Pilsudski's flat, and arrested both him and his wife. Both
were sent to prison.

Meanwhile Pilsudski had become the leading spirit of
the Socialist Party, which could hardly afford to lose him
for any length of time. An elaborate, uncanny plan was
formed to liberate him. As it would be easier to free him
from an asylum than from a prison, Pilsudski was to simulate
madness in order to be transferred to a lunatic asylum.

The authorities were hoodwinked, and he was duly sent to an asylum in St. Petersburg. After ten months of this exhausting pretence he was released with the help of a Polish doctor, who led him from the asylum one Sunday evening. Pilsudski fled from Russia to Austrian Poland, where he was safe from the agents of the Russian "Okhrana."

Pilsudski had now realized that the intellectual preparation of the people was not enough, and that Poland could only hope to win back her independence by resort to arms. He decided to form the nucleus of a Polish army. Military books and studies became his absorbing passion, and he studied most of the literature which was to be found in the military libraries of Austria. In a few years he acquired the military knowledge of a life-time. He substituted a fanatical enthusiasm and faith in his cause for the long experience of other military men. The new movement began modestly in the form of a rifle club, which could hardly afford to buy the necessary rifles. It met with some mistrust on the part of the Polish Intelligentsia of Galicia, where it was stationed. But Pilsudski's influence and iron will inspired the younger men, of whom more and more rallied round him. At the end of a few years the rifle clubs had grown to the dimensions of a small army. Meanwhile Pilsudski was building up similar military units among the Poles of other countries. He travelled to France, Germany and even Russia, lecturing on military matters, and collecting more money for the movement.

II

When war broke out in 1914 Pilsudski was the only Polish leader who had anything approaching an army. On the first day he mobilized his rifle clubs, giving them the ancient title of Polish *Légionnaires*, and marched at their head into Russian territory. For him Russia was Poland's greatest enemy. He hated and distrusted Russia so much that he almost forgot the alliance with Germany and

Austria into which he was automatically thrown. The Polish Legions were augmenting in numbers day by day, becoming an army which was to fight gallantly during the first two years of the war. Not without some justification, they prided themselves on being the reincarnation of the ancient Polish knights and warriors with their high ideals.

At first Pilsudski believed that the Central Powers would keep their word and would create an independent Polish State. When he realized that their sole object was to win over his Legions, in order to incorporate them in their own armies, he decided to disband his troops. He even planned a conspiracy against Germany, but the German Secret Service found out that he designed to fly to Russia, in order to found a Polish Legion there. Pilsudski, together with his best friend, Colonel Sosnkowski, was therefore arrested and interned in the fortress at Magdeburg. This act on the part of the German military leaders greatly increased Pilsudski's popularity. He came to be regarded as a national hero, as an almost legendary figure. Picture post-cards of the stern-faced man with the drooping moustache were treasured among the Poles along with the pictures of the saints and of former national heroes, such as Kosciuszko. The Legions worshipped him. The influence which he always had over men, the persuasiveness of his conversation and the simplicity of his manner helped to form a halo round his name.

Pilsudski's personal appearance was eminently suited to the part of the plotting military leader. Thick, bushy eyebrows overshadowed deep-set, dark, piercing eyes, which would at moments lose themselves in an expression of dreamy melancholy, turning sometimes even to gentleness. The presence of a child often had that effect, and it would also bring a smile to the determined mouth, hidden behind the moustache. High cheek-bones and an uncompromising jaw gave him almost the aspect of an Eastern warrior. He was suspicious of most things and of most people. His manner was usually short, but with his soldiers he was jovial;

MARSHAL JOSEPH PILSUDSKI

he enjoyed highly flavoured humour, and he was proud of his prestige amongst his men and their love for him. He had a passion for patriotic literature and, besides, he had a strong vein of mysticism. The extraordinary ups and downs of his adventurous career made him believe in the higher mission to which fate had called him. He discovered subtle relationships full of hidden meanings between him and things around him. His principal hobbies were chess and patience, both of which he accompanied with innumerable glasses of tea and endless cigarettes. He was convincing, but also uncanny. If he wanted, he could be both entertaining and charming. His romantic attitude gave him the air of a warrior in an ancient saga. His position as a national leader of the twentieth century was something of an anachronism ; but he was the perfect figurehead of a country that had lived and struggled for over a century under the almost Oriental rule of Russia, a country that had been forced to adopt at times almost Oriental methods of conspiracy.

When the German revolution broke out in November, 1918, Pilsudski was released, and appeared in Warsaw on November 10th. He was straightway acclaimed as the leader of his country and the commander-in-chief of her new army.

III

Paderewski was not attracted by what he heard about Pilsudski. He did not care for his method of conspiracy. In its mediævalism it seemed crude to a man who had been brought up on the logical architecture of Bach, the elegance of Mozart, the well-controlled passion of Beethoven, the spirit of Chopin, all of which were civilized and exquisite. In Pilsudski and his works there was hardly anything of that world of order which Paderewski had learned to appreciate in thirty years of hard work. There was nothing of the joyous light that was shed by art.

There was also between the two men a fundamental social difference. Paderewski, who came from a very modest milieu, had steadily worked his way up, and in the course of the years had acquired an exceptional position in society. Pilsudski, on the other hand, though poor, was the descendant of a family with the oldest traditions of nobility. He was not indifferent to his aristocratic origins, but he had deliberately descended from them and had chosen a career that for many years had made him an enthusiastic member of the lower classes. His present elevated position had no social but purely political and military foundations. It is very likely that the two men were conscious of the cleavage that their respective positions created, and that they were not quite free from contempt either for the origins or for the achievements of the other.

The purely political problems which confronted Paderewski were fairly simple, although not easy of solution. A Regency-Council, consisting of Prince Lubomirski, Kakowski, Archbishop of Warsaw, and one Ostrowski, after the flight of General von Beseler, the German Governor of Poland, handed over the affairs of the country to Pilsudski. Pilsudski became Chief of State ; the title of President was as yet unknown in Poland. On November 18th Pilsudski commanded the Socialist Moraczewski to form a Cabinet. One of its chief tasks was the creation of a legislative body : a *Seym* (Parliament) which should prepare a new Polish Constitution. New electoral laws were introduced ; the age of franchise was fixed at 21 ; both sexes were included and voting was equal and direct, based on proportional representation. The elements of the Right looked towards the National Committee in Paris, to Dmowski and to Paderewski, and were naturally hostile to Pilsudski and his Socialist ministers. Pilsudski notified the Allies in a wireless message of the " existence of an independent Polish State, uniting all Polish territories," long before those countries were willing to recognize the fact

Friends of English National Opera

present . . .

Dame Eva Turner as Turandot

'Ninety Years On'
A 90th Birthday Celebration
in honour of
DAME EVA TURNER DBE

Monday March 8 1982
The Auditorium, The London Coliseum
8 pm

peakers will include **Dame Isobel Baillie, Lord Miles, Roy enderson, Linda Esther Gray.** Recordings played will include tracts from an unpublished **'Turandot'** at a 1937 Covent Garden rformance. Chairman: **Harold Rosenthal**, Editor, OPERA agazine.

om 7.30 pm Dame Eva will sign copies of her **Golden Voice** cord, which will be on sale in the Stalls Foyer.

ckets: **£2** for guests and **£1** for Friends from the Box Office, at e door or by post from the Ticket Organiser, Friends' Office, The ndon Coliseum, St Martin's Lane, London WC2N 4ES.

Friends of English National Opera

Membership entitles you to Friends Priority Booking, Discount Party Booking Offers, Dress Rehearsal passes, free membership of the ENO/ROH Mailing list, regular meetings and a quarterly magazine.

embership/programme leaflets are in the Foyer, **The London** liseum. Join now and support English National Opera!

or to furnish that help, without which the new State would hardly be able to struggle on.   There was no Government machinery, no serious political or military organization of any kind.   The German military authorities had fled almost in panic, leaving the whole administration in a state of chaos.   Thousands of their unhappy soldiers were left behind without any instructions or the means of returning to Germany.   One of Pilsudski's first tasks was to arrange for their peaceful return.   The political future of the country was uncertain.   The National Committee in Paris insisted on being recognized as a *de iurae* Government. The French were willing to recognize them as such, and were only prevented by British caution from doing it. Such a recognition would have brought about the menace of dual government, which might have led to civil war. The country was divided into the landed and bourgeois classes who sympathized with the Entente on the one hand, and on the other, the mass of workers, small shopkeepers and soldiers, who followed Pilsudski.   Pilsudski could pride himself on holding Poland ; the Committee in Paris had the aid and the assistance of the Allies, and neither could exist without the other.   Paderewski would have to be the ambassador of peace who should bridge the gulf between Dmowski on the one hand and Pilsudski on the other : between Poland in the East and Poland in the West.

IV

A meeting between Paderewski and Pilsudski was arranged. It was to take place at Pilsudski's residence, the Belvedere. This was an eighteenth-century palace, backing on to Lazienki, the lovely rococo park of Poland's most delightful rococo king, Poniatowski.   The route lay through one of the main thoroughfares of the city, the long Ujazdowska Avenue, flanked by the elegant villas and mansions of Warsaw's plutocracy, and with rows of huge trees down the middle.   The trees looked black and bare under a lowering sky. Paderewski's car drove into the courtyard, which was neither large nor imposing. The Palace, built in the manner of the Greeks with classical columns supporting a Grecian portico, was in its austerity simple, almost poor, and there was little of the bright transparency of Greece. The Palace had been built in Russian days, and the simplicity of the Greeks had been transformed into Russian austerity. Soldiers were on guard, soldiers of the new army, in long grey overcoats and four-cornered forage-caps. There seemed to be a good many of them. But there were no butlers or footmen or other servants such as one might expect in the palace of the Chief of State. The soldiers looked with curious eyes at the man alighting from the motor-car. He wore a small brown felt hat and a costly long fur coat reaching almost to the ground, with a large sable collar and sable cuffs.

Paderewski was shown at once into the room in which his host awaited him. It was Pilsudski's private study next door to his bedroom. A sudden gleam of the late sun deepened the shadows in the room. Through the windows one looked into leafless trees and gravelled garden paths. Paderewski was determined that no selfishness or pride should mar their conversation. Both he and his host worshipped the same mistress : there was no reason why they should not combine forces to help her. He wanted to win over Pilsudski to some sort of collaboration with the National Committee. When his eyes became accustomed to the light in the room and he could clearly see his host, it was only by a great effort that he maintained the smile on his lips. " *Dziadek* " (Granddad) they called him in the army. But was there anything of " grand-dad " in those eyes, fixed upon Paderewski, determined to pierce through him? They were shadowed by thick black eyebrows and lashes ; the greying moustache, neglected and too long, did not conceal the fighter's jaw ; even the lofty forehead was militarized by the short, stubborn hair ; the grey tunic, without trimmings, without colour, was plainness itself : it was actually shabby. But Paderewski was determined to be conciliatory.

When both men rose after a long conversation, Paderewski knew that no understanding was possible, and not merely because of a difference of political opinion.   It was as though two planets had tried to revolve on the same orbit.

His car drove back through the cold dark streets with their dim, yellow lamps. Was it then possible that the same country, the same history, the same religion, the same ambition could produce two such antagonistic beings ? The exhilaration of the last weeks was waning.   A dark mountain seemed to overshadow and crush all Paderewski's plans and hopes. Were his lifelong efforts to be set at naught just because another man had reached Poland a few weeks earlier ? Was the sacrifice of his personal convictions not enough ?

The same evening Paderewski was told that Prince Sapieha and a few of his friends were preparing a *coup d'état* against Pilsudski and the Government. The conspirators tried to win him over, but Paderewski was horrified. His ambitions might be crushed, but he would not enter Polish politics on the treacherous wings of conspiracy. If he was to lead his country, it must be in broad daylight ; his personal feelings about Pilsudski had nothing to do with the matter. He immediately left Warsaw and went to Cracow, intending to proceed to Hungary. The Allies had accumulated a great amount of German and Austrian arms in that country, and Paderewski had been given permission to take some of them over for Poland. But he also wanted to await developments and to see in what way his services might be required in Pilsudski's Poland.

The night after his arrival, at about 3 a.m., Paderewski was awakened by loud knockings at the door. Strakacz, his private secretary, came into the room in night attire : " General Szeptycki has just arrived from Warsaw with special orders from Pilsudski." Paderewski jumped out of bed, threw a dressing-gown over his shoulders and went

into the sitting-room where Szeptycki was waiting, looking
even taller than usual in his long grey army overcoat. The
sternness of his greyish moustache and of his soldierly bearing
was relieved by their elegance and by the good manners of
the best Viennese tradition. The *coup d'état* in Warsaw
had been crushed ; the young adventurers who had succeeded in arresting the Cabinet had been in their turn
placed under arrest by Pilsudski, who had then released the
Prime Minister and his colleagues. Paderewski felt a great
weight lifted from his shoulders : thank God, they had not
succeeded ; a new country cannot begin life in conspiracy.
The optimism that had upheld him in the last weeks
gradually returned.

Though, both in its aims and its execution, the *coup
d'état* had been rather childish, it must have made Pilsudski
realize that it might be unwise entirely to neglect the existence of certain inimical elements in the country. He must
also have been impressed by the fact that Paderewski had
had nothing to do with it. He decided to compromise.
Through General Szeptycki Pilsudski was asking Paderewski
to return to Warsaw and form a Cabinet. Of course, he
would do it. " Helenka," he exclaimed, " we are going
back to Warsaw. Strakacz, see that the things are packed.
We are going with you, General, aren't we ? in a special
train ? Wonderful. General, you must be frozen dead.
Helenka darling, do have some tea made for the General :
he is frozen. Strakacz, are you ready ? Yes, darling, I
am dressing ; I shall be ready in a second. Another
cigarette, General ? I'll have one too. Oh, no, please let
me give you a light. When do you think we shall be in
Warsaw ? "

The special train steamed through the snow-covered
countryside, bearing the future Prime Minister, Ignace
Jan Paderewski, the Prime Minister's wife, General
Stanislaus Szeptycki, and Sylwin Strakacz, the private
secretary.

v

Paderewski was determined not to form a party Cabinet. He endeavoured to form a Cabinet of experts. In his manifesto to the nation he declared : " The new Government shall be free from any party tendencies. The Council of the Ministers who will willingly collaborate with me is composed of men who, be it in the posts and offices they hold or in the profession they exercised, have made themselves known for their remarkable ability and competence. . . ." He did not forget the world from which he had come to form this Cabinet, and he concluded the manifesto with the words : " Guardians of public order and security, we address a pressing appeal to those impatient ones who would fain realize their ideals by recourse to violence, and we urge upon them not to forget that the whole civilized world has now its eyes fixed on us. It behoves every loyal citizen that we should be considered as a people worthy of the liberty whose radiance now illuminates the Polish land."

Paderewski himself was to be Prime Minister, Foreign Secretary, and Poland's Delegate at the Peace Conference, together with Dmowski, who was still in Paris.

For the time being Paderewski settled at the Hotel Bristol, which, in fact, belonged to him. There were days when he hardly stirred from the hotel ; there would be visitors all day, secretaries and telegrams. How could one organize an office, when at every moment things turned up that were new and unprovided for by any routine which was anyhow alien to his nature ? What mattered to Paderewski was to persuade people to collaborate, to make them unite in a common stand at the Peace Conference, to prepare Poland's case for the Conference. He worked until three and four in the morning. Often he could not help getting up late, nor was it always possible for him to be punctual.

The worst obstacle of all was Pilsudski. The meetings with him were sometimes terrible. Paderewski recognized the force and the genuineness of Pilsudski's patriotism.

Of course he himself would be most loyal to the Chief
of State. If only he would change his habits ! Generally,
he would arrive late at night, when Paderewski was worn
out with fatigue ; or there would be a telephone message
from the Belvedere, asking the Prime Minister to come out
and see Pilsudski on a most urgent matter. Sometimes this
would happen at 2 a.m., often for no better reason than
that Pilsudski had had some surprising new ideas which he
wanted to place before his Prime Minister. But could one
trust Pilsudski ? Was he honest in his attitude towards his
Prime Minister ? Paderewski clearly perceived that Pilsudski was out to impress him. What other reason could
there be for the exaggerated simplicity of his appearance
which contrasted so strangely with the display of brilliant
adjutants and elegant officers ? Napoleonic gestures perhaps ? That would not have mattered had his mentality
not been so strange. His arguments seemed to Paderewski
complicated, long-winded, far-fetched ; he would talk for
hours, mixing fact and poetry, superstitions and political
planning. He was moved by mysterious impulses, he
would sometimes avoid the straight and narrow path,
and, worst of all, he would lose his temper. Paderewski
himself could no longer control his temper. He would
raise his voice, or become caustic. Pilsudski would pace
feverishly across the room, stop in front of Paderewski,
assume a Napoleonic attitude, gesticulate wildly with his
cigarette, and shout as though to his soldiers. When
Pilsudski finally left the room at about 5 a.m. thick
clouds of cigarette smoke curled slowly above the table.
Often an ash-tray had fallen to the floor ; the remains
of dozens of long Russian cigarettes lay on the carpet,
amongst messy heaps of cigarette ash. Paderewski too
would then leave the room, pale, exhausted, hardly able to
think or to feel. By God, there was something terrible in
that man, with his hypnotic eyes and his unkempt appearance ! One morning Paderewski turned to a secretary and
said : " You know, when he enters the room, there is a

smell of sulphur, as if the devil came in." Could they blame the Prime Minister in Warsaw that sometimes he did not get up until eleven in the morning ?

VI

On February 10th the first *Seym* was opened in great state. All the bishops, with the two archbishops of Warsaw and Cracow, were assembled. A Solemn Mass was celebrated in the old Cathedral of St. John. Paderewski headed the Government. But it was left to Pilsudski to open the *Seym* and to make the speech of the day. In striking contrast with the rich vestments of the clergy and the brilliant uniforms of the foreign diplomats and the generals, Pilsudski wore his old, unadorned tunic of the First Brigade of the Legions.

The *Seym* consisted of many parties. The danger of a revival of the old traditions of parliamentary particularism was present once more. However, on February 20th the *Seym* passed a vote of confidence in Paderewski, but also confirmed unanimously, with all its 305 votes, the position of Pilsudski as Chief of State. There was no doubt that Pilsudski's hold over the country was beyond challenge. Moreover, he had no need of daily dealings with the *Seym* or those petty affairs of State which filled the Prime Minister's days. The undisciplined parties in the *Seym* were a danger to Paderewski. He was able, however, to strengthen his position, when Herbert Hoover came to Warsaw to arrange for the supply of food from America. Poland was terribly poor, and in some parts on the verge of starvation. By the end of February large quantities of foodstuffs arrived in Poland from America, which was due in large measure to the prestige which Paderewski enjoyed in that country. Apart from this, the general and the political situations in Warsaw were by no means easy. Communist propaganda from Russia was increasing every day ; lack of discipline threatened to become a daily event; there were even active disturbances, hunger strikes and demonstrations.

On several occasions Paderewski had to come out on to the balcony of the Bristol and address the people. At first they shouted and they hissed, but in the end he would find the tone and the words to convert them and send them home. His power over the Polish people had not diminished, but he felt exhausted ; it was all much more difficult than he had ever anticipated.

When at last, early in April, the day of his departure to Paris arrived, he felt a sense of relief. The air in Paris would not smell of sulphur.

CHAPTER FOUR

THE PEACE CONFERENCE, 1919

I

WHEN the train arrived at the Gare du Nord, Paris, on April 6th, there were assembled most of the members of the National Committee, headed by Roman Dmowski. Up till now Dmowski had been the undisputed leader of the Nationalist Party. The man whom he had come to receive had been merely the delegate of the political body of which Dmowski had always been the head. But the man who now descended from the carriage was Poland's Prime Minister and Foreign Minister, and therefore Dmowski's chief.

Paderewski had been very loyal to Dmowski during all this time, and had not accepted Pilsudski's offer to become Prime Minister without first having consulted Dmowski. During all the years of his political activity he had looked upon Dmowski as the legitimate head of Polish affairs in the Western world, and no vital decision was reached, no change of policy accomplished, without an exchange of lengthy telegrams between the two men.

They went straight to the Hotel Wagram, where the Polish Delegation had its headquarters. Paderewski, Dmowski and a number of other members of the Committee seated themselves in the elegant sitting-room, and without delay Dmowski began to give an account of the events of the last weeks. He was completely pessimistic. He sat there describing the situation, his eyes as cold as ever, the tenor of his remarks being that the Polish question was practically settled and that, mainly through the opposition of the head of the British Delegation, Lloyd George, many of the Polish demands had been refused. Whenever Paderewski interrupted him, enquiring after certain details as to frontiers, national rights or unsettled territories, Dmowski's invariable answer was : " That has been already decided," or " There is nothing more to do about it," or " There is no more hope for it." Paderewski was as anxious as Dmowski, but he could not believe that the situation was as hopeless as Dmowski painted it. One could not hope for success at the very outset. Moreover, the Treaty was not yet signed, negotiations were still in full progress.

II

Dmowski had presented the Polish case on January 29th. He had spoken for five hours, first in French and then in English, claiming all Polish territories which had Polish majorities, Danzig and far-lying frontiers in the East. He had presented his case in a dignified and statesmanlike manner, and when he finished, Clemenceau had shaken hands with him, saying : " You have presented the Polish case in a masterly way." Even President Wilson had been impressed. He authorized Colonel House to tell Dmowski that he quite realized that Danzig ought to be Polish and that he was " one with Poland in that question." Although many of Dmowski's claims were the logical result of the Thirteenth Point, they naturally aroused the opposition of the peoples affected by them : the Bolsheviks, the Germans, the Lithuanians, the Czechs and the Ukrainians. A month later Dmowski sent two long notes, dealing in detail with the frontiers claimed by Poland. But vital differences between Wilson, Clemenceau and Lloyd George, and ceaseless intrigues in unofficial quarters made the acceptance of Dmowski's plans problematical. The Supreme Council dispatched to Poland an Inter-Allied Commission which was to study the problems on the spot. Headed by Noulens, this Commission collaborated with a Commission on Polish affairs, which was sitting in Paris under Jules Cambon, the former French Ambassador in Berlin. On March 12th that Commission sent its report to the Supreme Council, and its recommendations were in striking agreement with Dmowski's notes. Although both Wilson and Clemenceau were willing to accept them, Lloyd George strongly opposed them. There were certain political reasons for this opposition, and for his sudden apparently pro-German attitude. But it seemed as though it were produced in the main by his obvious dislike of Dmowski. He had been told that Dmowski had accused him of being influenced by the Jews and that he was circulating a number of stories about him. So Lloyd George never spoke to Dmowski. Dmowski's anti-Semitism had shocked some of the Jewish members of the British Delegation, and it is doubtful whether they found it easy to remain quite impartial when the Polish question came under discussion. Much of the effect created by Dmowski's intelligent and accomplished presentation of the Polish case was indirectly ruined by his anti-Jewish attitude. Whilst Clemenceau, Wilson, and at times even Arthur Balfour, agreed to the proposals of the Commission, Lloyd George was violently opposed to them. Having achieved what he wanted for his own country, he thought it would be wiser to show a more conciliatory attitude towards Germany. The case of Poland was of no interest to him whatsoever, more especially as the whole world looked upon France as the chief advocate of the Polish cause. In a heated discussion on March 18th President Wilson fought for that cause, as presented by the Cambon commission. Lloyd George's attitude, however, was such as to be called " outrageous " by two of the chief members of the American Delegation : Gordon Auchincloss, Colonel House's secretary, and D. H. Miller, the American legal adviser. Actually Lloyd George's knowledge of Poland and her problems was rather limited. His fundamentally cheerful outlook made it hard for him to get to the roots of a problem that throughout its very history had always been serious and

10

dramatic. It could scarcely be solved by a jovial antagonism. Even the prospect of Paderewski's arrival in Paris hardly changed Lloyd George's preconceived attitude. All he could say about the arrival of one of the most unselfish and patriotic statesmen in the whole Conference was : " What can you expect from a country that sends as her representative a pianist ? "

Through Lloyd George's opposition the recommendations of the Cambon Commission were referred back and had to be revised in a way that was recognized by impartial judges as being unjust to the Polish cause.

III

It was therefore desirable that the Polish problems should be discussed once more, and without that atmosphere of hostility created by the Polish delegate around the British spokesman. Paderewski appreciated the real situation, and where his own work would be effective. He would have to try to persuade the Allied leaders to reopen many of the Polish questions and to start afresh when there was an opportunity. Although the general lines may have been decided upon, everything was still in a fluid state. He had arrived at the right moment, a moment when personal influence could be of the greatest use. Even among those statesmen representing the smaller nations, such as the Greek delegate, Venizelos, or the Czech, Dr. Benesh, most of their successes were obtained through personal influence. Paderewski realized that an official approach and the use of purely legal argument would be of little avail.

Paderewski decided to call without delay on the President of the Conference, Clemenceau, whom he did not know and whose support would be of paramount importance. He went to Stephen Pichon, the French Foreign Minister, at the Quai d'Orsay to ask whether it could be arranged for him to see Clemenceau ; he knew well how busy the Prime Minister was, but he felt it his duty to pay him his respects on his very first day in Paris. Pichon was willing to arrange a meeting, and he asked Paderewski to wait a while. He himself disappeared to another room from which he returned after a few minutes. As was known later, he had gone to the other room to telephone to Clemenceau, who, though busy, decided to come directly to the Foreign Office to meet Paderewski, whose name he had known for a great many years.

Hardly fifteen minutes had passed before a door was opened and Clemenceau appeared in the room. He remained at the door looking at Paderewski for a second or two ; then he said : " *Vous venez d'exprimer le désir de me voir. Me voilà.*"

He held out his hand in its traditional grey cotton glove, and putting his head slightly on one side as though examining his guest, he said with a mischievous giggle which a few people provoked in him : " *Est-ce que vous êtes cousin du fameux pianiste Paderewski ?* "

Paderewski appreciated the thrust and answered with well-assumed seriousness : *C'est moi-même, M. le Président.*"

Clemenceau raised his bushy eyebrows in mock surprise, and, shaking his head once or twice, he said in a resigned voice : " *Et vous, le célèbre artiste, êtes devenu Président du Conseil ? Quelle déchéance !* "

He chuckled. And then they both laughed.

Clemenceau was a cynical old man, but he had outlived that stage in cynicism which revels only in bitterness. He had experienced bitterness for too many years not to enjoy a good joke at the age of almost eighty. Paderewski believed in Clemenceau's deep sincerity when the latter tried to bring about a real peace in Europe. He admired his host's strength and determination, even the cynicism which he wore like an armour in his fights.

Clemenceau was not the only one of the Big Four from whom Paderewski found a good reception. He got in touch with President Wilson, who asked him to visit him immediately at his house in the Place des Etats-Unis. Meeting Wilson was not the same as seeing at the Quai d'Orsay the old man of whom enemies used to say that a pair of cotton gloves meant more to him than faith in God and humanity. Here was nothing of the atmosphere in which geniality was nourished by sarcasm and patriotism was matched with disbelief. Paderewski felt for Wilson both gratitude and admiration ; the American President was to him a statesman of true greatness. Paris already had its stories and criticisms of Wilson's coming over from the States, of his ceremonial visits to London and to Rome, of his mind and of his methods as disclosed during the Conference. For Paderewski Wilson was not the Nonconformist preacher, the puritan, the autocrat, egotistic, conceited and fanatical, a bad diplomat confusing ethics with politics, but the man whose name was spoken by peasants, miners and workmen in Poland and in other countries with a veneration accorded to the names of the saints. He was the man who in a world of extreme nationalism, himself without national vanity, conceived his Fourteen Points ; the man who had the sense of the moral responsibility of being the leader of a great country ; the man who for the cynicism of the professional politician substituted the faith of the true Christian. Would not a future generation put him on a higher pedestal than that on which the Paris Conference placed him ?

Wilson must have felt the wave of sympathy that radiated from his guest. His serious face was marked by the struggles and disillusionments of the Conference ; it was becoming a heavy mask, scored with bitter lines. His former faith was gradually turning to resignation. But his face brightened up as he shook Paderewski warmly by the hand. At the end of their conversation Paderewski knew that several Polish problems would be dealt with again, and that he would be their spokesman. Wilson reassured him of his attitude towards the Thirteenth Point ; Poland's prospects were no longer so gloomy.

Paderewski even had an interview with Lloyd George. The two men knew each other, having met in London a few years earlier at luncheon at 10, Downing Street, when Asquith was Prime Minister. Nevertheless Paderewski noticed in Lloyd George a changed attitude towards Poland. But before long the British Premier must have come again under the spell of Paderewski, and his antagonism towards Poland began to melt away. Although the heads of the Supreme Council could not commit themselves, there was little doubt that they were willing to help Paderewski, and that Lloyd George became more sympathetic about Poland than he had ever been before.

IV

Thus the important men of the Conference were won over. Once the atmosphere surrounding the name of Poland had been changed, there was more hope of success. Paris would have to think kindly of the name of Poland, which no longer must evoke memories of a clever man, admired by many, but liked by few.

The French Foreign Minister, Pichon, gave a dinner for Paderewski. This was one of the first occasions which was to tighten the bonds between the Conference and Poland. A speech at a dinner with most of the important delegates present would have to be more than just a polite answer to a toast or to a political declaration. Paderewski never prepared speeches in writing. He hated being tied down; but similarly he disliked improvising at an important occasion. He would think out carefully what he was going to say ; he would foresee the climaxes of his speech ; he would build up beforehand certain sentences or expressions which he sometimes even learned by heart ; little was left to chance. On this occasion, after his first few words, the guests realized there was a new note in the speaker's words. The Polish Premier hardly spoke of politics or of Poland, as everyone had expected that he would ; he spoke instead

of the wonderful destiny of Paris that had become the house
of the most important Conference in history ; he spoke of
human and spiritual tasks that must form the real foundation
for the daily problems of the Conference. The delegates,
who in the course of the Conference had become blasé,
were unaccustomed to that note of deep conviction ; even
the most cynical amongst them detected a sound which
they but rarely heard in after-dinner speeches or during
the Conference. A new note had been struck. Paderewski
was no longer the representative of one of the smaller
Powers, but an individual, who stood on his own exalted
pedestal. Poland, too, emerged suddenly from an atmosphere of daily Conference quarrels into one of dignity.
One or two more speeches like that and Paderewski would
become one of the important men of the Conference :
not through the power of his office or of his country, but
through the power of his personality. In fact, a few weeks
after his arrival in Paris there was among the delegates
of the smaller Powers only Venizelos who enjoyed a prestige
equal to his.

Shortly after his arrival in Paris Paderewski appeared
for the first time before the Jules Cambon Commission
for Polish Affairs, with the result that the Commission
reaffirmed its statement that Danzig ought to be Polish.

v

Soon after that Paderewski left the Hotel Wagram and
moved to the Ritz. His days were fuller than ever. His
evenings were so late and so protracted that only rarely
could he rise before ten o'clock the following morning.
Sometimes he was not ready until midday. While he was
dressing there would be delegates, colleagues, friends and
secretaries to be seen. Office routine in Paderewski's
rooms was somehow less organized than it was in the headquarters of other delegations, and many things were im-
provised. Only when Paderewski had to make a speech on

the following day would he work in his room in the evening, studying his subject, collecting the necessary data, working out his actual speech. As he disliked writing a memorandum or even a letter, he would outline his ideas to one of his secretaries, who would prepare a draft. When the latter was ready Paderewski would go over it with the secretary, suggesting alterations here and additions there, and would then take it to bed with him, and here and there insert a correction in his own hand.

At the end of April Paderewski had to go to Poland, but he was soon back in Paris. During the summer he had to pay one or two visits to Warsaw, but otherwise he spent the early parts of summer in Paris. A number of times he was called upon to present certain Polish claims to the Big Four or to explain sundry points before the Commission for Polish Affairs. Sometimes both he and Dmowski spoke at the same meeting. While Dmowski stressed certain details, pressed his claims and tried to force definite promises, Paderewski created the atmosphere in which Dmowski could be heard sympathetically and the one in which Poland could hope for success. He still showed some of his declarations to Dmowski ; he exercised the same loyalty to his former chief as in the days gone by ; but the relations between the two men had changed. Dmowski was undoubtedly jealous. In his heart he probably considered Paderewski an amateur, while he himself had been responsible for the whole outline of the Polish scheme, the details and the arguments. From Poland's point of view both men were important in the parts they played. But whereas Dmowski's activities were limited to the Polish problem, Paderewski was able to pursue his even outside it. His friendship with Clemenceau, Foch, Wilson, House, Balfour and other leading statesmen brought him into contact with them outside both the Conference room and the negotiations about Poland. Most of them liked to discuss topical political questions with him, and they often asked his opinion and advice. As Paderewski had a profound understanding both of the French and the American viewpoint, Clemenceau would sometimes ask him unofficially to explain to the Americans the French attitude, while Wilson would ask him to do the same with Clemenceau in regard to the American viewpoint.

VI

Such success as Paderewski was able to achieve during the long negotiations in Paris was due to the very personal way in which he was wont to approach music, politics or life in general. His speeches, his relationship with other politicians, his methods, all showed clearly that the human element was the basis of his whole political career. Unlike to most members of the Conference, political or legal scheming was unknown to Paderewski, but his artistic adaptability enabled him to identify himself with a problem that stirred in him feelings of pity or indignation, justice or love. In the ordinary meaning of the word he was not a good politician. Politics were for Paderewski not a profession built up on the emotionalism of a fighter as they were for Clemenceau, nor a moral doctrine as for Woodrow Wilson ; and, above all, they were not a shifting game as for Lloyd George and most of the members of the Conference. Paderewski believed neither in changing one's fundamental opinions nor in involving oneself in political intrigue. Politically he was much too childlike to pursue such methods ; he still possessed the idealistic enthusiasm of the young politician who on first entering Parliament believes that he can lift politics to a high moral plane, thus reforming the entire political life of his country. Almost anyone else with Paderewski's idealistic outlook would have been a hopeless failure ; but Paderewski, instead of trying to force elements that were alien to his very nature, contented himself with replacing them by his own individual power—the human appeal. His artistic disposition and his personal connections made possible the success of such a method. From another's

PADEREWSKI

From the bust by Sir Alfred Gilbert

lips some of Paderewski's utterances would have been unconvincing ; but the prestige which he enjoyed automatically put his appeal on a unique basis. As most of the leading men at the Conference felt a deep affection for him, they came to interest themselves in the cause which he represented. They knew of his personal sacrifices, and his altruistic character was as much admired as had been his artistic achievements earlier in the century.

VII

In a joint letter signed by Wilson, Clemenceau, Lloyd George and Orlando, the Big Four expressed unanimously their opinion of the Polish Prime Minister, stating : " No country could wish for a better advocate than he. . . . " Jules Cambon, the former French Ambassador in Berlin, who, as President of the Council of Ambassadors and President of the Committee for Polish Affairs, had more opportunities than others of judging Paderewski's political career, and who admitted that he had the professional diplomat's natural distrust of the amateur, expressed in a personal conversation with the author his opinion that " nobody could have done better in Paris than Paderewski. Even had he not been Paderewski he would have achieved a lot with his political talents. . . . Lloyd George laughed about the pianist turning politician. But he was the only one who took that attitude. Later even he changed his opinion, and, like all the others, he became a genuine admirer of Paderewski's political gifts." In fact Lloyd George was to prove one of the most helpful supporters of Paderewski and thus of Poland. This was especially evident when the question of Danzig had once again come before the Big Four, who had received a report about it which was not favourable to Poland. On the morning of that day Lloyd George personally rang up Paderewski, warning him that he had something important to tell him and that no time was to be lost. Lloyd George was so busy

that day that he would be able to see Paderewski only in
the evening at a concert of the bands of the British Guards
at the Trocadéro which the British Premier had to attend.
In the evening Paderewski, meeting Lloyd George in his box
at the Trocadéro, was given further details of the report in
question and was advised to do all he could to have the
report altered.

The most striking change of attitude was, however, that
of Robert Lansing, American Secretary of State, who
started with a profound distrust of the Polish delegate.
In his book, " The Big Four," he states : " My original
impression was not one of a complimentary nature. . . .
When the famous musician came to see me at my office at
the Department of State I could not avoid the thought that
his emotions were leading him into a path which he was
wholly unsuited to follow. In truth, I thought that he
was making a mistake. . . ." A few pages later Lansing
writes : " My second impression,—and it is the impression
that I still hold,—was that I.P. was a greater statesman
than he was a musician. . . . He was wonderfully re-
sourceful and apparently had an instinctive sense of the
possible. . . . He held his imagination in leash as he did
his emotions. . . . His views were essentially sane and
logical. What M. Paderewski has done for Poland will
cause eternal gratitude. . . . His career is one which
deserves to be remembered not only by his countrymen, . . .
but by every man to whom love of country and loyalty to a
great cause stand forth as the noblest attributes of human
character. . . . In history as in memory there will live
two Paderewskis,—Paderewski, the master of music, and
Paderewski, the statesman of Poland."

Colonel House, who possessed a particularly intimate
knowledge of Paderewski's political work, wrote years after
the Conference : " Paderewski came to Paris in the minds
of many as an incongruous figure whose place was on the
concert stage and not as one to be reckoned with in the
settlement of a torn and distracted world. He left Paris, in

the minds of his colleagues, a statesman, an incomparable orator, a linguist, and one who had the history of his Europe better in hand than any of his brilliant associates. Had he been representing a power of the first class, he easily would have become one of the foremost of those whose decisions were finally to be written into the Peace. As it was, he played a great part nobly, and gave to the world an example of patriotism and courage. . . . ''

Such appreciation on the part of the other politicians created conditions in which the personal character of Paderewski's statements did not sound strange or senti-mental. Such words as " humanity," " freedom," " right," did not strike the listener as the meaningless clichés of a second-rate orator. The leaders of the Con-ference never gave him a downright " no " for an answer.

VIII

But Paderewski's method would have been doomed to failure had it not been based on a thorough knowledge of his subject. The systematic work of his musical career had taught him to identify himself with successive details until the whole structure was his own. It was the same now. He did not rely solely on information from experts, as did some statesmen in Paris, for example Lloyd George ; he did not turn a deaf ear to his advisers, as did Woodrow Wilson, but listened to everybody, and acquired information wherever he could, his marvellous memory being of the greatest assistance to him. There was probably no statesman in Paris who possessed such an extraordinary memory as Paderewski. There were many striking examples of it. One day the Polish General Haller sent Paderewski a long telegram, asking him to obtain help from the Allies for the Polish army which was hard pressed on the eastern fron-tiers. In his telegram the General quoted the precise numbers of the arms, munitions, uniforms, boots and other supplies which he needed. Paderewski decided to go personally to the Council of Ambassadors and to read them General Haller's telegram. After he had begun his speech it was discovered that his secretary was under the impression that Paderewski had put the telegram into his pocket, while Paderewski understood the secretary to have brought it along with a number of other documents. Actually the telegram had been left at the Ritz. Although the document was missing, Paderewski quoted all the figures from it. Later in the day they were checked, and it was found that he had quoted every one correctly, although he had read the telegram only once.

IX

Undoubtedly Paderewski's close contact with some of the most important men in Paris was one of the main assets of the Polish cause. These contacts were helpful not only where great issues were concerned. The vastness and complexity of the Conference involved hundreds of minor details, which could only be dealt with through unofficial channels, through personal relationships and with the help of friends. Meetings with other statesmen had to be arranged unofficially ; certain documents had to be got hold of ; private secretaries and experts had to be seen, advised, questioned or persuaded. In all this varied work no one helped Paderewski more than the little girl whose duty it had been thirty years earlier to entertain him in a large Roman studio while her father, Laurence Alma Tadema, painted his portrait. The friendship and loyalty which Paderewski inspired were rarely more fruitful than in the case of that Englishwoman, who, devoted to him, became one of the most powerful advocates of the Polish cause in England. Miss Alma Tadema had been an intimate friend both of Paderewski and of his wife throughout the years of their married life ; she usually spent the whole summer at Riond Bosson and often travelled with them. Officially she was almost unknown in Paris ; she did not visit those brilliant functions at which the vanity of the women present was only surpassed by that of the politicians ; her name appeared neither in political leaders nor in the gossip columns of the boulevard newspapers. Brought up on the highest moral principles, an intelligent writer, a poet of distinction and having a character of rare purity, she became a very vital help to Paderewski in the exhausting days of the Conference. During the war she had worked in London, organizing help on a large scale for Polish refugees, collecting money for them, arranging schools for Polish children and homes for Polish mothers, lecturing about Poland and spending her private fortune for the Polish cause. Her library of Polish books and rare Polish maps was one of the most valuable collections of its kind in Western Europe. Polish politicians would come to her house and study in her library. She was often approached by British authorities, being the most trustworthy expert on Polish affairs. Some people called her Poland's first Ambassador at the Court of St. James, and there was much truth in the remark. During the Paris Conference she talked to the private secretaries and to the men who were working on various committees. She gathered round her many of the less famous, nevertheless important members of delegations, advisers or experts, creating in her simple hotel room a centre for Polish affairs. Paderewski knew that he could always trust her, that her advice would be careful and well-balanced. She possessed considerable knowledge, yet retained a simplicity of outlook which saved her from becoming a blue-stocking. She knew and understood Paderewski better than practically anybody. By a natural affinity she was able to perceive the deeper meaning of things. Thus she was never in danger of being swamped by the many petty jealousies which are rife in any great man's entourage. She had definite beliefs, but she was not dogmatic, which made her convincing without rousing opposition. She had been a wonderful daughter ; she was a wonderful sister and friend. Her friendship brought with it moral and intellectual support. But Paderewski found in it even material help, which was not without its importance during the Conference. In her collection he was certain of finding such documents and books about ancient Poland as might exist nowhere else and which could be of assistance to him. Actually on two separate occasions he remembered certain important books which he had seen at her house in London and which would disclose certain facts that could not be proved otherwise. Twice Paderewski chartered an aeroplane so that books from Miss Alma Tadema's house in London might arrive in time.

x

One of the reasons for Paderewski's popularity among the statesmen at the Peace Conference was the fact that his national strivings never made him forget the bigger, the international issues. Colonel House testifies : " Paderewski was one of the few at Paris who had an outlook wider than his own country. While he was for Poland and her needs if she was to become an important State, yet he was for Europe as a whole—a Europe that could live in peace with itself. Many and constant were his proposals looking to the safeguarding of the rights of minorities in the old and the newly created States. Unlike other representatives at Paris, he never asked for Poland more than he thought was just or more than he thought that she could digest. His recommendations to those having the deciding voice, if accepted, would have brought a fuller measure of peace, not alone to Poland, but to Continental Europe as well. He saw clearly and with vision, and had the courage to combat public opinion at home and abroad . . ."

xi

The human element in his political dealings helped Paderewski to retain two of the highest qualities in a statesman : not to press a point which has been won, and not to give way to personal animosity. These qualities impressed friend and foe alike. In the negotiations concerning the Polish-Czechoslovak frontier, particularly in connection with Teschen Silesia, Poland's position was very difficult. Pressing the fact that they had been pro-Ally all through the war, while in Poland Pilsudski had fought with Austria and Germany against one of the Allies, the Czechs had received from Clemenceau a number of definite promises. At one of the meetings of the Conference of Ambassadors the argument between Paderewski and Dr. Benesh, the Czech Foreign Minister, became particularly heated, the difference consisting mainly in a divergency of figures quoted by the two speakers.

After Paderewski had emphatically stated the Polish version of these figures, Dr. Benesh, no longer able to find a convincing argument, retorted sarcastically : " It is known to you, I suppose, that Polish statistics are mainly faked ? "

The big conference room fell silent. Even Clemenceau seemed to rouse himself from his lethargy, looking with curious eyes towards Paderewski. It was not easy to answer to such an accusation.

Paderewski rose and said quietly : " I shall not go into this personal offence against my country and myself." Raising his voice and turning towards the heads of the meeting, he added : " But I beg that my figures be taken down, and I also beg that the accusation of Dr. Benesh be taken down." Benesh agreed.

Paderewski rose again, no trace of excitement showing in his face. When he spoke he was not loud or sarcastic, but he accentuated every word distinctly and solemnly : " I shall tell you where my figures come from—from the man who is one of my most admired friends, and who worked harder in America during the war for the suppressed nations, such as Czechoslovakia or Poland, and for the general peace than almost anyone I know. We all here assembled love and esteem him." Paderewski stopped, taking a book from his pocket. Turning to Dr. Benesh, he proceeded : "The figures come from this book, which, however, Dr. Benesh must have found no opportunity to read. I shall allow myself to make a present of it to him." Paderewski advanced towards the Czech delegate.

Before he reached Dr. Benesh, he spoke once more : "The book was written and supplied with the most accurate statistics by my esteemed friend Dr. Masaryk, the President of the Czech Republic."

He handed over the book to Dr. Benesh and returned to his place to continue his speech. Although the effect of his last words could not have been more striking, he did not pause to enjoy his victory. He went on, but on an entirely new note. He spoke of the historical friendship between Czechoslovakia and Poland and of the necessity for mutual work and sacrifice. Now he was no longer aloof ; his words were warm and moving.

There was scarcely a movement in that gathering of delegates, ministers, secretaries and translators. "When I was on my way to this Conference," said Paderewski, "miners from Teschen Silesia came to see me in my train. They wore their mining kit and their leader must have been well over seventy. He came up to me and said : 'You'll see the Czechs in Paris, Sir. Tell them that we all look upon them as our brothers. We don't want to fight with them. And tell them that we all will work every Sunday, and that we will send them that coal for nothing, so that they may have all the coal they need or they want. But our soil, Sir, that they don't need.' "

When Paderewski sat down the whole Assembly was impressed, Clemenceau making a gesture as though he were wiping away a tear. The atmosphere of enmity and bargaining had left the heavily gilded room. It seemed filled with human understanding, dignity and strange beauty.

XII

Not only in speeches but also in letters Paderewski often
tried to solve his difficulties by a human presentation of the
case. This happened at another stage of the fight for
Poland's Czechoslovak frontiers in the case of Spisz and
Orawa. The question of these two small districts was finally
settled in favour of the Czechs, and there was not the
slightest hope of having it reopened. Paderewski felt the
Polish defeat very acutely. He came back to the Ritz late
at night, after having had to attend a dinner where there
were good wines but indifferent speeches. His principal
secretary and collaborator was still working in the room
next door. Paderewski paused in this room as though to
say something.

He was looking tired. These days in Paris were more
exhausting than the earlier days of long tours and tiring
concerts. The divine exhilaration after a concert was
missing ; he felt worn out ; he was tired of endless dinners
and speeches. And yet these dinners and speeches were the
occasion for much useful work : they were one of the main
channels for the Conference activities.

Suddenly he said : " Mr. Jan, we must reopen the
question of Spisz and Orawa."

The secretary looked up in surprise : " But, Mr. President,
you know quite well that is impossible."

Paderewski went on in the same tone : " It must be
possible. We will approach Clemenceau directly. Draft
me a letter to him." Then, as though remembering the
late hour, he added : " It won't take you long. You
always draft such wonderful letters, Mr. Jan."

The secretary sat down to work. After an hour's work he
had exhausted every legal, political or geographical argument, no matter how far-fetched. All the other arguments
had been used during the official negotiations on the subject.

He went into Paderewski's room and showed him the
draft. " No one could have done it better, my dear Mr.

11

Jan." Paderewski never criticized any of his collaborators directly ; he never made them feel inferior or inefficient. " But don't you think you could improve one or two points ? " He proceeded to show which points he meant.

His secretary returned after rewriting the letter, but even so it was not right. Four times he had to redraft the letter. Of course, by the end there were no arguments left.

Suddenly Paderewski said : " Please write." It was only rarely that he dictated. On this occasion he dictated only a few sentences, but they took the place of most of the long arguments of the previous drafts. He mentioned the visit of Polish peasants from Spisz and Orawa, who had come to Paris to beg for a reunion with Poland. He had received them, he had listened to them ; he had tried to explain the hopeless position to them ; he had even taken them to see President Wilson, who was much moved by the visit of these simple peasants in their picturesque costumes.

Referring to their visit in his letter to Clemenceau, Paderewski dictated : " *Lorsque je leur ai dit que la question était résolue et ne pouvait pas être réouverte, ils m'ont demandé naïvement s'il était jamais trop tard pour faire justice. Je ne pouvais pas leur repondre. Et alors, M. le Président, je vous demande si vraiment il est trop tard pour faire justice.*" [1]

This was not an argument of a political kind ; coming from a professional politician it would have seemed ridiculous ; but Clemenceau felt the human sorrow that spoke. The Tiger was a confirmed cynic ; but deep down there must have been some hidden well of tenderness, apparently dried up, but which now in his old age sometimes gushed forth again. Few people knew of its existence. The question of Spisz and Orawa was reopened.

XIII

June 28th.
Would the Germans sign the Treaty ?
Like everyone else during those last few weeks Paderew-

---

[1] Quoted from memory.

ski heard all the rumours as to whether Germany would sign or not.   The German Cabinet resigned ;   Scheidemann had refused to sign ;   Erzberger and Noske now decided to sign ;   Brockdorff-Rantzau, who a few weeks before had presented Germany's reply to the text of the Treaty, refused to sign ;   eventually Hermann Müller and Dr. Bell were appointed to sign for their country.

Paderewski heard all the rumours about the " bad peace." Among the younger generation there was strong opposition. In fact, no one was spared from attacks.   Woodrow Wilson sacrificed most of his principles in order to save the League of Nations.   Neither Rumanians nor Yugoslavs, Czechs, Greeks, Turks, nor even Italians were satisfied.   Poland, too, felt that she had achieved less than she believed herself entitled to.   But it was the first official international and general acknowledgment of an independent Polish State.   And it was to be signed by Ignace Jan Paderewski.

XIV

Paderewski's car drove through the streets approaching Versailles.   Besides Paderewski there were in the car Mme Helena, Paderewski's two principal secretaries and his military A.D.C.   The streets were not crowded, but at every corner there were posted poilus with little red flags, and they examined every car that went towards Versailles. It was very hot.   At Versailles the crowd was dense.   Many people recognized Paderewski and shouted : " *Vive la Pologne !* "   The car drove towards the palace down a wide avenue, flanked on either side by mounted soldiers wearing steel helmets and the familiar blue uniform.   In the Court of Honour some of France's generals were already assembled: one-armed Gouraud, Pétain, Mangin, and a number of exotic-looking delegates in shiny top hats, and young secretaries, looking hot and bored and without their usual dispatch-cases : for the first time during the Conference their services would not be required.   Many of them recognized Paderewski ; one or twice he waved his hand and smiled.

Giants of the *Garde Républicaine* lined the imposing stairway and saluted with their silver sabres.

The vast *Gallerie des Glaces* was full. Someone showed Paderewski to his seat. In the middle of that huge apartment was the small table, on which even the Germans would now sign the document that recognized the new Poland. For a moment Paderewski's eyes were focused on that little table. The movements and the agitated murmurs of the assembled crowd transformed the huge hall into a restless wave of many colours and exciting rhythms. Paderewski waved his hand and nodded to a number of his friends.

At the head of the room, at the long table, with the huge mirror at their backs, sat Clemenceau, looking small and yellow like his own effigy in wax ; Woodrow Wilson ; Colonel House, kindly yet silent ; Balfour, distinguished-looking, aloof and absent-minded ; Lloyd George, smiling, chatting, pleased with himself as ever ; Pichon ; and Venizelos, intelligent, with a finely-cut face and a white beard. Suddenly the myriad murmurs ceased. Clemenceau's voice was heard : " *Faites entrer les Allemands.*"

The Germans entered the glittering room. Two thousand eyes followed their self-conscious steps. They were the first to sign the Treaty.

After this delegate upon delegate formed up in front of the table, each waiting his turn to sign the document. Paderewski advanced to the table. He wore a long black morning coat, a white waistcoat and a white bow tie ; his old-fashioned buttoned shoes were small and neat. A young man received him : a familiar face, an official from the Quai d'Orsay. He pointed to the place where Paderewski was to sign his name. Suddenly a number of people applauded. They had applauded when Clemenceau and Wilson and Lloyd George came to sign ; now they applauded once more when Poland's delegate took up the pen to write :

I. J. Paderewski.   He wrote his name with a golden quill with which he had been specially presented for the occasion. The signature looked impressive on the costly white paper. The two initials " I " and " J " had a vigorous swing, full of life, and the capital " P " dashed forward decoratively and with courage.   The small letters were neat and clear, like the notes on a sheet of music.   After they were written, Paderewski underlined the whole with an elegant ornamentation that supported the whole name like a handsome pedestal.   It consisted of two long flourishes that balanced each other, as though symbolizing the two professions of the writer.   A shorter line, ending in a small flourish, cut across the two loops of the first ornamentation, suggesting another ambition in this twofold life.   Next to his signature Paderewski stamped the document with the seal which he carried on his watch-chain.   It consisted of three lines crowning each other, very like the three lines of his signature, and surmounted by a heraldic crown and goat.

Was it not the marriage certificate between Poland and Paderewski signed in the presence of the world and witnessed by the world ?

xv

It was late at night.   One could still hear the hooting of the taxicab horns from the Place Vendôme.   In all their noise there was a definite rhythm, drumming, dashing, squeaking, sounding like some Hungarian Rhapsody, and evoking picture after picture in a tired mind.   Had not Clemenceau's gloves been blue to-day and not grey ? President Wilson's shoes had been tidy as always, buttoned and somewhat old-fashioned.   Some said he was a broken man, and all the French newspapers had repeated it.   They also said that Lloyd George had lost his last friend, and that the man who won the war had lost the peace.   Was Clemenceau pleased with his Treaty ?   It legalized Poland.

The blanket of the night gradually turned to ashy cotton-wool. Things in the hotel room were even less real than they had been before. Was the new Treaty real? What was real? Warsaw was real, and Parliament : the *Seym*, the strange *Seym* with its hundred peasants, its workmen, and its rabbis with their long side-locks and their strange pronunciation. The Treaty would have to be defended before the *Seym* ; the *Seym* would certainly attack it, as it attacked everything. It would be tiring in Warsaw ; more tiring even than playing thirty pieces of music a night. But a pianist's hands had helped to shape the new Poland after it had ceased to exist for more than a hundred years. Pilsudski, too, would be real. A clock was striking. The light was changing to palest pink. Poland, Poland above all, was real.

CHAPTER FIVE

PRIME MINISTER OF POLAND

I

ON several occasions during the Peace Conference Paderewski returned to Poland, but these visits were only short, and did not bring him into close contact with people or events. Their main purpose was to defend before the *Seym* the policy of the Polish Delegation at the Conference. Paderewski did not finally return to Poland until the beginning of November, and the situation by then differed from that of the day in January, when he first stepped on to Polish soil. In those days one of his main obstacles had been Pilsudski, who for the majority of the Polish population was the national hero. In the east of Poland war reigned, and it was natural that the military leader should become the central figure in the life of the nation. Meanwhile Paderewski was held responsible for a number of things that Poland had been unable to achieve in Paris. Ignorant of international negotiations, many of the deputies at home seemed not to realize that a Peace Conference was like an Eastern bazaar, a matter of bargains, and so they blamed Paderewski when any of the frontier questions agreed about by councils of experts in Paris did not satisfy their own ideas. The first *Seym* consisted largely of party politicians, often without any clear policy and without a definite party behind them. There were about fifty provincial clergymen among them, many Jewish rabbis, a number of workmen and peasants, some of whom could not even write or read ; most of them had no knowledge of the parliamentary system.

The deputies came from the Austrian, German and Russian parts of Poland that for more than a hundred years had forced upon the population entirely divergent systems of work or education. The methods of the various politicians had therefore very little in common in education or practice. Members of the same party coming from the Russian, Austrian and German section of the country differed often more from one another than from the political adversaries coming from their own province. It needed time for all those differences to melt away before a common national aim.

To make himself understood in his speeches Paderewski had often to descend to what he considered the level of the *Seym*. Nevertheless, his personal presence often impressed the *Seym* as little as did the particular character of his intellect. While his important parliamentary speeches generally had some effect, he was rather helpless in parliamentary debate, to which he was unaccustomed. He also found it quite impossible suddenly to stoop to the use of such weapons as personal enmity might dictate. Many deputies failed to understand both his motives and his methods, while Paderewski himself seemed reluctant to accept the fact that the majority of his political adversaries were not experienced politicians, but beginners without even the rudiments of political knowledge.

Outside the *Seym*, too, opposition to the Prime Minister was increasing. The Socialists and Pilsudski's military adherents constituted by no means the only antagonistic groups. The powerful Jewish elements associated Paderewski with Roman Dmowski in whom, forgetting his accomplishments, they only saw their most hated detractor and enemy. They did not realize that in Paderewski there was no room for racial or religious prejudices ; they also forgot that, all through his life, some of his best friends, whether in England, America, France or any other country, had been Jews. Each day brought fresh attacks on him. People complained of the Prime Minister's lack of punc-

tuality, of work that was delayed, of the inefficiency of
the Prime Minister's office, of its lack of organization ;
they complained of the long hours wasted in awaiting an
audience ; they complained that the Prime Minister was
often surrounded by the wrong people, people who should
not have been allowed to come near him.

II

Poland and the state of her politics cannot alone be
blamed for Paderewski's lack of success at home.   Certainly the *Seym* did not behave towards him in the way
that a more experienced Parliament would have done.
However, the *Seym* had but little to do with the battle that
ultimately led to the Prime Minister's downfall. Paderewski seemed incapable of constructing the bridge that might
have spanned the gulf between him and Polish politics.
He found himself as though in a vacuum where other
political laws operated.   Individual romanticism was common to other Polish politicians ; but they did not see it in
Paderewski in its purity, but only in that distorted form
which was in themselves.   It would probably have been
more helpful if, instead of his artistic temperament,
Paderewski had been able to bring to Polish politics a Western
system of organization, such as he had acquired in the field
of music, and which would have impressed his countrymen
by its very efficiency.   Certain habits that might have been
harmless in private life were a positive hindrance in the
routine work of public affairs.   Paderewski never cared to
dictate either his letters or his memoranda, preferring to rely
on his memory and on his talent for improvisation.   He
never spoke on the telephone, however urgent or imperative
the occasion : the buzz of the telephone affected the sensibility of his hearing.   No one was allowed to touch his
writing-table ; he preferred to follow an impulse rather than
work in conformity with a definite programme.   Had the
Polish Constitution supplied him with a Vice-Premier, who,

while himself attending to the necessary routine work of his
office, would have allowed Paderewski to follow his own
impulses, he might have been as successful as Prime Minister
as he was as Foreign Secretary. He liked to act as the fancy
took him, though sometimes this would happen at a moment
when more urgent though duller tasks called for his atten-
tions. The Prime Minister's work did not consist only of
important negotiations with foreign Governments and
diplomats, of duties that needed the resources of his patriotic
devotion or of speeches in the *Seym* on great occasions. In
such cases ideas seemed to come to him from nowhere, and
he gave himself up to them whole-heartedly until they were
moulded into definite shape. But those were only the high
spots in his political life at home. The main problem of his
Premiership seemed to lie not only in the perpetual conflict between the East and the West, represented by the
national spirit and Pilsudski on the one hand and Paderewski himself on the other, but rather in the divergence
between that particular East and Paderewski's individual
artistic conception of the West.

III

It was plain that Pilsudski, as Chief of State, would come
foremost among Paderewski's obvious difficulties. The
meetings between the two men became more and more
like the meetings of two alien elements. They no longer
took place in the familiar atmosphere of the Bristol Hotel,
but in the old Royal Castle on the banks of the Vistula, a
part of which had been turned into the Prime Minister's
quarters. Often they took place at Pilsudski's residence at
the Belvedere. There were divergences not only in the
political or intellectual standpoints of the Prime Minister
and his Chief of State, but everywhere else. Even in their
unpolitical activities they were diametrically opposed. Both
Paderewski and Pilsudski liked playing patience, but whereas
Paderewski liked having someone in the room, Pilsudski had

to be by himself ; Paderewski enjoyed a sociable game of
billiards or bridge ; Pilsudski lost himself in the individual
joys of secret scheming at chess.   He was in close touch
with the spiritualist Ossowiecki, with whom he would carry
out mystical experiments in secrecy and seclusion.   In his
hobbies as well as in his art Paderewski joyfully accepted
things as they were, without trying to go beyond them.

Even when the chance came for an understanding
between the two men, it would be upset by people around
them.   Paderewski and Pilsudski each represented for his
followers a definite method and a school of thought.   For
most of them a deeper collaboration would have meant the
sacrifice of their particular comfortable creed, and so they
did everything in their power to prevent that.   At times a
human understanding seemed almost possible ; but their
followers would not have it.   Gossip and intrigue were
hard at work to prevent it, promptly exaggerating any
difference that arose.   On Paderewski's part it was by no
means a personal animosity.   He was made to believe that
Pilsudski was Poland's greatest danger, and so he saw in
him the cause of any national failure.   He was beginning
to hate Pilsudski, not so much as the Chief of State, but
rather as the dark power that would ruin Poland.   And yet
there existed vital points of community and understanding.
Both Paderewski and Pilsudski were striving towards the
same goal ; both worked for it without personal selfishness,
with similar devotion and patriotism ; both were men of
such outstanding gifts that, left to themselves, each might
have appreciated the qualities of the other, forgetting
differences of opinion.

IV

It was the opinion of many that Paderewski's political
career in Poland would have been somehow different if
his wife had been able to play a different part.

Madame Helena Paderewska took in her husband's new-found political activities the same interest that she took in anything else connected with him. When they first arrived in Warsaw in January she had no definite ideas as to what Warsaw and the near future would bring, but she was determined to make a success of it. Paderewski's new activities gave her greater opportunities than ever before. After all, the essence of her husband's life till now had been his music, a one-man job, and there had not been much left for her to do. Niuncio's way had been determined long before she entered his life. Now, however, it was different, and every day was bringing new activities. In the last few years she had learned how important it was in political life to see to such small matters as Niuncio might forget : it would be her job to see that he did not neglect any of his many duties. For herself she had no ambitions, although she cared a great deal for the furtherance of her charitable undertakings.

Her life in Warsaw had became as busy as that of her husband. Not only was she Paderewski's, she was also the Prime Minister's wife. She lived at the Hotel Bristol, and later at the Castle, on the same floor as he, and usually her work started some hours before he got up. Generally she would rise as early as seven o'clock, and while in her bath would make plans for the day's work. Those were the only peaceful moments of her day, when it was possible to concentrate and when ideas would come. She worked, with numerous secretaries, in her two rooms as though they were an office. A morning's work meant strenuous hours of receiving callers, dictating letters, reasoning with ministers, soldiers and beggars ; going backwards and forwards into her husband's room, advising him, reading letters for him, interviewing people whom he did not want to see. In the afternoons she would go to individuals and organizations ; trying to collect money for her various charities ; seeing widows of fallen officers for whom she was establishing a home ; visiting the school which she had started. Her main activities consisted of the White Cross for Polish

soldiers, which she had initiated in America during the war,
and for which she had collected very large sums of money.
She had also founded a home for the widows of professional
men who had fallen in the war, and she started a school
for girls, in which they could learn the latest agricultural
and business methods.   She felt very strongly about all her
charities, not from any sense of social or other ambition, but
because all the misery in this new struggling country caused
her acute suffering.   When in 1919 the Polish army endured
terrible ordeals, fighting without proper clothing, boots or
ammunition, without medicines or antiseptics, she herself,
on her own responsibility, went to Paris and saw Marshal
Foch, and begged and pleaded and persisted for so long
that finally she was given a train, made up of thirty-seven
coaches, laden with all the necessary medical and surgical
appliances.

Apart from her personal charities, there was always the
one great urge : to help her husband and to glorify him.
She was not really interested in politics and in her husband's
job as Prime Minister, but she realized what it meant to his
position and how it enhanced it.   It was often she who
had to stimulate his interest and even to advise him ; not
because she wanted to take part in politics, but simply because such stimulation seemed essential for him if he were
to climb as high on the political ladder as he had on the
artistic.   Things that lay outside Paderewski's individual
diplomatic or artistic scope had often to be forced upon
him, and no one could do this better than his wife.   Nevertheless her desire to make his Premiership a real success
was misunderstood by his enemies, who talked of her as
though she were burning with personal political ambitions,
while in reality, for her, the whole world revolved so much
around her husband that she simply could not see things in
the light of their intrinsic importance.   It never entered
her mind that she might be called indiscreet or interfering,
although her attitude naturally enough brought about
situations which were considered wrong by people un-

accustomed to her ways. Almost every day brought about little scenes, insignificant enough in themselves, but obvious proofs of her unorthodox behaviour, and giving rise to exaggerated gossip. One day in January, 1919, soon after the creation of the new Polish State, a special courier from the Polish representative in Berlin was sent to Warsaw to hand over to the Prime Minister in person some very important documents. During the night he had crossed the frontier, where the activities of war were still proceeding, and he arrived in Warsaw just before noon. He went straight to the Prime Minister's apartments at the Bristol to deliver his documents. Paderewski was only half-dressed. He was sitting in the big corner room playing patience, and Mme Paderewska was with him. When the young courier entered the room it was she who greeted him and asked him about his journey and the conditions in the war zone. The question about which the envoy had been sent from Berlin did not interest Paderewski at the moment. A number of most important things had to be decided, and he had been working well into the early hours of the morning. Before he could question the visitor, Mme Paderewska asked : " Where are your papers ? " After some hesitation, the young man handed over the documents. It was she who opened the sealed envelope and began to read its contents. When she had finished, she turned to her husband with the words : " Niuncio, you ought to read this."

There were often similar incidents. In reality they only showed her eagerness to make sure that nothing was forgotten in the affairs of State, but they helped to spread the legend of her political intrigues. As she had no political ambitions or conceptions of her own, she accepted those of others who happened to be near her. People who knew how to approach her and to win her heart could achieve a great deal. Her natural desire to help was coupled with her strong, unsatisfied maternal instinct, and both were taken advantage of, provoking antagonism against her over and over again. She would try to find jobs for people who had

won her heart ; she would ask her husband to place them in
various State offices ; she would try to help them with a
motherly kindness.   Yet the most incredible stories were
invented about those deeds of pure altruism.   Newspapers
that were unfriendly to the Prime Minister would accuse her
of trying to interfere with the machinery of State by putting
into office people who were entitled to their appointments
solely by the sympathy that the Premier's wife lavished upon
them.   Her personal appearance no longer helped her to
popularity.   There were still traces of her great former
beauty, but they were overshadowed by a certain careless-
ness in her appearance which made her look heavier than
she actually was.

Although on State occasions she appeared in a flowing
garment that possessed great dignity, in everyday life that
dignity was not always maintained.   Her beautiful dark
eyes acquired an expression of dreamy vagueness which was
generally taken for lack of interest.   An insignificant detail
of that sort helped to make enemies.   Even if conversation
interested her, her expression would become listless, and it
seemed that her thoughts were far away.   Her guests would
get the impression that she was not interested, and few
things offend people more than an obvious lack of interest.
Her chin, once so imposing in its determination, became
heavy, without losing its autocratic air.   All the peculiarities
of her behaviour became the more striking if her husband
was in the room.   No greater contrast could be imagined.
Whereas he would rise from his seat, his face radiating
smiles of pleasure, his hands outstretched in welcome to his
guest, paying compliments and urging the visitor to the
most comfortable chair, Mme Helena would remain seated,
staring vaguely beyond her visitor's head, and would put
out her hand to be kissed, with a gesture which seemed to
some dignified but to others haughty.   Such guests who
did not know her intimately would forget during the short
moment of that particular gesture all that they had heard of
her kind heart, her good intentions, her genuine devotion to

charity and the endless services she rendered to her husband.
Her manner of speech was in equal contrast to that of
Paderewski. His conversation was keen, vivid, entertaining,
lively and intensely human ; Mme Paderewska's remarks
were slow, long-drawn-out, impersonal and rare. Visitors
saw in them the reflection of a sense of superiority, though
this was not intentional on her part. Warsaw, a somewhat
gossipy town, did not care for that sort of thing. People
made fun of her, and the stories about her grew daily in
number.

No one was able to formulate the slightest accusation, but
her lack of political instinct coupled with her fanatical
devotion to her husband made her do things that were
bound to create bad feeling. She still looked upon Paderewski as a private individual who was entitled to lead the
same life as before his succession to office. The room at the
Bristol or, later, the room at the Castle, where ministers or
foreign diplomats would meet for conferences, was for her
not the Prime Minister's conference chamber, but the
private drawing-room of M. and Mme Paderewski. All her
life they had entertained together. As her husband's hostess
she had received ministers, diplomats, kings and generals
before. Why should it suddenly be different ? Her
husband's colleagues or foreign ministers were to her just
friends of the house, and therefore personal guests. Often
she would open the door behind which a conference was in
progress, and would drop in to say how-do-you-do to the
members. She knew most of them, and considered it the
right thing to stop for a little chat. She would also drop in
if she considered that Niuncio had had a tiring day and
must be rescued and made to rest. She would approach
the conference table and plead with the ministers : " Have
pity on Niuncio, gentlemen. Can't you see how tired he
is ? He simply can't go on. You must stop now." Generally
her entreaties would succeed, and Paderewski, although
possibly feeling that there was something wrong about his
wife's methods, would be grateful at heart for her continued

care and love.   Nevertheless, and especially if they were
alone, he realized that her remarks and her interference
were often out of place.   He would turn on her and cut her
short in so emphatic a manner that she dared neither
contradict nor apologize.   But he cared for her too much not
to be sorry immediately.   Sometimes she would come in
and say : " Niuncio, you must come and have something
to eat " and would compel him to go into another room ;
or else she would ask all the ministers to come across into
her room and have some food.   Nothing but love and
traditional hospitality prompted her actions, but rumours
about these actions would be spread about the cafés of
Warsaw, and in the most distorted forms.   Only few individuals knew the real motives of her actions.   Yet any
café-gossiper felt entitled to judge her by deeds existing
merely in his own imagination.   Her only interests were
her husband's well-being and her charities.   Even her
social duties she performed only if one of her two interests
in life required them ; otherwise she did not care for entertaining the wives of her husband's ministers, or for being
amiable to women who had social ambitions.   Therefore
in those circles, too, stories were invented about her.
Others who sought revenge by inventing calumnies were
those whom she prevented from seeing her husband.   It
was most important that the Prime Minister should not be
overwhelmed by the many petitioners who sought to obtain
a hearing, and Mme Paderewska was a most efficient guard
in such circumstances.   In time, however, that habit made
her antagonistic to any visitor who had ever been received
by the Prime Minister without her previous knowledge.
When Paderewski's attention was drawn by some friends to
a young pianist to whom his advice might have been of
decisive importance, he impulsively asked to see the young
man at once.   The pianist arrived and played.   Paderewski
was much interested, and was just starting to talk to him,
when Mme Helena, who had not been consulted about the
visitor, entered the room.   She took in the situation at a

12

glance and cut the conversation short with the words :
" *Monsieur le Président*, the country before everything. The
Republic awaits you."

When newspaper articles of a very offensive nature
finally came to her notice, and she realized for the first time
the reaction of her behaviour, she was deeply shocked, and
burst into tears. Why should she be blamed for something that was done entirely for the good of Poland's
Prime Minister, and therefore of Poland ? It was terribly
unfair to attack her at all !

Paderewski, who felt very keenly how much he owed to his
wife in his daily life and work, suffered even more acutely
under those accusations. He knew how much she had
done for the Prime Minister of Poland, how she had worked
from morning till night for Polish soldiers, beggars, mothers,
children and widows, and how she had sacrificed herself
during the tiring months of his Premiership. Usually his
natural optimism prevented his being oppressed by
occasional disappointments, but the wound made by the
accusations against his beloved Helenka was not easy to
heal. It seemed as though the same power that prevented
his final happy reunion with his country must also strike at
the being nearest to his heart. The two great loves of his
life, his love for Poland and his love for his wife, had been
deeply wounded by the same power of fate—by Poland.

v

Paderewski would not believe that his country's antagonism against him and what he represented was genuine.
He thought he would be strong enough to fight against
intrigues and petty spitefulness. Even now he did not care
to identify himself with party politics. He continued to
follow his idealistic altruism, hoping that in the end such an
attitude was bound to succeed.

The National Democrats with whom he was associated
had been steadily losing ground during the year. Pader-

ewski still believed that the straight path was the best, but
he forgot that he was not dealing with the political machinery
of a highly experienced country.   In a speech in which
he defended his attitude, he summed up his policy in words
that he hoped would set an example to the *Seym* : " Some
people tell me that Poland is crawling on the right flank ;
others that she is crawling on the left flank.   But I tell
you that Poland is marching forward, but only along a
straight road."   For the majority of the *Seym*, however,
he was by now not an outstanding individual but a politician
connected with the National Democratic Party.   When
Paderewski arrived in Poland in January the National
Democrats hoped they could use him, as their instrument.
When they found out that he was not a party man and that
he would not be directed by a body with a limited party
programme, they began to desert him, hoping to find someone more willing.   The parties of the Left considered
Paderewski, not without reason, a man of the Right.   The
necessary party support could come only from the National
Democrats, and without their party help the Prime Minister's
career was doomed to failure.   Paderewski found himself
left more and more in the air.   Pilsudski, though more
preoccupied with the army and the war than with the
political machinery at home, understood the attitude of the
Seym much better than Paderewski.   He knew its thoughts
and methods and he could speak its language ; he also
knew that abuse could be more effective with the *Seym* than
civility and gentleness.   Most important of all : Pilsudski
seemed, at that moment, to represent the spirit of the
country.

The Home Secretary, Wojciechowski, was a friend of
Pilsudski's ; so was Skrzynski, the Under-Secretary for
Foreign Affairs.   An open conflict between them and
Paderewski broke out.   They were joined by the Finance
Minister Bilinski, a former Minister of the Austrian Emperor
Francis Joseph.   One after another Paderewski's ministerial
colleagues left him.   Yet he would not accept defeat.

Without his knowledge the Speaker of the *Seym* announced on November 27th that the Prime Minister had resigned. The Speaker knew only too well that the National Democrats had dropped Paderewski, and as Paderewski could no longer count on any support in the *Seym*, he had no power to hold his office. Paderewski rushed to the *Seym* to contradict the Speaker's announcement, but it was of no avail. The country no longer saw in him the Prime Minister.

Paderewski felt that he had no right to give up his mission. Personal enmities did not seem sufficient reason for resignation, and he would not allow himself to admit that his nerves were overstrained and that he was physically exhausted. He felt that he must go on, no matter what happened. No doubt he would have acted differently and would have perceived the situation more clearly had the personal atmosphere around him been otherwise. For a number of people he had become the focal point for their own political and personal ambitions and affairs, but Paderewski, accustomed to believe only in the highest motives in human nature, saw in these people only unselfish patriots, working like himself for the same supreme goal. There were certain new friends, some of whom had been brought into the Prime Minister's circle by his wife, and who had no political wisdom, no real knowledge of the situation. It was they who created an atmosphere of alarm and distortion, which blinded Paderewski. They came and they went, bringing alarming news, imploring Paderewski to go on sacrificing himself for the nation's good. One afternoon in the beginning of December a friend burst into the room, crying : " Mr. President, if you don't stick to your duties, there will be a revolution in Warsaw and Bolshevism in Poland within three days." At that moment a shot rang out—it did not come from across the river, but seemed to have been fired actually outside the Castle. Madame Helena rushed into the room : " Niuncio, you cannot give up, Poland needs you ! " She was overanxious for him, but she also felt that, as the wife of a hero, it was her duty to show him where his place was. The telephone-bell rang. A friend in the army insisted upon seeing the Prime Minister without delay, as it was of the utmost importance. Paderewski stood in the middle of the room when the officer arrived ; he was pale and haggard, and had aged considerably during the last few months ; the customary keenness in his eyes had become anxiety and nervous expectation. Yet even now there was that dignity about him that no circumstance could shake. The guest exclaimed : " Mr. President, Pilsudski wants to arrest you. He has ordered the army not to give you protection if the Socialists try to attack you. You must either fly or remain Prime Minister." More people entered the room, most of whom were National Democrats, afraid that Paderewski's resignation would mean their own political downfall, maybe even their arrest. Who could tell what a man like Pilsudski would do ? Their voices were raised in one general pleading : "Without you the country is doomed to anarchy ; you must stick to your task ; you must save the nation ; you are the only safeguard of Poland's existence ; it is your duty towards your name, your prestige, your patriotism. "

It was all very theatrical, looking much more dangerous and of greater importance than it really was. And yet the force behind which was responsible for the many events of the last days was composed merely of usual parliamentary intrigue, of political enmities and of muddled political tactics. For the last few weeks, however, life in the Castle was never quite without a suggestion of the theatre before the ringing down of the curtain. In the confusion of the situation the overstrained nerves of Paderewski were no longer able to discriminate between the tongues of gossip and those of truth.

More than ever Paderewski felt it his duty not to abandon his ship. He did not realize that his ship had long ceased to respond to his commands ; another hand was at the helm. The one unmistakable fact was the vast shadow of the Chief of State darkening the whole atmosphere within the castle on the Vistula. Now that Pilsudski was assured of the *Seym's* final victory over his most dangerous competitor, he was no

longer in fighting mood. He waited quietly, sure of the
army, sure of the workers, sure even of the *Seym*, which
would hardly dare to oppose him. He watched the frantic
efforts of his Prime Minister, he even achieved a sort of queer
sympathy for him, and when on December 5th Paderewski
eventually realized the futility of his efforts and resigned
officially, Pilsudski, sure of the other's defeat, asked Paderewski to become once again head of a Government.
Paderewski still hoped that the best conservative elements
in the land would support him, particularly as the Archbishop Teodorowicz and the Conservative Speaker of the
Seym had approached him, asking him to form a new
Cabinet. Pilsudski knew better. He agreed to all
Paderewski's suggestions about the formation of a new
Cabinet, but after Paderewski had gone, turned to one of
his officers and said : " Sooner will hair grow on my hand
than he will succeed." Paderewski represented the losing
cause, and no one likes to join a losing man. He tried and
tried in vain. His usual clearness of vision deserted him in
these days of strain and anxiety, and he found everyone's
hand against him, and no one who would collaborate. It
was no good; Poland had failed him, failed him cruelly.
He would leave his treacherous love, he would go back to
Riond Bosson, back to the shores of Lake Leman. How
peaceful and calm and lovely Riond Bosson was. He was
so tired, so very tired.

VI

Was it not natural that Paderewski should be defeated
in Poland by Poland ? Other powers than those he represented overshadowed the fate of the new country. They
were the powers of a nation only just reborn and trying to
find itself, a nation that had to go through all the pains and
convulsions of a political rebirth. Paderewski's fate was
certainly to glorify Poland, but to glorify her through his
particular medium and in his particular world. Poland

claimed Paderewski spiritually, but physically he belonged to another world. His mission did not seem to require physical contact with Poland, but it required the intimacy with the Western world which he understood as well as it understood him.

There is always an inner meaning in an historical success or failure. Either of them is generally too complicated to be explained by a simple formula, but the main tendency can often be deducted without artificial construction or speculation. It is as yet too early to find the ultimate reasons for the failure of Paderewski's political reunion with his great love, with Poland. Nevertheless, even to-day we perceive reasons deeper than those that politics can supply. Was it permissible for Paderewski, who so perfectly sublimated his strivings after an ideal, to achieve the material as well as the artistic consummation? The argument that an artist could not possibly achieve supreme success in a world that was not his own will not suffice for explanation. Such an explanation would even be untrue : we know that he achieved an outstanding political success, and the greatest political experts agreed that no other living man could have done more for Poland at the particular period than he did. Whatever the deeper reasons may have been, higher powers than accidents of circumstance forced him to relinquish his intimate connection with Poland. Practically all his days in Warsaw brought him worry, misunderstandings and unhappiness. As seen from the West, Poland had worn a crown of beauty on her youthful head ; at close quarters she had become a quarrelsome, exhausting termagant.

There is grandeur of classical tragedy in Paderewski's career in Poland. No man could have worked for any ideal with greater devotion and love, with purer intentions, with greater sacrifices —yet his highest ambitions were defeated by a fate that selects the dearest to deliver the fatal blow.

PART THREE

A GREAT MAN

CHAPTER ONE

REBIRTH OF THE PIANO

I

THINGS in life are not real so long as we are not conscious of them. Had Paderewski's political career come to an end at the moment when he became conscious of the fact that it offered no further possibilities ?

Riond Bosson had opened its peaceful gates, and once more Paderewski's life was bounded by the shores of the Lake of Geneva. The end of his Premiership had not meant the end of his personal sacrifices for the cause of Poland. He was deeply disappointed by the way he had been treated in Poland; he had been planning a number of reforms for Poland which he had no hope of ever realizing, and he was conscious both of the magnitude of his own devotion and of the comparative pettiness of his success while actually in Poland. Nothing hurt him more than the way Mme Paderewska had been slandered in Warsaw ; but personal disappointments were not allowed to govern his actions. He consented to become Poland's first delegate at the Council of Ambassadors, and when Poland's new Foreign Minister, Prince Sapieha, begged him to serve Poland with his enormous prestige and knowledge of international affairs and to become his country's first delegate at the League of Nations, Paderewski accepted. His disappointment in Poland must in some measure have been compensated by the popularity which he enjoyed amongst the representatives of most other countries of the world. At Geneva he was looked upon by everybody as a great patriot and the distinguished statesman. When he first rose to make a speech before the Assembly, the vast

187

gathering of foreign ministers, ambassadors, secretaries, interpreters broke into prolonged applause. His speeches were considered among the finest oratorical achievements of the League, and they carried much greater weight than they ever would have done in Warsaw. The audience which assembled to foster international ideas was impressed by the humanitarian, international outlook of the Polish delegate. He seemed to embody the ideals for which they were fighting. In September, 1920, during the dispute between Poland and Lithuania, Paderewski made the great gesture of friendship towards Lithuania, treating her representative, Prof. Valdemaras, as a friend. He thus gave an example of a new spirit of peace and international understanding, and the enthusiasm of the League knew no bounds. Paderewski felt more at home here than in the atmosphere of suspicion which pervaded the *Seym*, but even now he did not always find it possible to co-ordinate his own political opinions with those of responsible men at home ; he was becoming more and more conscious of the inadequate support he was finding in Poland, and of the resulting lack of a success commensurate with his endeavours. Although he went on taking the keenest interest in the activities of the League, and although he used to drive out to Geneva every day to assist at the sittings of the League, he resigned the post of Poland's representative and contented himself with remaining solely a spectator in the visitors' gallery.

Did this mean that the statesman was going to be replaced by the musician ? Science tells us that a man renews himself every seven years. His skin, his blood, every molecule of his body is replaced. Even his heart, even the cells of his brain, are renewed. But it is not only the scientists who have discovered that the number seven is of supreme importance in man's life. It is supposed to be a unit complete in itself, full of mystery, and as indivisible as the more sacred three. Paderewski's seven years of politics were drawing to an end. His first professional appearance in the political arena had been made in 1914 ; in 1921 the

PADEREWSKI AND MUSSOLINI
(In the Palazzo Chigi, Rome)

seven years would be over.   Precisely seven years after his
first speech on a political platform on Poland's future freedom, seven years after the unveiling in 1910 of the
Grünwald Memorial, President Wilson had assured him
that there would be a free and independent Poland
vouched for in the coming Fourteen Points.   It took
Paderewski's political declaration seven years to acquire
significance for the whole world.   There is something
terrifying in the logic of fate, though we discover its
wisdom only after its manifestation.

.   .   .   .   .   .

II

No stage was set for a new beginning in Paderewski's
life, and nothing dramatic happened.   The year 1920 was
ending in a bustle of activities.   Most of the leaves on the
trees had been scattered by autumn winds ; the grapes
had turned into wine and the peaches had been gathered.
There had been much work in connection with the League
of Nations on account of the disputes, the negotiations and
the signing of the treaties concerning the new status of
Danzig.   Even the usual game of patience was in progress.
Mme Helena and Mme Wilkonska, Paderewski's sister,
and several members of the household sat round playing
patience.   Paderewski himself was walking from player to
player, looking over their cards, stopping for a while,
giving advice.   Eventually the evening came to an end and
Riond Bosson went to bed.   A full moon floated slowly
above the lake, silently shifting the deep shadows of the
trees in the park.   Paderewski had gone upstairs and
locked himself into his study.   Then all at once came the
sound of a Chopin Nocturne.   In that house deprived of
music for many years the sounds were strange and unreal ;
there were no hesitations ; the music flowed without
interruption as though resumed after only a moment's rest.
On the staircase was sitting Jan Rosen, Paderewski's

young A.D.C., a soldier and political worker by circumstance and profession, but a painter and a student of art by talent and vocation. He scarce dared to move. He was devoted to his master, and anything vitally connected with Paderewski became vital to him. If this were a dream, then it was a wonderful dream, brought perhaps by the moon that sailed on endless waves of Chopin's music across the waters towards the mountains. But it was not a dream ; it was those seven years sailing towards their end.

When Paderewski appeared next morning, he was silent about this sudden unsealing of the fountain. He locked himself up again in his study, and played four hours. Was he practising, or was he calling back the spirits that were waiting for the word of invocation ? He did not play regularly, although he realized from the very first day how difficult it was to find the way back to his former technique. The members of the household at Riond Bosson may not have noticed a difference between the master's playing before the war and now ; but Paderewski knew only too well how stiff his fingers had become and what pains he would have to take to acquire once more the old mastery of the piano. Meanwhile the piano was the bridge between two worlds. When the last piece of skin, the last fibre of his nerves had been renewed, then it would be time to take up the former profession.

III

This exchange of political for musical tools was not dictated only by Paderewski's free will. There were more compelling causes. The years of war had swallowed the vast private fortune which Paderewski had accumulated in the preceding twenty-five years. His political and charitable generosity had known no limits, and now, at the age of over sixty, he found himself deprived of financial means. A musical career was the obvious solution. After a prolonged visit to Paso-Robles, his ranch in California, where he underwent a cure, he began to work regularly, preparing a repertoire and practising for many hours a day. As in former years, he hardly ever played through a whole piece but studied individual fragments and left the composition in its entirety to the inspiration on the platform.

Having lived for years in a style in which lavishness and generosity were the daily accompaniments of life, he did not care to change those standards. Riond Bosson remained a centre of hospitality. Even when Paderewski was away, guests were entertained, and sometimes ten or more would be asked to lunch or dinner. Admirers from America, South Africa, Australia or New Zealand felt compelled on their European tour to see their idol in his domestic surroundings. Often the music-loving traveller would be accompanied by an equally enthusiastic spouse, and perhaps by a number of sons and daughters, with whom he would present himself at the gates of Riond Bosson, considering it to be almost the duty of the great man, whom they had travelled so many miles to see, to receive them. Indeed, they generally were received. Often, if they were fortunate enough to arrive at the appropriate moment, they were asked to stay for lunch or dinner, or for tea, if by mischance their railway time-table would not allow of a more substantial reward for their musical devotion. The enthusiasm of these gentlemen or the excited ladies and their blushing daughters was touching, but as meals at Riond Bosson were elaborate and richly cooked, they were also very costly. Paderewski enjoyed those visits if the guests were cheerful and if they could appreciate the quality of his food and his wine, and he liked them to eat and drink plentifully.

IV

Paderewski still enjoyed eating and drinking ; he ate abundantly, but not to excess. His days now were more peaceful than they had been while he was engaged in politics. During the greater part of his life the climax of each day was not reached until the evening ; even now he concentrated more on the later than on the earlier part of the day, and seldom rose before eleven. The first person who was allowed to see him in the morning was Marcel, the French valet who had been with him a lifetime, first as the companion of Paderewski's son Alfred, and since Alfred's death as Paderewski's personal servant. Alfred's premature death some twenty years earlier had been a tragic blow to Paderewski, and since that day he had become very attached to Marcel, who was one of the few men whom he occasionally embraced with affection. Marcel had a real passion for those brown *petits pains* which are served instead of bread at some Paris restaurants, but he was also dignified, he enjoyed good music and he was devoted to his master. When Marcel entered his master's room, it was time to get up. There followed the daily morning exercises, the bath, a prolonged dressing, a breakfast which consisted only of fruit and tea with lemon. Paderewski would remain in his study until about two o'clock, when he would come downstairs for lunch. Meanwhile the household assembled in the hall, waiting for him to appear. His coming down the staircase and joining the rest of the party was always a sort of ceremony. Luncheon was rarely finished before four o'clock, when Paderewski retired into his study to practise again. Between six and seven o'clock there was tea, at which he confined himself to some fruit and a cup of tea. After tea he liked going into the garden to see the peaches, the pears or the vines, and to talk to M. Dolezal, the Polish head gardener, who was considered one of the greatest fruit and gardening experts in Switzerland. Monsieur Dolezal's talents had enabled Paderewski to grow grapes that normally would grow only in certain parts of Algeria, Italy or the South of France, and peaches for which the richest Californian orchards might envy Riond Bosson. Grapes and peaches were still Paderewski's chief hobbies. He would stay to admire

the long trellises on which M. Dolezal had tied and arranged
the branches of the peach trees as though he were composing
a Japanese picture. In the long hothouse he would enjoy
the impressive picture of endless bunches of grapes, many
of which weighed three or four pounds. Paderewski was
proud of his fruit, and he liked to hear the admiring ex-
clamations of his guests the moment the enormous peaches
were brought into the dining-room. There was often some
joke or some little story in connection with the peaches.
One morning, for instance, M. Dolezal had found to his
dismay that three of his finest peaches, weighing almost a
pound each and left unpicked on purpose so that the master
himself might eat them, had been taken during the night.
No member of the household would have dared to pick
them, and it must have been one of the guests who had found
them hard to resist. M. Dolezal knew that Paderewski's
guests went in awe of their host, and he was determined to
expose the culprit ; but before he was able to do so Marcel
arrived in the garden, saying, with the self-restrained dignity
that never left him : " *Monsieur le Président* wants you to
know that last night, when nobody could see in the dark,
he picked three large peaches. He thought somebody else
might try to do it, and as he wanted Madame to eat them,
he preferred to do it himself."

Everybody referred to Paderewski as " *Monsieur le
Président*," which title he of course possessed since his
appointment as Prime Minister of Poland. His presence
at Riond Bosson affected everyone from his wife and his
sister down to the kitchen-maids and the garden-boys.
Everyone tried to be at his best ; people were no longer
given up to jealousies ; they adopted some of that hospitality and that generosity which characterized the master
of the house. The luminosity of a knight-errant which
Burne-Jones and others in London had seen in him more
than thirty years earlier was there, affecting everyone who
came in contact with him.

13

V

In 1923, when Paderewski's career as a pianist began once again, the years of political efforts were nothing but a memory. All the intoxicating details of a virtuoso's life were back again : preparation of programmes, travelling, the new concert halls, the interviewers, and above all, the crowds. But his public had to be conquered anew. Paderewski's political career confused the issue in many people's minds. Some people thought that a man of his age would not be able to take up a musical career again ; the younger generation had almost forgotten that the only Polish statesman whose name was really familiar to them had once been a great pianist, and they looked upon his artistic past as on a beautiful legend.

Mr. I. Bowman recalls that when asked one day if he found it difficult to face the crowds of Warsaw on his first appearance there in 1919 Paderewski said that though he expected to have stage fright, actually he felt quite at ease, and that he supposed it was due to experience in facing audiences during his musical career. "You know I used to play," he said. "Yes," replied his listener, "I used to hear you."

Although Paderewski's political career diminished his prestige in Poland, it heightened his position abroad. He was, after all, the only pianist in the world who had also been a Prime Minister and one of the great men of the age. People who did not care particularly for music went to hear him in order to see the famous man. He reconquered his world, the Western world, in the shortest space of time.

Many things remained as they had been many years ago ; others were different. Above all, there was still his old stage fright. Years of conferences, of speeches at distinguished gatherings or before tremendous crowds, all his varied political experience, had not killed the old disease. It was as though he were still a beginner afraid of breaking down in the middle of his piece. He would reach the artists' room long before the concert, hoping to conquer his stage fright. This would often take the form of acute pain in the arms, the shoulders and the back, and Paderewski would stretch out his arms and twist his body, hoping that such exercises might relieve the pain. Besides the French tuner, M. Dolmetsch, who had to look after all the technical details, one person only was allowed to enter the artists' room before the concert. This was Marcel, who was also left in the room during the concert, and who would be there when Paderewski returned from the platform after the last encore, the final bow. Exhausted with fatigue he would throw himself into an armchair, his eyes closed, breathing heavily. Marcel stood at the far end of the room, watching his master out of the corner of his eye. When he thought that the worst exhaustion was past, he would advance slowly, saying in his quiet, respectful voice : "*Monsieur le Président, un peu de champagne, s'il vous plaît.*" The glass of champagne restored his master's strength, and now he could think of the second part of the evening. Behind the door he could already hear the voices of all those friends and admirers who wished to be admitted. However, before anybody was allowed into the room, Paderewski would have to change his clothes. Generally, he came back from the platform drenched with perspiration, his shirt, tie, and collar one wet shapeless mass ; his coat and trousers, too, were creased and damp. Marcel was there with clean clothes, and he helped his master into them. The last thing which Marcel had ready was the black overcoat which prevented Paderewski from catching cold. Often the doors outside the artists' room would be open, and draughts and sometimes icy winds would sweep into the overheated atmosphere of the little room. It was a long opera-coat that he wore, with a cape attached to it, very Edwardian, very practical and most impressive. After having looked into the mirror, Paderewski was ready to receive his guests, who had to be announced by card or by name, and who were admitted one or two at a time. When the door was thrown open, Paderewski was standing in the middle of the room, his face slightly flushed, his general appearance even more impressive and elegant than usual. Smiling, and with an inviting gesture of the hand, he advanced towards the door. In the background stood Marcel, anxious lest his master should overtire himself, a little jealous perhaps and extremely proud of the evening's success.

After the last guest had gone, Paderewski would exclaim : " I am simply famished ! " It was time to get home for supper. Supper after a concert was a large, substantial affair, during which Paderewski talked incessantly, joked, told stories, and gave accounts of the various people who had been at the concert ; he was radiant, brilliant. Through his conversation he was establishing a more intimate contact with the world around him, but the somewhat absent expression of his eyes revealed the fact that his mind still lingered in the distant world in which it had lived for the last three hours ; it often seemed as though he had not yet found his way back to earthly surroundings. Sometimes one or two guests would be invited to supper, especially if they were good bridge players. The end of dinner meant the approach of the climax of the day, which would be sheer enjoyment. While to the first part of dinner all the time was given that a gourmet's meal required, Paderewski became impatient now that the end was approaching, and before coffee was served he would turn to his guests, saying jokingly : " Let's do something for our living, gentlemen. Let's start." The game of bridge would begin.

Bridge had become Paderewski's chief distraction. Patience, chess, billiards, endless after-dinner conversations, all were replaced by bridge. If there was only one guest, Strakacz, the secretary and Marcel had to join the party. When no guests were available, the three of them played with a dummy fourth. Paderewski also played bridge in other people's houses, but bridge being for him not a social function but an important part of his very existence, he enjoyed bridge parties at home more than anywhere else. He disliked playing for money. Concerts always left him very wide awake : it was as though the music which he had accumulated before the concert had not been entirely used up in these two or three hours on the platform ; but it had been released from its inner storehouse, and it went on playing in Paderewski's head with a thousand voices. It simply had to be worked off. If it was impossible to get a game of bridge, he would sometimes pace up and down his room for hours, until towards dusk the music would be tamed once more, allowing Paderewski to go to sleep. Before that it was impossible for him even to lie down on his bed or to remain quiet. Bridge gave him a wonderful feeling of peace and quiet pleasure ; finally, it enabled him to get to sleep. But even so, after the guests had gone and the last rubber had been played, occasionally, before going to bed, he would have to play a game or two of patience.

Paderewski was a good bridge player and made his decisions quickly. He disliked bad players, but he did not show his displeasure by losing his temper. His partners felt his wrath more than his opponents did ; their mistakes would occasionally be referred to in some sarcastic little remark. But he loved praising them if they had played well. He was superstitious to a certain extent, and he did not like changing packs during the game ; blue cards were his favourites. His game of bridge was one of the few things in life to which he looked forward with impatience and which he hated to miss.

VI

His game of bridge after his concerts was not the only difference between the pre-war and post-war habits of his career as a pianist. Even his stage fright, though it still existed, was finding a new safety-valve. For the first time it left him entirely when in 1923, at his first post-war recital at the Queen's Hall in London, the whole audience rose as he appeared and remained standing until he had sat down, while deafening applause continued for several minutes. This spontaneous tribute touched him very deeply ; he could hardly keep the tears from his eyes, and he felt a great sense of happiness and gratitude. The wonderful feeling of human warmth brought about by the outburst of this London audience seemed to wipe out any feeling of stage fright. Similar tributes were repeated spontaneously in many other towns and other countries after the war. When Paderewski planned his first post-war tour in the United States no insurance company was willing to take the risk, thinking either that his political career had destroyed his artistic capacities or that as an artist he was forgotten. But when Paderewski appeared on the platform of Carnegie Hall in New York, all the boxes intended for four people had been made to seat eight ; the prices were higher than ever, and the whole audience rose to their feet like one man. The same happened at all his fifty concerts between the Eastern and the Pacific Coast, and by the end of this tour Paderewski had earned half a million dollars. Even in his career such a success was unique.

The homage of people all over the world was not the only thing that was different in Paderewski's new life as a pianist. He no longer practised for twelve or more hours a day as he did before the war. During a concert tour he hardly ever practised more than four hours a day ; if not on tour, he hardly practised at all, remembering only too well the strained hand of pre-war days. In later years he even told his pupils not to practise for more than about five hours a day. His hands were treated with the greatest care, and after he had been practising Marcel had carefully to massage his fingers, his hands, and even his arms. At times Paderewski would practise with such abandoned physical vigour that the finger-tips would get wounded and bleed. It was Marcel's duty to cover them up with special leather finger-stalls which had to protect the fingers during the day.

Paderewski now played mainly on a Steinway piano. His connection with Steinways was almost as old as that with Erards. Just as many legends were invented about that relationship as about his connection with his French piano-makers. Too-clever journalists discovered that the wood and the ivory used for Paderewski's pianos were of a very special kind, and that Steinways, too, employed special work-men who were bound by oath never to disclose the secret of the unique mechanism which they had created for the instruments which were to be played by the Polish pianist. In reality, Paderewski played on an ordinary Steinway Concert Grand, but as he liked a hard and rather crisp tone, essential to certain of his orchestra-like effects, the felt on the hammers of the pianos used by him was treated in a way that made them particularly brilliant. The "special workmen" consisted of one tone regulator from the firm's headquarters, who would go to Riond Bosson to tune Paderewski's Steinway pianos there and who would travel to England to attend the piano played by him on his English tour. But it was no secret knowledge or superiority over his colleagues that accounted for the regulator's visits to Morges and to England. It was simply that Paderewski disliked few things so much as new faces. He liked to see around him people whom he had known for years and whom he knew he could trust, and as this particular man had looked after his pianos for many years, the firm paid Paderewski the compliment of letting him have the same man throughout his English tours.

Ingenious musical agents or musicians would often men-tion sums of money that Steinways were supposed to have spent on Paderewski in the course of years. No famous pianist is ever safe from stories and gossip of such a kind. In reality, the relationship between Steinways and Paderewski was that of friends, and Steinways did not pay Paderewski a penny. This kind of financial arrangement

would have run contrary to Paderewski's fundamental
principles and to his very high opinion of the profession of
a virtuoso. This perhaps accounts for the excellent relations between Paderewski and his piano-makers and for
the fact that he was loved by all the managers, tuners,
regulators and piano-shifters of the firm both in New York
and in London. When the firm of Erard gave up their
English depot several years after the war, Paderewski played
on a Steinway also in England. In France he still used an
Erard ; in his hotel apartment in Paris there was always an
Erard upright, and at Riond Bosson in his study there
was an Erard upright and a small grand. When he went
to the United States, he had a Steinway piano in his
cabin.

During his frequent voyages to and from America, he
used to stay most of his time in his suite, practising, reading,
writing letters and playing bridge with friends who might
be travelling on the same boat. Generally he had his
meals served in his own rooms, and he would take his
walks mainly in the evening, when there was less danger
of being approached by admirers, strangers, or autograph-
hunters.

VII

Paderewski's personal prestige was still on the increase.
People with whom he had worked during his political career
remained his friends. Clemenceau, Franklin Roosevelt,
Colonel House, Masaryk, Briand, Herbert Hoover, Pichon,
Arthur Balfour, Wickham Steed, Norman Davies, Marshal
Foch were still his hosts or his guests. When he went to Rome
he was the guest of the King, of the Prime Minister, Mussolini,
with whom he spent long hours in political conversations, and
of the Pope Pius XI, with whom a friendship had begun soon
after the war, when the Pope, then Achille Ratti, had been
Papal Nuncio in Warsaw. In the capital of the United
States he stayed at the White House as the guest of the

President, no matter whether his host's name were Herbert Hoover or Franklin Roosevelt ; in Brussels the King and Queen went to the station to meet him, as one of their oldest friends. King George of England, who had known Paderewski for a great many years, remarked after decorating him on June 25th, 1925, with the Grand Cross of the British Empire, that he thought Paderewski was one of the greatest men he had ever met. Paderewski's friendship with Arthur Balfour was of a particularly intimate kind, both men having the greatest admiration for each other. In a way Paderewski represented for Balfour something that he himself might have been, but never achieved. Here was a man with a particular talent and yet with an all-round intelligence that enabled him to talk brilliantly about practically any subject, serious or frivolous ; a first-rate statesman who had not needed to sacrifice his artistic integrity and intellectual ambitions to achieve his political aims ; a man who could enjoy the quiet appreciation of the few whose judgment he valued more than anything in the world, and yet one who could dazzle vast crowds. Balfour once said in a conversation : " Paderewski is one of the very few people to whom the word genius can be applied."

In England Paderewski was now especially popular. His rigid political fairness appealed to the English ideas of political decency. What made his career as a statesman particularly attractive to the English was the fact that its predominantly English qualities were coupled with a personality that had many of the typically Continental traits which the English adored. The picturesqueness that would have been considered affected in an English artist was admired in Paderewski. Brilliance of conversation and obvious intellectual keenness in an Englishman met with a certain suspicion ; in a Pole they were acclaimed. Paderewski realized that, and it seemed that in England his sense of humour let itself go even more than ordinarily. He did not forget it in England even when on a concert platform. One day when he played at Oxford the hall was

somewhat stuffy and two ladies sitting on the crowded
platform quite near Paderewski insisted upon some windows
being opened. A violent draught blew down Paderewski's
back, and after he had finished playing an item he turned to
the ladies and said : " Excuse me, I must insist upon the
windows being closed again. You can't possibly have both
pleasures at the same time : listening to good music and
killing the pianist."

Women were delighted with an introduction to Paderewski,
now almost seventy. He was one of the very few men in
post-war society whose compliments actually made them
blush with delight. They adored being told charming, old-
fashioned things about their youthful appearance, their
complexion or their clothes by one who was considered the
most spoiled of men. Every friend at a party was treated by
Paderewski as though he or she were the principal guest of
the evening. He still possessed the gift of finding the right
answer even if taken by surprise. One day Lady Oxford,
when introducing one of her guests to Paderewski, realized
for the first time that Paderewski lived at Morges, a little
town of a few thousand inhabitants. She exclaimed
enthusiastically, " You live at Morges ? Then you must
know that dear friend of mine, Stravinsky. Don't you
agree that he is the greatest composer ? " Considering
that Paderewski's intense dislike of modern music was
almost proverbial, and that his inborn suspicion of any
member of a race that had oppressed Poland for more
than a hundred years was one of the best-known traits
of his nature, the question found him rather unprepared.
Nevertheless he answered : " M. Stravinsky and I
used to bathe at the opposite ends of the lake ; so we
never met in the water. And as Morges is such a huge
place we never met on land either." Even when exhausted
after a recital Paderewski never seemed too tired to find the
proper reply. When an enthusiastic admirer in order to
get near Paderewski jumped down from his box into the
stalls shouting excitedly : " Mr Padrousky, you have sent

me to heaven," Paderewski smiled down, answering with a gentle voice : " I am so glad to see that you have come back to earth again." His acute sense of words, whether in his own or a foreign language, had not left him even in the troublesome months in Poland when he had been Premier. Once he had to dine with Mr. Hugh Gibson, the American Minister in Warsaw. It was in the days when the Polish mark was beginning to depreciate and the printing-press was working night and day producing more paper money. Paderewski as Prime Minister had been busy all day, an evening conference had prevented him from arriving on time, and he was an hour late. When the butler eventually announced him, Mr. Gibson crossed the room to receive his distinguished visitor at the door. Shaking hands, he said with a smile : " Mr. Prime Minister, we are here on American territory, and, as you know, in America time is money." Without a moment's hesitation Paderewski answered : " My dear friend, don't you know that I am Prime Minister of Poland, and that in my country time is only paper ? "

VIII

Paderewski the pianist and Paderewski the man were once again celebrated in the whole Western world as only few men before him ; but it was also to Paderewski the statesman and patriot that the Western world paid homage. In 1928 a tribute was paid to Paderewski in the United States, which was an official acknowledgment of his work as a statesman and which was expressed through the mouth of America's most distinguished men. Had it come from Poland it would probably have meant more to Paderewski than most of the achievements of his life. The tenth anniversary of the independence of Poland was chosen for the occasion, and a reception was arranged in New York which, though general in its scope, developed into a tremendous demonstration for Paderewski personally. The list of those who in personal speech or in a written message put their feelings for Paderewski into words reads like a roll-call of America's most distinguished citizens. It was headed by the President and three ex-Presidents of the United States. Calvin Coolidge, the President at the time, spoke of Paderewski's " outstanding devotion to the advancement of humanitarian and cultural causes." Words of a similar kind were used by Franklin Roosevelt, Hoover, Taft, by General Dawes, Kellogg, James Davies, Lansing. Of the present twenty-four Governors of American States one said : " I admire Paderewski more than any other great man of our time " ; Elihu Root, the " great old man " of American political life, used similar words ; Nicholas Murray Butler, President of Columbia University, referred to Paderewski as " one of the chief ornaments of the public life of our time . . ." and Charles E. Hughes, the Chief Justice of America, said : " Creative power has rarely had such an opportunity, and rarely has opportunity been so nobly used." Norman Davies considered it " an honour to pay tribute to the great liberator of Poland." The tributes of Bishop Manning, of New York, of John D. Rockefeller, of General Pershing and of a score of other leading Americans were equally flattering or affectionate.

As impressive as this list of America's leading citizens who combined in their tribute of the Western world to the Polish pianist was the list of the honorary degrees and decorations, that showed what the world thought of him. Almost every year some university honoured itself by investing Paderewski with a degree. He was Honorary Doctor of the Universities of Oxford, Yale, Cracow, Lwow, Columbia, Southern California, Poznan, Glasgow, Lausanne, New York. He held the Grand Cross of the British Empire and high orders of a number of other countries. He even possessed the two highest Orders of Poland : the White Eagle of Poland, and the Grand Cross of Polonia Restituta.

CHAPTER TWO

ANGER OF THE GODS

I

THE envy of the gods had been roused. To feed their anger the gods had chosen the most vulnerable parts of a victorious life. First they had robbed Paderewski of his mother, then they had killed his young wife, then again his beloved son. Now Mme Helena was gradually withdrawn from their previous intimacy. In the twenty-five years of their married life she had been the focus of Paderewski's search for human intimacy. The unity of purpose which directed the whole of his existence ruled even his most intimate relationships. All his life he was sensitive to feminine beauty and the influence of women; he was worshipped and spoiled by them; nevertheless, during all these years, he remained passionately devoted to the woman who was his wife. Both were no longer young, yet their mutual devotion still retained the warmth and the tenderness of earlier years. Paderewski must have been conscious of certain of Mme Helena's actions that affected her popularity unfavourably—but they did not influence his gratitude and affection.

Was it the impeccability of his private life that was responsible for an almost puritanical attitude towards moral problems? Paderewski's ideas about morals were very much opposed to what one would have expected in a man who enjoyed all the good things in life, who was broad-minded, sensuous, vital. This attitude was especially noticeable when there was the danger of some scandal in his own entourage or when someone had taken a step which in Paderewski's eyes was not strictly reputable. At times it would be simply a mild flirtation between some of the younger guests at Riond Bosson. In such a case the master of the house would summon the unfortunate culprit, and would walk with him up and down his study or along the terrace, delivering a very stern lecture, putting the whole prestige of his personality into his argument, and ending with grave and fatherly advice. Paderewski expected in others his own high moral standards.

But few things roused his anger more than the slightest signs of disrespect towards Mme Helena. Even a casual word that lacked admiration or appreciation could make him an enemy. One day a guest recalled an incident that had happened many years ago, remarking : " But after all your wife is much older than yourself." The expression on Paderewski's face resembled that of a lion who might at any moment become dangerous. Carefully emphasizing every word, Paderewski said : "You are grossly mistaken, Sir. My wife is much younger than myself. But I also want you to know that I still consider her the most beautiful woman I have ever seen." Turning to his sister, he said in a whisper which was loud enough to be heard in the farthest corner of the room : " That man must never be asked again." Such remarks about Mme Helena were amongst the very few which roused Paderewski to forceful retaliation, when his engaging smile turned to the alarming expression of a satyr. Afterwards he was always sorry. But his feelings about Mme Helena were so strong as to make complete self-control impossible.

II

Paderewski had escaped the danger of creating around himself that magic circle common to many great artists, in which self-centredness and a detachment from everyday life reign supreme. Without himself realizing it, he became the centre of another circle, which, but for his strong

PADEREWSKI WITH MME HELENA
At Riond Bosson (1929)

common sense, would also have removed him from the world of reality. It may be that a man whose mind is constantly active, who works very hard and with more concentration than ordinary people, requires for the little activities of everyday life an entourage of much smaller people than himself. Most great men would be perfect if it were not for their followers and their immediate circle. Daily intercourse with smaller people does not call for much mental effort ; they belong to the routine of everyday. So it was with Paderewski's domestic life. It consisted to a large extent of adoring women with but little sense of proportion, without any very close contacts with the world of reality and with a natural tendency to emotional exaltation. These women judged and saw the world as though Paderewski were its centre. Everything that was not hero-worship in its purest form was sacrilege. They would not admit the slightest fault in their hero. Everything he did, said, felt or thought was superior to the action, word, feeling or idea of anyone else in the world. The man of flesh and blood, intensely alive, exquisitely human, fully conscious of the tiniest detail around him, was already looked upon as a god with a halo of divine wisdom. The language these women spoke and the feelings they expressed had but little to do with reality. When at dinner, one hot summer's evening, Paderewski wiped his forehead with a handkerchief, one of them turned to a guest and murmured : " Look at him. Doesn't he look like Our Lord ? So pale, so tired, so weak." But the man who was so pale, so tired and so weak, was at the moment enjoying a very substantial cutlet and an excellent glass of wine which were to be followed by other dishes and wines of equal excellence.

Besides Mme Helena there was Paderewski's devoted sister, Mme Wilkonska, whom we have seen in an early photograph, sitting with an air of childish superiority between her father and her piano-teacher. Now, as an elderly lady, she was full of pride, handsome with her white hair and her keen face, energetic, a busy housekeeper, but devoid of any sense of reality in regard to her adored brother. She had married as a young girl, but the marriage had not been a success, and after the war she had come to live with her brother and run his house for him. There was a lady secretary who had become a confidential friend of the family ; her old mother also moved into the house. And there were one or two other women in some way connected with Paderewski or his wife. The rooms and the world in which Paderewski lived were for them sanctuaries that could be opened to a stranger only if he approached them in a spirit of perfect worship.

Paderewski himself could hardly have been conscious of all this. He took his domestic circle for granted without bothering too much about the details, though their oddity might strike a stranger. Yet occasionally even Paderewski must have had a feeling of discomfort. At times it looked as though he were trying to escape from the grip of life at home, suddenly finding excuses that, if only for an hour or two, would enable him to absent himself.

For example, his Spanish lessons. Paderewski had a genuine interest in Spanish. When he lived during the war in the United States, he had started taking Spanish lessons. He liked the peculiar style of the language, and the intonation and music of spoken Spanish appealed to him. He owned a property in South America. On his Californian ranch he had often come across Spanish traditions and customs. Certain Spanish words had roused his interest as much as did the origins of certain Spanish proverbs and superstitions ; he wanted to know where they came from. He was eager to read the Spanish classics in their own language. He was horrified when he was told that a man like Henri Bergson was incapable of reading the German philosophers in their own language. He, Paderewski, always sought for first-hand information and original versions. There were enough obvious reasons for his decision to take Spanish lessons.

He started taking them seriously in 1924. As he did

not like preparing lessons at home, he decided to have
five lessons a week, of two hours each. His teacher was a
young Spaniard who lived at Lausanne. Either Paderewski
went to Lausanne or Señor Carrasco would come to Riond
Bosson. But wherever the lesson took place, it invariably
lasted longer than its prescribed time, and no one in the
household was allowed to interrupt it. During the Spanish
lessons the magic circle of Riond Bosson was broken.

Paderewski was equally fluent in Polish, French and
English, and in any of these languages he could make a
speech or write a book. He had a perfect knowledge of
Russian, and his German was excellent, although he disliked
talking German. Now he was going to add Spanish to
his linguistic storehouse. After beginning in 1924, he
took up his lessons again in 1926 and in 1929. By then
he was able to read all the Spanish classics ; he could
converse easily in Spanish and even make a speech in it.
At times it appeared as though his thirst for Spanish was
only one reason for his lessons : these lessons furnished an
excuse which otherwise could not easily be found.

III

Was Paderewski afraid of his home circle ? Did he
anticipate that the tragic blow of his life would come from
there ? There had been thunder in the air at Riond
Bosson for a number of years. The inhabitants of the big
house felt it daily, but they hoped that the clouds would
soon disappear and that the master of the house would be
saved. He must have seen the clouds as clearly as anybody.
Increasing from day to day, the tragedy had been approaching now for so long that the final strike was almost a foregone
conclusion. Mme Helena had been in indifferent health
for some time, and she was becoming more and more
sensitive. It was not, however, till 1929 that her poor
health required that for the first time Paderewski should go
on a tour alone. For thirty years neither of them had ever

14

undertaken a journey without the other's companionship, and for weeks Mme Helena had been nervous and anxious. She had been crying the whole morning. She was conscious of all the help that she had been able to offer her husband on previous occasions, and the idea of letting him go alone appalled her. Paderewski was to leave Riond Bosson soon after lunch, and they sat down to their last meal together. As usual Paderewski and his wife sat opposite each other while several members of the household sat with them along the table. Suddenly Mme Helena burst into tears and turned to the person nearest to her, exclaiming with sobs : " I should not have let him go alone. I should not have let him go. . . ." An expression of intense anxiety came into Paderewski's face. He leaned forward and said in a soft voice as though trying to pacify his wife : " But, Helenka darling, I am still with you." Although no greater blow could have been struck at Paderewski, no one was allowed to see how much the gradual loss of his life companion meant to him. More gold streaks in his hair turned white. Otherwise he remained the same hardworking, brilliant, genial companion. In the afternoon, however, when nobody was about, he would steal quietly into the rooms which were left entirely at Mme Helena's disposal and would tell his most intimate friends afterwards that he had tried to re-establish a contact which higher powers had attacked. He would sit facing her in a chair and would take her hand and talk to her ; he would be sweet to her as to a child and as though he hoped that his words might fall on fruitful ground. If Mme Helena responded to his tender words he forgot all the wretchedness of his situation ; he would come down and join the others as cheerful as though something wonderful had happened.

In reality his high spirits must have been a comedy played for the benefit of others ; inwardly the tragedy grew more and more intense.

IV

On September 21st of the same year Paderewski was seized with an unfamiliar pain. The family doctor, M. Masson from Morges, was called in and diagnosed appendicitis. Never before had Paderewski been ill ; chills and colds were all he had allowed himself. In the late evening the state of the patient became worse : it was as though the suppressed mental suffering of the past months were seeking relief in physical outbreak.

Dr. Jacques Roux, a surgeon from Lausanne, was called in. He confirmed the diagnosis of his colleague : it was a clear case of appendicitis. But both doctors felt the responsibility of operating on a man of Paderewski's age and fame. They were also well aware of the mental torment which their patient had suffered during the last few months. The two doctors went into another room to decide on their plan of action. Dr. Roux was the calmer of the two : a self-possessed, quiet man with the matter-of-fact manner of the surgeon. Dr. Masson was more excited ; he was the family doctor and could call himself an intimate friend of the patient. Neither of the two men dared to make the final decision, and ultimately Dr. Roux decided to consult his uncle, César Roux, one of the most celebrated surgeons in Europe. César Roux was rung up on the telephone and advised an immediate operation.

Paderewski was willing to be operated on without further delay. He had spent the last few hours in arranging his papers and in settling business matters with the notary from Morges, who was his financial adviser. The doctors realized that his pain was increasing every minute, but they were the only people who were aware of it. Nobody else in the house was allowed to know that the master was in pain. Paderewski went to everyone in the house and shook hands with each one individually, and at half-past two in the morning he called his two doctors, saying : " *Messieurs, je suis prêt.*"

Before three o'clock a motor-car with the patient, the two doctors and Marcel was speeding through the dark towards Lausanne. Paderewski walked to the operating-table in quiet and cheerful mood. Soon after three Dr. Jacques Roux performed the operation. It was a complete success.

v

It seemed that his mental suffering must seek further expression in bodily ailment. In October Paderewski developed swellings in both legs and a particularly bad form of phlebitis, which forced him to remain in the nursing-home for months. He left it just in time to spend Christmas at Riond Bosson, but he was still far from well.

After a short stay at home he decided to go to Nice ; but even there he did not recover and there were days when the pain of the swelling in his legs prevented him from walking. As playing the piano was still a financial necessity to Pader-ewski, and as for many months he had not been able to touch that instrument, he decided to go to Paris without further delay, though it was doubtful whether he would be restored to health in time to start another tour the same year. But the old stubborn pride prevented him from giving way or betraying his real state of health.

This characteristic was demonstrated very strikingly on the day Paderewski was to leave for Paris. He wished to leave Nice quietly and did not disclose the date or hour of his departure to anyone. His swollen legs were paining him considerably. Unwilling to betray his condition to anyone, Paderewski did not even carry a stick. When he appeared on the platform accompanied by two or three friends there was quite a crowd of admirers waiting to see him. Somehow the news of his departure must have leaked out. As a rule Paderewski took kindly to ovations, but on this occasion he became really alarmed. Each step gave him pain. As long as he walked on level ground he could contrive to walk without limping or suffering unduly ;

but to climb the few steep steps into the railway carriage
without showing signs of pain would be quite impossible.
The bell rang. The sweat on Paderewski's forehead was
the only thing that betrayed the nervous strain through
which he was passing. No, he could not possibly climb
these steps ; rather would he let the train go without him.
On the second when the train actually began to move, he
jumped up the three steps with all the vigour of a young
man. But his friends on the platform could not see that
inside the carriage Marcel had just picked up his master on
the verge of collapse, his face distorted with pain and almost
unrecognisable.

In Paris M. Blondel, one of Paderewski's oldest friends,
suggested the name of a doctor in Orléans who was beginning
to become famous for his unorthodox and outstanding cures.
Dr. Choussou had the reputation of being something of a
character. He was of a retiring disposition. Paderewski's
confidence had been shaken by the fruitless cures he had
undergone. Nevertheless he decided to see the doctor.
Dr. Choussou immediately adopted an entirely different
method ; he allowed his patient to move about instead of
remaining motionless in bed, and bandaged the legs in a
particular way. After a few weeks' treatment Paderewski
was able to go walking unattended. When the time for the
autumn tour arrived, he was cured and ready to start on his
strenuous professional journey across the Atlantic.

CHAPTER THREE

IMMORTALITY

I

ALTHOUGH in the opinion of some people Paderewski's post-war playing no longer possessed all its former qualities, his popularity on the concert platform did not suffer at all. Crowds may be bad judges of the subtle arts of piano playing or of politics, but they are very sensitive to signs of true greatness. Paderewski may no longer have been the greatest pianist, but he certainly was still the greatest man that had ever been a pianist. The crowds flocked to see him.

Paderewski even now played as no one else could the Beethoven Sonata Pathétique, many of Chopin's Polonaises, some of the shorter Schumann pieces and, above all, Liszt's Hungarian Rhapsodies. When he played the Hungarian Rhapsodies it seemed hardly possible that it was only one piano which filled the Albert Hall, or Madison Square Hall ; the piano seemed to become a huge orchestra, and the audience clutched the arms of their chairs with excitement. In the opinion of some critics, on the other hand, Paderewski's individuality of style, which once had been the sign of his powerful independence, now took excessive liberties. They said that his *tempo rubato*, once responsible for the incomparable richness of his interpretation, was rendering it unintelligible ; that his exaggerated pedalling was drowning the clearness of the detail ; that his forte too often became fortissimo and his presto prestissimo. The younger generation of musicians criticized particularly his broken chords, which since the war were out of fashion. But

Paderewski still produced by their means effects that nobody else could approach. He broke his chords if the right and the left hand were playing two different melodies because in such cases the unbroken chords in the right hand masked the tune in the left. By accelerating or delaying one hand by the infinitesimal part of a second he was able clearly to produce both melodies. This gave his playing a full melodic richness, which was often responsible for Paderewski's orchestra-like qualities. Likewise Paderewski was still the master of a rare technique which enabled him to play a crescendo with one hand while the other faded away in a diminuendo. Such independence of the two hands produced the strangest harmonies and colours. Without realizing whence they came every audience succumbed to their effects.

And yet it was often said that all these subtle methods, instead of being the invisible undercurrent, were becoming the main substance of Paderewski's art. Nevertheless his post-war audiences were amazed at his virile and youthful playing. More than anyone Paderewski confirmed their idea of " playing from the heart." This was due to the fact that he would forget himself entirely when he was playing, and that at such moments the composition became the whole essence of his existence. If certain passages of a composition made the audience sad, or even made it weep, it was because Paderewski himself suffered acutely and because he too wept. Even his masterly self-control could not prevent him from showing outward signs of the deep effects which the music had on him. At many concerts he would actually cry over certain passages ; he would utter deep sighs, his mouth would tremble, an expression of agony would come over his parted lips, as though he were going through all the sufferings of the composer himself. Perhaps this was one of the many reasons why Paderewski could play only in a darkened hall. Even so, listeners in the front rows could often perceive the signs of emotion that all his will-power could not control. Sometimes they would see

large tears stealing from under his closed lids.   Some people
condemned all this as mere sentimentality.   In reality it
was the force and the human character of Paderewski's
musical reaction.

It was by no means only the older people who in those
years after the war filled the big halls in order to hear
Paderewski.   The younger generation could not resist the
indefinable fascination of his playing, even though they
often did not approve its details.   They realized that he
had powers which could not be judged by standards of mere
piano playing.

II

For years Paderewski had looked upon himself as the greatest pianist alive.   He considered his own musical knowledge
so much more mature than that of any critic, and the newspaper opinions so often disagreed with the reality as he
himself saw it, that he did not feel he could pay any attention
to press critiques.   What mattered to Paderewski were the
people he played for ;   not one particular critic or a select
group.   While he could rouse the frenzied enthusiasm of
such varied crowds as those at Toronto and Birmingham,
Cape Town and Barcelona, Paris and Buffalo, Brisbane and
Lausanne, he did not bother about what the gentlemen of
the local papers in those towns had to say.

Paderewski was very definite in his belief that his playing
could not be judged by musical standards only.   Some critics
argue that in music only musical standards hold good.
But the meaning of musical standards has not yet been
clearly defined by the critics themselves ;   presumably
because it is an impossible task.   An artist who can appeal
to the deepest emotional faculties has gone beyond the
limitations of purely musical criteria.   Human or racial
elements may enter in which cannot be easily defined by
professional canons.   Though he never actually said so,
Paderewski must have believed strongly that the pedestal on
which he stood was higher than that of any other virtuoso,

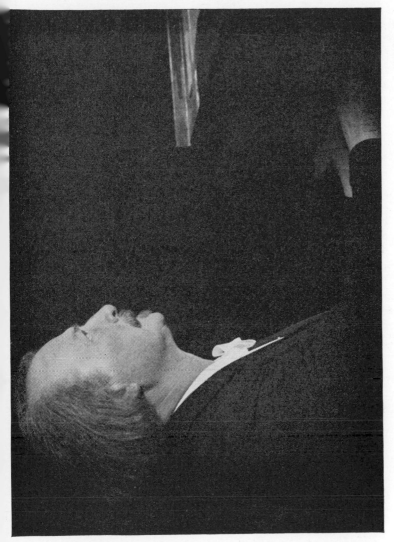

PADERERWSKI AT THE PIANO

PADEREWSKI AT THE PIANO
(London, 1925)

(By courtesy of J. G. Adlington, Esq.)

216]

including even Liszt and Rubinstein. But he himself was only partially responsible for this attitude of supreme pride, the chief responsibility resting with the world in which he lived. The behaviour of the crowds, of crowned heads, of statesmen, of artists, who all pursued him and sought his company, openly admitting that their love for the man equalled their admiration for the artist, formed as it were a magic carpet which carried him year in and year out, and which gave him this consciousness of superiority. The admiration of the crowds was like a reserve of power from which his playing drew qualities that no other pianist could possess. One day after the war the pianist, Ossip Gabrilo-witsch, the son-in-law of Mark Twain, said jokingly : " We had better all become Premiers and then come back to music ! " He was actually not far short of the mark. Pader-ewski's premiership was one of the many phenomena that were responsible for his pianistic superiority. It may be true that after the war Paderewski played less distinctly or that his playing was noisier than that of younger pianists. But there was an even greater maturity and depth in it than there was before the war ; and none of the younger pianists roused the very musical audiences at the Carnegie Hall, the Queen's Hall or at the Théâtre des Champs Elysées to such a pitch of exaltation. Some critics wrote that they could not understand why this should be so. It may be that in some critics the ordinary emotional response is so overlaid with purely musical considerations that they are no longer able to perceive the " non-musical " powers of Paderewski's playing. When asked about critics, Paderewski said : " Between the artist and the critic stand the public. If the public acclaim me, it matters little what the critics have to say."

III

It was not surprising that by now Paderewski was but little interested in other pianists, and that he went to hear them only on very rare occasions. It was more than mere lack of interest.   It is only in his youth that a virtuoso is anxious to possess himself of the secrets of other artists. Later the consciousness of his own achievement directs his curiosity towards himself, and makes him seek to understand his own talent fully to perceive the pattern of his own fate.   At less than forty years of age Paderewski was already on a dazzling pinnacle of perfection.   For thirty years the world convinced him that no other artists could give greater power and subtler beauty to the piano.   By the time the post-war generation of pianist appeared, Paderewski's musical ideas were definitely set.

There were other reasons for his apparent lack of interest in the younger pianists.   He could hardly be expected to enter whole-heartedly into the spirit of the era they represented.   An almost boundless gulf separated them from each other : it was as though Paderewski's artistic achievement and that of Iturbi, Horowitz, Poulenc, Levitzky, Gieseking and Fischer were of different worlds.   The younger pianists may have been more " purely musical," if by that is meant that their interests are centred in the pure quality of the instrument they play and not in the emotional possibilities for which it might be used.   To the younger generation Paderewski was old-fashioned ; they called him romantic, which after all he was.   He believed in the poetry of music, while they believed in the music only, the word poetry evoking in them a feeling of slight embarrassment.   Another point was that Paderewski was the last representative of a generation of pianists that did not consider the piano as a limited instrument like the violin, but acknowledged the fact that it could be used as an orchestra.   As long as *tempo rubato*, individual accentuations and artistry in using the pedal enabled him to produce more colour and a wider range of effect, for Paderewski they were legitimate means.   Liszt, Rubinstein and Paderewski " conducted " the piano, while Iturbi, Stravinsky or Poulenc just " play " it.   To the younger pianists the music that they play hardly represents more than the score itself : an ingenious

accumulation of sounds, rhythms, accents, colours, syncopa-
tions and harmonies. Just as light strikes the eye or as an
electric shock reaches the nervous system, so the sounds and
rhythms of the modern pianist have to reach the emotions
of the listener. They are not meant to evoke the listener's
response until they awaken his emotional or intellectual
associations. Paderewski, on the other hand, shed tears
over Chopin's nostalgia ; the Polish rhythm of Mazurkas
or Cracoviennes were not simply musical forms to him like
Etude or Nocturne, but were instinct with humanity.
Life and music were one. It may be that the musical
background which Paderewski sensed and recreated was
nothing but an illusion and that he was an illusionist.
Nevertheless his illusions were as vital to him as was their
super-realism to the younger generation. Paderewski did not
exhibit a single manifestation of life, but the whole of life
as he knew it ; he identified himself with the music while
the young pianists were mostly content with interpreting it.
If the art of the younger men was a transparent crystal,
Paderewski's was a diamond flashing and fiery. The piano
sang for Paderewski ; for the younger men it sounded.
Paderewski meant to sing ; they meant to play. They
were not better and they were not worse, but they
worshipped at different shrines.

IV

The desire for immortality is one of the natural instincts
of men. All possess it, though not all agree as to the form
in which they would like to see it cast. The most general
instinct strives after physical immortality through children ;
artists dream of achieving it through their work ; others
hope to find it in heaven, or in Nirvana, or in the endless
cycle of reincarnation.

Paderewski's only child was dead. The art of the virtuoso
dies with the man himself. The circumstances of Paderewski's life had forced him to give up composition, his most

obvious claim to immortality. He had always known that in order to reach the heights in piano playing one had to devote one's life to it. There was little time left for other things. Nevertheless, for a long time he did not abandon the hope that one day he might be able to come back to composing to make of it the essence of his work. While he was Prime Minister a friend asked him whether he would ever take up piano playing again, to which Paderewski replied : " Never, but I shall start composing again ; I shall give myself up entirely to composition." But that was not to be. The piano was forced upon him by fate and circumstance, there remained no time for composition, and he realized that it would be vain to cherish the hope of a new creative spell as a composer. One evening at Riond Bosson he said to a friend : " As a composer I am a corpse now, just a corpse." His ambition as a composer was never to be fully realized.

Paderewski hardly needed to worry about his immortality. Even in politics his name was chiselled too deeply ever to be forgotten. The new Polish State bore his name and his spirit in its very foundations. On the other hand, it was the work of many makers and it would immortalize his name only together with the names of others.

It is doubtful whether thoughts of this kind ever entered the mind of a man who was much too active to waste time over metaphysical speculations. But Fate does not ask whether we are conscious of her commands or not. A deep instinct compels us to do things for which we find enough excuses later, believing that nothing but accident dictated our doings. If a famous man of nearly seventy, a man full of occupations, worshipped by his friends, gifted with the most varied of accomplishments, if such a man almost for the first time in his life sets out to teach a group of young men all the ideas and methods which he himself made triumphant ; if he gives himself up to this instruction with all the devotion of mature age and all the vigorous enthu- siasm of youth—then it seems legitimate to say that he is

also seeking after a self-realization which will last beyond
the grave and which will bear his message to generations
still to come.

Paderewski had often been asked to give lessons. Besides
his few regular pupils of former years, the American
composer, Ernest Schelling, the pianist Harold Bauer, or
the Polish composer Stojowski, he would occasionally give a
lesson to a friend or to someone who had been recommended
to him. But after Strassburg and his success as a virtuoso
he had never had a group of pupils with whom he worked
year after year ; in whose careers he had a personal interest ;
whom he coached in those ideas and methods which were
responsible for his own success : pupils, in short, he intended
to be the real heirs of his art. Almost ten years after the war
and at the age of nearly seventy he found himself for the
first time confronted with such teaching as a reality with all
its excitement and all its importance. On several occasions
after the war he had come across young Polish pianists who
had impressed him sufficiently to evoke in him the desire
to make them his pupils. That desire was fulfilled in a
group of five youngish men. Occasionally they were joined
by one or two pianists, but primarily those five were
selected to become the legitimate heirs of Paderewski's
musical method. They were men of varied abilities and
varying ages ; at first there was no clear-cut plan or
time limit. Soon, however, the indeterminate beginnings
developed into regular work, which was to continue for a
number of years. Not all the pupils were able to afford a
long period of further education without the means of
earning their living, and Paderewski decided to help two
of them so long as they remained under his tuition. It
went without saying that all of them must be Polish.
During the months in which the lessons took place, that is
to say, between June and the late autumn, when for
Paderewski a fresh concert tour would begin, his pupils
came to live in or near Morges.

V

Paderewski gave his lessons once a week. During the rest of the week the five Poles had to work and to prepare for the lesson. The lesson was generally on Saturdays, and Saturday became an enchanted day for them. They looked forward to it as to a feast ; they counted the days ; they strove to be at their best when the day should come round, and they were so much under the spell of their teacher's personality that when eventually Saturday arrived, their love and their admiration for Paderewski turned to a state of nervousness which can only be described as sheer terror. One of them never played so badly as he did on Saturdays when he sat down at the piano in the study on the first floor at Riond Bosson. Paderewski must have been conscious of the effect of his personality upon his pupils. Although invariably kind to them, he never forgot the importance of the impression he made upon them, even though the proper staging of his personality actually increased their fright. After all, his pupils were an audience, and an audience always had to be impressed. Familiarity, joviality, equality found no place in his system of teaching.

The pupils generally assembled in the big hall at three o'clock. If luncheon was not quite finished, they had to wait. Then Paderewski would appear in the hall, smoking his post-prandial cigarette. To all seeming he was not in that state of nerves into which a concert was wont to put him. Nevertheless there was a perceptible nervousness which implied that the lessons meant almost as much to him as they did to his pupils ; his geniality and kindness were transformed into an impatient excitability and abruptness of manner.

Paderewski led the way. The five pupils followed him through the hall, with its many pictures and portraits, up the wooden staircase into the study. For them this was the room in which for the last thirty years all the mysteries of the Liszt Rhapsodies, the Beethoven and Mozart Sonatas, the Chopin compositions were finding their final shape, where the art of the virtuoso reached its crown. That consciousness alone intimidated them. The room was large and high, with walls of a faded pinky colour and with old-fashioned, undistinguished furniture. Against one wall was the upright piano on which Paderewski used to practise; in front of it stood a low chair covered with worn red leather. On the piano was a small portrait of Chopin, and above it hung two reproductions of drawings by Burne-Jones made the same day as the famous profile drawings of 1891 ; but though Paderewski had served as their model, they represented armed knight-errants of dreamy and expressive air. In the middle of the room stood an enormous writing-table, covered with innumerable papers, letters and books. The light streamed on to it through a large window looking over the lake and gardens, backed by Mont Blanc. Between the writing-table and the window there was a glass case filled with Chinese *objets d'art* : a few carved pieces of greenish jade, more mellow than stone and less outspoken than emeralds, but fuller of character than either ; some unpretentious china vases of the Ming period, almost painfully convincing in the simplicity of their shapes and their plain, unblemished glazes ; cloisonné jars, ostentatious and overdressed in such an aristocratic company, and, as the radiating centre of the collection, a few pieces of the costly glass *Jaune Impérial*, of which the rare and intense yellow colour seemed to embody Eastern mystery as though coming from the very centre of the Forbidden City.

In the corner of the room next to the window was the grand piano on which the pupils were to play. A small pen drawing representing Liszt as an elegant young man was hanging on the wall, and above it there was an original sheet from a Liszt composition. These musical documents created the real atmosphere of the room ; the glass case with the Chinese collection was only a guest, for all its beauty, distant and strange. Above the piano there was also a large old-fashioned photograph of Paderewski as a young man in the clothes of the eighties, and an even bigger photograph of his son, Alfred, as a boy of ten or twelve. Those many eyes looking down from their large frames on each piece of fingering, each passage, each tiniest mistake must have affected the sensitive nerves of the five pupils.

VI

Before the lesson began chairs were placed for those four of them who had to wait. The chairs were placed in such a position in front of the window that the young men could see from them both the hands of Paderewski and those of their fellow-pupil. Paderewski himself settled down at his upright piano, but he would turn his head towards the window to watch the pupil who was seated at the other piano.

The first pupil began. It was the tensest moment of the afternoon. Paderewski said hardly a word ; thunder seemed in the air, though no sound was heard, and no one dared to move. The first notes of a composition, practised incessantly for six long days and sometimes for many nights, rang through the room. Sometimes Paderewski would not utter a word even after his pupil had finished playing. In silence he would just take a small golden cigarette-case out of a pocket, open it rather slowly, extract a cigarette, put back the case, take out a flat gold match-case and light the cigarette. That was terrifying. It was more terrifying even than the sudden interruptions that sometimes came from the upright piano :   " So that is how you play it ! " Paderewski would suddenly say in a quiet, sympathetic voice which, however, did not entirely conceal the undertone of sarcasm. At other times he did not even pretend to be nice and kind. At such times he would say pitilessly and in biting tones : " Is it the piano, Mr. Brachocki, that you are playing? "

Paderewski the teacher was very formal and polite even when his tone of voice was not. During a lesson he never

addressed his pupils by their Christian names and he never
omitted the Polish " Pan " or " Panie," which means
Mister. Crowned heads could not have wished for more
respectful treatment. But the formality of his remarks made
their undertone of irony doubly alarming. Sometimes he
would deliberately address his pupil in a certain way which
was more biting than any sarcasm : " You pretend that
you have just played Chopin. It was beautiful, was it not,
Panie Dygacie ? " he would ask his pupil Dygat. It was
the correct formal manner of addressing the unfortunate
gentleman whose name happened to be " Pan Dygat "
(Mr. Dygat). But in that particular case the grammatical
form had a provocative sound that would bring a flush to
sensitive cheeks. As Pan Dygat was small, rather girlish
and very sensitive, he not only blushed, but he forgot what
the master's question had been and whether what he had
been playing had really been Chopin and beautiful.

Paderewski's impatience and irony were nothing but
a form of nervousness. As time went on, this nervousness
diminished. He became less ironical and less personal,
and the pitiless teacher was transformed into a loved and
honoured friend. From being for him the causes of a
nerve-racking performance, his pupils became new and
exciting instruments that Paderewski began to experiment
with, to " play," to bring to perfection.

There was a short interval for tea in the dining-room,
during which Paderewski read the afternoon mail. After
tea Paderewski's earlier nervousness would have worn off.
Whereas his pupils began to get tired, he became keener.
No longer did he sit at his piano, to all appearances taking
but little interest in the proceedings, and only occasionally
interrupting the pupil with a remark. Now interruptions
followed one another. Paderewski was no longer thinking
of his pupils or of the lessons, but of the playing, of the
audience, of the concert which would be the eventual
outcome. " No, you are not playing for yourself, you are
playing for three thousand people who want to hear you

15

from the farthest seat in the gallery" he would exclaim. He would then stop the pupil in the middle of his passage and play it himself in such a way as to be really audible to the farthest hearer in the gallery.

These were the joyous moments of the lessons. His pupil's terror was transformed into a musical lust after achievement and into boundless admiration for the man who was disclosing one secret of his art after another. " Everyone must hear you. Piano playing is like a speech. It has to be clear, articulate, distinct. Everyone must understand what you have to say."

Paderewski did not wish his pupils to forget that their ultimate goal was to play for audiences, and not for egocentric dreamers who happened to be virtuosi. He had the highest respect for the audience. In later years, after one of his pupil's concerts, he made the following criticism : " You have played well, but you have made one gross mistake. When bowing to the audience you did not show them enough deference. You treated them as though they didn't matter to you, which is an unforgivable mistake. You must treat your audience with the utmost gratitude and modesty. The audience is a great lady and has to be treated as such. You ought to prepare your bows beforehand ; you ought to study them if necessary in front of a mirror."

Literary meanings or explanations found no place in these lessons ; the only language being the language of music. Musical standards and laws were the only ones that applied. One of the most important things for Paderewski was touch. He insisted upon his pupils playing without moving the hand more than absolutely essential and without raising the fingers. Neither hand nor finger must fall on the keyboard, as such a method produced harshness. The finger-tips must remain in constant touch with the keys ; they must have enough time to manipulate the key even before its hammer strikes the string. This gives them a chance of modulating the tone within extremely fine limits and it creates subtle effects which could not otherwise be obtained. The motion must come from the finger, almost from the finger-tip alone, which must remain on the keyboard ; the hand, the elbow or the arm are there to create the necessary resistance to the efforts of the finger-tips. The sensitiveness and power of the finger-tips were of essential importance to Paderewski. On the other hand, at times he would strike a tone with his whole fist or rather with the joint of the thumb clenched in the fist, this producing a power and brilliance of sound which could not be obtained from the finger alone. Equally important as the touch and the power of the sound was the proper fingering. Often Paderewski would get up from his chair, walk towards the other piano and direct the fingering of every individual note ; then he would take a pencil and cover page after page with the right fingerings.

Never were the pupils allowed to forget that they would have to capture their audience not only once, but over and over again. " Panie Tadlewski, we are not at a race meeting. This is supposed to be piano playing. Haven't you learned yet that speed is of no account whatsoever ? It may impress your listener once, but it will bore him a second time." And Pan Tadlewski was forced to play the passage again, and again, and again, till eventually Paderewski himself played the composition at the speed he desired. Such interruptive criticism was followed by lengthy explanations of the musical structure, of the meaning of the composition and of the particular passage. Each note, each accent, each nuance was explained and eventually forced upon the pupil. Occasionally Paderewski would allow his pupil to adopt an individual interpretation of a composition ; on the whole, however, the master's interpretation was compulsory. Paderewski's attitude was that a pupil has to be practically a slave deprived of all individuality and free will. The pupil can learn from his master only if he believes in the latter's infallibility and if he tries to copy the master in every way. After the period of discipleship the pupil is allowed to forget what he has learned, to give up the things taught by his master, to evolve his own methods and interpretations. As long, however, as he is a pupil, he has to remain a slave.

If ever Paderewski heard a sound outside, he would jump up from his chair, hurry silently to the door and throw it open with one swift movement, expecting to catch the culprit who had dared to listen outside the door. He hated anybody to listen outside his study while a lesson was in progress. Most of the actions of his life took place in the open and in full view of the world ; but when it was a case of special concentration or preparation he strongly resented any intrusion upon his privacy.

It must have been their admiration for their teacher, together with the strength that emanated from him, that helped these young men to keep going to the end of the lesson. The nervous tension, the continuous concentration, the intensity of the initial anxiety and the ultimate pleasure, the strain of the actual work were so great that by the end of the lesson they were all worn out, with the exception of Paderewski himself. Their highest reward came to them if during the lesson Paderewski saw fit to use one of his rare sentences of praise : " Panie Sztompka, that wasn't at all bad." Towards the end of the lesson Paderewski's criticisms would tend to be made in a humorous vein. One of his pupils whose nervousness grew in direct proportion to the amount of trouble that Paderewski took to correct him made more and more mistakes as the lesson went on. After half an hour's fruitless efforts Paderewski began to lose his self-control, but instead of flaring up with devastating candour, he only exclaimed : " Panie Szpinalski, if you go on persistently taking no notice of my instructions, you won't be given any soup at dinner to-night." The spell was broken. The men in the background roared with laughter : Pan Szpinalski was noted for being devoted to the pleasures of the table almost as much as to the joys of music.

VII

At times the lesson lasted till after nine o'clock, and as everyone dined together, the rest of the household would have to wait until the lesson was over. The host, himself in high spirits, appeared in the dining-room followed by the five nervous wrecks from Poland. They were not in the habit of dressing for dinner, and it was all quite informal. The nervous tension of the lesson had passed, and Paderewski was now in that bland mood in which he made jokes and puns. He now looked upon his pupils as though they were members of his own family. They lived in Lausanne or in Morges, near enough to be summoned whenever it was considered necessary. They had to be there if ever Mme Wilkonska needed help in entertaining guests or in getting up a party ; they had to be there if one of the guests were suddenly prevented from coming and somebody had to take his place ; they had to come if it was discovered that there were thirteen about to sit down to dinner. Although Paderewski laughed about it, his own superstition grew with the years. It may not have been very profound—his general outlook was too rational for that—but at times it gave one the impression that there was still some inheritance from his distant forefathers, in whose lives superstition had played its part. Thirteen at table was impossible, and often one of the five young men was summoned, and even if his own evening meal was already over, he had to put on a dress-suit and appear as the fourteenth person at dinner. If they failed to find a fourteenth, Jodko, Paderewski's Polish-American adopted son, would have to leave the big dinner-table and sit at a small table apart where he would be served. Paderewski would also never allow three people to light a cigarette from the same match.

VIII

After a few years a pupils' concert was arranged at Riond Bosson. There was a large and distinguished gathering of friends, many of whom had come from distant parts of Switzerland and even from abroad. Paderewski was as excited as if he had been going to play himself, but when he heard the spontaneous applause of his guests he felt as though a great battle had been won.

The main test, however, did not come till 1933, when his pupils went on tour to carry the message of Paderewski's art and work to Poland. Paderewski must have felt very anxious about this tour ; every new contact with Poland threw him into a state of tremendous excitement. It is difficult to know whether, after he had carefully read all the press notices, even the smallest critique from some Polish provincial newspaper, there were only thoughts of music in Paderewski's mind. There had been some feeling in Poland against the tour. Certain political circles saw in this tour a means of political propaganda by which Paderewski sought after renewed popularity in Poland ; others were opposed to the tour on principle. In various musical sets there was a feeling that Paderewski did not do enough for musical charities in Poland, and that he confined himself to helping the musicians of all the foreign countries which he visited regularly. When questioned one day about the reasons for that, he answered with great solemnity : "Poland must not only know how to take, but also how to give." Even the Jewish press was determined to boycott the concerts, blinded still by the old legends of Paderewski's anti-Semitism. The younger generation of Polish musicians did not care for the school which Paderewski represented ; they mistrusted all forms of romanticism and believed only in a matter-of-fact method, which consisted in serious and realistic musical reading and interpretation. Most of them knew Paderewski only by name ; even in earlier years he had very rarely played in Warsaw, and on most of those occasions in private houses. The general surprise was therefore great when it was discovered that, even when judged by the most modern standards of piano playing, some of Paderewski's pupils had to be acknowledged as musicians

of distinction. The tour was an outstanding success ;
the power of the name Paderewski coupled with considerable
curiosity in musical circles swept aside all obstacles, and at
a time of severe economic depression the tour proved to be
one of the rare musical occasions in Poland which enjoyed
not only an artistic but also a financial success.

The Polish tour was the crowning event of Paderewski's
educational experiment.

CHAPTER FOUR

THE TRAGEDY OF GREATNESS

I

RIOND BOSSON was still a centre for a number of people. Between autumn and late spring Paderewski was away on tour. Since he had once more taken up his career as a pianist, he had fulfilled a number of engagements in the United States, South Africa, South America, Australia and in most of the countries of Europe. Even when he was away the house was kept open and the great household went on with all its lavish expenditure. When Paderewski was at home many people would be invited to stay at Riond Bosson, and at times the household would be as crowded almost as an hotel. Besides Marcel, who during the summer months was rather a major-domo than a valet, there would be Paderewski's personal valet, an Austrian ; there were Marcel's wife and daughter ; there were a butler and two parlour-maids, three house-maids, a chef, two cooks and two girls in the kitchen, an Italian chauffeur, two laundrywomen, a number of gardeners. Before Mme Helena's illness there had also been a German chicken breeder. As Mme Helena's sister with her son and the son's governess also stayed at Riond Bosson, hardly ever fewer than ten people would sit down to a meal. On Sundays the house would be thrown open to any native of Poland who happened to be in or near Morges and who cared to see the home of his most distinguished compatriot. Paderewski might invite old friends from Poland and from other countries, his pupils, often with their wives and children, relatives of the various

RIOND BOSSON

secretaries, his agents or piano makers, some music critic
from New York or Paris, former political collaborators.
The day of St. Ignace was still celebrated in great splendour,
though, even so, not quite so gaily as in the years when
Riond Bosson still had its real *châtelaine*.

For most of the visitors Riond Bosson had become a name
which stood for much more than just an hospitable house
with a fine garden, or the home of a celebrated artist. It
was a spiritual centre, and the symbol of a certain period
of musical history of the nineteenth and of political history
of the twentieth centuries. For some people Riond Bosson
was what Wahnfried was for any devout Wagnerian ;
for others it was the realization of something that they had
come across only in Russian fiction. Though magnified
and Westernized, it was for them a mansion such as they
had read about in Turgeniev or in Tolstoy. There was
a constant coming and going ; unexpected guests and
whispered conversations ; the flushed cheeks and exaltation
of hero-worshippers ; motor-cars sent with telegrams to
the post office at Morges or with guests from the League of
Nations to Geneva ; dinners that began an hour or two late
because important conferences were taking place in the host's
study ; rooms crowded with furniture ; endless cigarettes
and endless tea ; picturesque men and highly strung women;
discussions in Polish, French, English or Spanish ; plans
altered many times a day and servants stranded in the
midst of their work on account of contradictory orders.
Though there was often high tension in the air, there was
never gloom or depression. When guests were staying in
the house there would be two tables laid in the dining-
room, one for guests and the older members of the household, the other for the sons and daughters of guests, the
pupils and the secretaries. The meals, lasting for hours,
were the main events of the day, and to some guests they were
not less entertaining and exciting than a visit to a theatre.
Paderewski, sitting at the head of the bigger table, led the
conversation, stimulated everybody and was feared by

most. Whether he was right or wrong, no one dared to contradict him. His presence gave not only focus and essence to these gatherings, it also brought harmony and equilibrium into the bustle and excitement of the household. For most guests a visit to Riond Bosson was an intoxicating experience, a rare adventure, a play in which it was sufficient glory to be allowed to act even the smallest part.

II

The cinema had become one of Paderewski's favourite pastimes. When he had old friends to dine with him in London, Paris or New York and it was not a ceremonial occasion, he liked asking them to an early meal and then going on to a cinema. There was no sophistication nor æstheticism about his cinematographic taste, and while the picture flickered across the screen, he liked to believe that the events of the film were real. There seems to be a decided analogy between his attitude to a cinema and to that of his more serious preoccupations. All through his life Paderewski's sense of reality was based on a peculiar kind of faith : it was faith in all the illusions of life which furnished it with an aspect of greater beauty. He had achieved his political successes through his firm belief in ideals that for other politicians had been only illusions. In a way, he was also trying to create illusions on the piano. When a thunderstorm with its vivid lightning and its torrents of rain raged on the screen, Paderewski, half in fun and half automatically, would turn up his coat collar and shiver. It was rarely that a film did not call for his whole attention. In such a case he would relapse into his traditional finger exercises, which consisted of little trills or passages played on the arm of his chair. It was an unmistakable sign of the dullness of a film, if, indicated by an occasional glance from the corner of his eye, the fingers of a hand resting on the balustrade or on a knee were seen to be raised in turn by the fingers of the other hand.

III

In appearance Paderewski no longer resembled the exotic being charming audiences under the dim light of one or two gas-lamps in Victorian concert halls ; the bewitching smile no longer played about the lips of a Burne-Jones youthful knight-errant. Paderewski's face had become sterner, even more awake and in its keenness at times almost frightening. His resemblance to a lion was very striking : there was the same powerful demeanour and dignified poise.

His love for good conversation remained as strong as ever, and he still took the same interest in all linguistic matters. With advancing years he developed a peculiar sensitiveness to his own pronouncements or speeches, and he was almost unhappy if one of his speeches or remarks was falsely reported or some particularly apt phrase or bon mot put into commonplace language. Even when he was Prime Minister and Poland's delegate to the Peace Conference, his oratory and his style were to him as important as the actual point in question. One day, after he had made a speech before the Supreme Council, he was visited at his hotel by the Paris correspondent of a foreign newspaper, who showed him the translation of the French speech which had been wired to the correspondent's newspaper. When Paderewski noticed that certain of his expressions had not been translated adequately, he was very perturbed and kept the journalist with him for almost an hour, trying to persuade him to telegraph a new and improved translation to his newspaper. He could hardly bring himself to accept the excuse that the speed at which it was necessary to work during a most intricate international conference made an exact stylistic rendering almost impossible. This attitude did not change in later years when politics had ceased to be the centre of Paderewski's life. One of his most important political speeches after the war was delivered on May 18th, 1932, at a banquet in his honour in New York. His speech was a brilliant exposition of the real state of affairs in the so-called Polish Corridor and one of the most enlightened surveys of the complex problem of Polish-German relations throughout the history of both nations. The speech was reported in all American newspapers, repeated and reprinted. Although the presentation of the matter could not have been more convincing, Paderewski was very worried when he was shown the uncorrected shorthand reports of his speech and when he found that certain of his sentences and some of his expressions would not pass for perfect English ; and when an adviser helped him to eliminate those slips, he was anxious that the originality of his style and the richness of his vocabulary should not be sacrificed. In the matter of literary style Paderewski in some ways resembled his compatriot Joseph Conrad : he knew the subtle values of the English language, and he shared Conrad's love of rare words, new metaphors and original description.

This speech of May, 1932, in New York also showed that Paderewski's political interest was by no means dead. Poland was constantly at the back of his mind, and he never missed an opportunity of helping the cause of Polish politics abroad or of making propaganda for his native land. This work was never affected by the fact that Paderewski disagreed with the existing political state of affairs in Poland, which with only short exceptions had been guided throughout all those years by Joseph Pilsudski.

Under Pilsudski's unorthodox but beneficial rule the country was growing stronger from year to year. From a " Saison Staat " (Season State),—as the German called it soon after the war,—Poland was becoming one of the important powers in Europe. Pilsudski's methods may often have been obnoxious to Paderewski, but they suited the existing conditions admirably, and they showed an almost uncanny instinct for the opportune policy. Pilsudski consolidated his country with the same success with which he saved it—and with it the whole of Europe—from the Bolshevik invasion in 1920. While he was the real moulder of modern Poland, Paderewski could claim to be Poland's unofficial spiritual Ambassador in the Western world.

IV

And yet life was not just as it had been even quite recently. There was growing peace and calm in Paderewski's daily existence. Though he would hardly admit it, it was plain that since Mme Helena's illness a greater balance had come into his life ; the nervous excitations which Mme Helena used to cause in her husband's life were lacking. Even Paderewski's anxiety before a concert was no longer so acute as it had been : he was less nervous about the instrument on which he was going to play, about the height of the chair he was going to sit on, about the lighting in the hall ; he was no longer so restless during the hours preceding the concert. Little details that in former days used to assume colossal proportions before a recital were reduced to their proper dimensions. Paderewski had even developed a sense of time which in the days before Mme Helena's illness had been of small importance in his daily life. Now his concerts began most punctually ; his appointments and his engagements were all kept to the minute ; he was even punctual for meals. When an intimate friend would occasionally dare to make a remark about this new-found sense of time, Paderewski would smile in answer. Once or twice he said : " I am more punctual than I used to be, they tell me," and then looking at his companion with a quick, amused glance, he added : " Am I really ? " In conversation many subjects were still taboo, especially illness and death. While actual need invariably evoked a desire in Paderewski to help, he never allowed himself to be sentimental. He disliked speaking of his own help as much as he disliked speaking about the ailments of people who were far away or whom he could not help. A smug enjoyment of sorrow was foreign to his nature, and at times his lack of sentimentality would shock people who did not know him well nor the working of his mind. He hated pondering over things that belonged to the past and could not be altered, his mental attitude being pre-eminently masculine and realistic. One day during a lesson a telegram arrived, announcing the death of the Polish 'cellist Adamowski, one of Paderewski's old friends. Paderewski put the telegram away and sat down on a chair. For two or three minutes he did not say a word ; there were no tears in his eyes, no particular sadness in his face ; it looked rather as though he were concentrating very hard. After a while he got up, turned towards his pupil and said in a voice so normal as to be almost impatient : " Where did we stop ? Please go on." The friend's death was not mentioned, either then or later.

It was always Paderewski who selected or dictated the topic of conversation, the private affairs of his life being only discussed if he so wished. His childhood, his family, business, his practising and his music, his reactions to other composers, his feelings before and after a concert, his days in Poland after the war, were only mentioned on the rarest occasions, and then only to a few old and privileged friends. Paderewski's frankness and open-mindedness did not prevent a certain secretiveness. The subjects that he did not care to discuss lay in the same anxiously guarded shrine as did his physical pains and his sorrows, and hardly anyone was ever allowed to catch even a glimpse of them. This secretiveness, in which some people saw a peasant character-istic, others a Polish inheritance, was in the main a form of emotional self-discipline. Nevertheless it often made it hard for people to get any first-hand knowledge about Paderewski's life, and there were probably more rumours in circulation about him than about any other living man, and they were not only circulated by strangers and casual acquaintances but even by Paderewski's friends, who would repeat stories that they knew to be only remotely connected with actual fact. On the whole it was a natural desire to create a legend round the life and name of a famous man.

V

The circle in which Paderewski lived was becoming more and more impenetrable. Paderewski, it is true, had a great number of friends, hundreds, even thousands of acquaintances and many more admirers, and he enjoyed their friendship or admiration—but his life, filled as it was with endless activities, had not left him much time for making any very intimate human contacts, contacts that should pass beyond the ordinary admiration for a great artist, beyond social relationships. His secretary Strakacz and Marcel were among the few people with whom Paderewski was at all intimate. Even his relationship with Mme Helena had not had the character of a simple human bond. The love and devotion of husband and wife had moved for well over thirty years on a stage where exaltation was the accompaniment of a private life on which the spotlight of publicity played without respite, and there was not much room left for a simple relationship that should be an end in itself. Even in Paderewski's domestic existence almost everything was bound up with his career, with his political work, with his charitable activities, with the pathway of fame on which his feet were set. Paderewski could be a man's father-confessor, his teacher, guide, helper, collaborator—hardly in the ordinary sense his friend.

Outwardly Paderewski showed few signs of loneliness, perhaps on account of his active and optimistic mind. Occasionally, however, a chance remark or expression of sorrow would betray the fact that he must sometimes have been conscious of solitude. The very greatness of a famous man separates him from the world at large. An Englishman might have had a dog for company ; Paderewski, a Pole with a nervous disposition and an intensely active mind, could not draw much consolation from the company of a dumb animal. He hated cats ; he had not been able to ignore the animal world that surrounded Mme Helena ; but his interest in her Pekinese dogs, in her parrots and her chickens was mild and impersonal. He preferred dogs and horses to most animals. He acknowledged one faculty in animals which most people deny or ignore : their sense of music. In Paderewski's opinion animals, or at least some of them, had a sense of rhythm not very different from that of men. He could bring forward a very convincing proof of his argument. One day, when he was playing Chopin's " Etude en Tierces," he saw a spider coming down from the ceiling of the room, and noticed something that made him keep an eye on it, while still continuing to play. The spider descended from the ceiling or retreated towards it at certain intervals. The "Etude en Tierces" consists mainly of a number of passages which run up and down the keyboard. After a short while Paderewski discovered that whenever he played a passage which went towards the bass, the spider came down from the ceiling into the room ; when Paderewski played up towards the higher notes, the spider hurried back again towards the ceiling as though trying to get there before the pianist's hands reached the upper end of the keyboard. There could be no doubt about it : the spider was musical ; it had a rhythmical sense which caused a most intelligent reaction to the rhythms of Poland's greatest composer as interpreted by Poland's greatest pianist. Musical spiders, however, are not enough to compensate for the loneliness of fame and of approaching old age.

At times there was something pathetic about Paderewski's efforts to find a way of escape from his exalted position. Occasionally he would put his head on the shoulder of one of his pupils or of a younger friend and say a few affectionate words ; or he would choose the most beautiful peach produced by M. Dolezal's loving care and would insist on passing it to someone perhaps at the far end of the table.

The most significant expression of his desire for direct and genuine contacts, however, was his enthusiasm for helping those in pain. Disease as a topic of abstract conversation was loathsome to him. Not so the direct contact with an

ailment that he thought he would be able to relieve. Anyone
complaining in Paderewski's presence of a sleepless night or
of a pain would be eagerly questioned about himself and
his symptoms. Eventually Paderewski would run upstairs
to his bedroom and hurry back, bringing with him some
little bottle or a box of pills. If it was a more complicated
matter he would insist upon special treatment, and in cases
of greater seriousness, especially if he knew that the patient
had no financial means, he would not only suggest the
particular cure, the visit to a well-known specialist or the
appropriate spa, but he would insist on making the gift of
money that would make the cure possible. In such cases
Paderewski could forget his position and his enforced
self-restraint, and it was as though he eagerly sought to
retrace the path that led to an almost forgotten land.

One day during a lesson, he noticed that one of his pupils
was playing particularly badly ; he also noticed a strained
expression on the pupil's face. " What is the matter with
you to-day ? " Paderewski enquired, and there was a look
in his eyes as though he expected the answer that actually
came. With some hesitation the pupil explained that he
had not slept during the night and that he was suffering from
an almost unbearable headache. Paderewski leaped up
from his chair and exclaimed : " But why didn't you tell
me so directly you came in ? There is no need for anybody
to have a headache. Come, I will cure you instantly."
He led the young man into his own bedroom, seated him
on a chair, placed himself behind it, and began to massage
the back of his pupil's head and neck. Feeling rather
embarrassed, the young man after a few minutes averred
that the pain had gone. But Paderewski's only answer
was : " Nonsense, dear boy. You are not telling the truth.
You are thinking that I have had enough. I know quite
well that your head is still aching." There was nothing to
be done ; the pupil sat back in his chair and Paderewski continued the massage for another twenty minutes.
His expert treatment actually did cure the young man's

16

headache. Paderewski was delighted with his success, and his good humour did not leave him during the rest of the day.

As Paderewski did not care for new faces or for new people, he had hardly any new friends, but his devotion to the oldest of his friends was unwavering. Nevertheless his immediate circle was contracting. While touring the United States in the spring of 1933 he received the message that Marcel, who had not been well for some time and who had not been able to accompany his master on this voyage, was desperately ill. Paderewski straightway hurried back to Europe ; he got to Paris and proceeded thence directly to Morges. When he arrived at Riond Bosson he was told that Marcel was very ill indeed, but had just gone to sleep ; it would be better not to see him until the morning. Marcel had been asking incessantly after his master and when he would be back from America. Paderewski's first instinct was not to wait until next day but to wake Marcel then and there, but he was persuaded not to interfere with his valet's rest. Early next morning, when Paderewski was hurriedly dressing to go across to the gardener's cottage where Marcel lay, the news was brought to him that Marcel had just died.

Nobody dared to enter Paderewski's room that day, and even his most intimate friends felt that any expression of condolence would be totally inadequate.

VI

Neither increasing age nor the sundry shocks sustained during the last few years had any effect on Paderewski's amazing generosity. Even at seventy years of age he would think nothing of giving innumerable long and exhausting recitals for charity, even though it entailed journeys of many hundreds of miles and material sacrifice to himself. Early in 1933 Paderewski played at the Albert Hall in London before almost ten thousand people for the benefit of English unemployed musicians, and the concert brought in nearly four thousand pounds. Soon after that he gave a number of similar concerts in the United States ; and on June 28th he gave a recital in Paris, the charitable purpose of which clearly showed, once and for all, how wrong all the gossip-mongers had been who in previous years had connected Paderewski's name with religious or racial prejudice. The recital at the Théâtre des Champs Elysées was given for Jewish refugees from Germany who on account of perse-cution had been compelled to leave their country. Although the tickets were expensive, they were sold out weeks before-hand. In the same week Paderewski played for another charity at the Salle Hercule at Versailles. That gilded hall, built by Louis XIV, had not been used for almost fifty years, and the concert had the character of a great social event the brilliance of which had been rarely surpassed even in Paris. Not more than two hundred tickets were issued to specially chosen guests ; Paderewski played only Chopin, and after the recital was over all the members of that distinguished company approached Paderewski one by one to pay him homage and to be introduced to him by Prince Poniatowski, the organizer of the concert.

It became more and more evident that the motto of Paderewski's life was : service, service for Poland and, indeed, for anyone in need. Chopin had been content to sing his love for Poland in his compositions. In Paderewski's hands both Poland and music became the instrument of service.

Is it then surprising that his work as a composer has never been completed ? The supreme egoism that actuates the artist in Paderewski gave way to service. From Poland's point of view this was an act of sublime greatness ; from Paderewski's it was the tragedy of his life.

POSTSCRIPT

CONVERSATIONS AT RIOND BOSSON

I

THE manuscript of this book was practically completed when the author received a letter from M. Strakacz, Paderewski's private secretary, inviting him to Morges.

It was almost three years since I had seen Paderewski, and I accepted the invitation with gratitude and pleasure. Nothing is more dangerous for the biographer of a living man than too intimate contact with his subject. It may disclose many details otherwise hidden from the biographer's eye, but it also robs him of the necessary impartiality. Nevertheless I appreciated the chance of talking to Paderewski with greater intimacy and at greater length than ever before, more especially as it seemed important to be aware of certain of his ideas and opinions which even protracted conversations with his most intimate friends had failed to reveal. There were also a few aspects of his political career which had remained obscure, of which even his closest friends, his collaborators and his secretaries were ignorant, and on which Paderewski alone could throw light. I proceeded to Morges without delay.

II

To reach Riond Bosson you have to walk through the charming old town of Morges, with its picturesque streets, its sixteenth-century castle with its huge window boxes gay with flowers, its Town Hall of late Renaissance construction and its general air of contentment and peace.

Before reaching the hill on the top of which stands Riond Bosson, you pass a large, open, grassy space, bounded on one side by the lake and on the other by the main road on which motor-cars hurry between Geneva and Lausanne. Goal-posts had been put up at either end and a number of boys in bathing-suits were punting a football about. A few cotton-wool clouds sailed gently across the blue sky, and by the goal-posts sheep were grazing. Except for the lake and the Alps in the distance, it might have been a village green in Sussex or in Kent.

There was some anxiety in my mind about meeting the man with whose life I was so familiar and whom I had encountered only a few times before. In the biographer's mind the model and his image of it become fused into one unit which, for all its resemblance to the original, becomes a new and intensely personal creation. The Paderewski whom I had known a few years before had long been replaced by " my own " Paderewski. Would " my " Paderewski stand between myself and my host at Riond Bosson ? Such thoughts filled my mind as I walked up the hill towards the wide gates of Riond Bosson. Masses of bright-coloured geraniums and hydrangeas were banked on either side of the broad path that led to the house. A big dog was chained at the door, but instead of barking, he wagged his feathery tail and insisted on being stroked and patted. Suddenly a voice said in Polish : " There you are at last. We have been waiting for you for the last half-hour." Paderewski was standing in front of the opened glass door that led into the front hall. Owing to a mistake on the part of his secretary, I arrived later than expected —but my host's greeting dispelled my recent anxiety.

Paderewski was wearing a dark-blue suit, a white waist-coat and tie, and in his button-hole the ribbon of the Grand Cross of the Legion of Honour. After a few words of greeting he led me on to the large terrace above the gardens, with a magnificent view of the lake and the mountains and of Mont Blanc which rose in front of us beyond the lake. Paderewski pointed towards Mont Blanc, saying : " Did you know that from here you get the most beautiful view of Mont Blanc ? I believe even Baedeker mentions that." Across the lake one could clearly see Evian and Amphion, and the names of Paderewski's old friends in this part of the world came to my mind. I mentioned the Princess Brancovan and her daughter, Anna de Noailles, who had died only a few months earlier ; and I remarked how fortunate Paderewski had been in knowing that exceptional woman when she was only a girl. " Yes, I knew her when she was twelve," Paderewski answered; "her sister was one year older; and then there was also Alexandre, an older brother ; but Anna was the most beautiful one of the whole family. Such hair, such incredible eyes ! And there was always a strange, an almost tragic expression in her face. She was a marvellous conversationalist ; but if you allowed her, she talked far too much, and at times it was exasperating. *Tout à fait comme un robinet*," Paderewski added laughingly in French, " *un robinet qu'on ne peut pas fermer*. But let's go in to lunch now. We are quite by ourselves, and my poor ladies must be famished, having waited all this time."

We went back into the drawing-room, and after shaking hands with Strakacz, whom I had met several years before, I was introduced to Paderewski's sister, Mme Wilkonska, to his lady secretary and her mother, and to another old Polish lady who often spent the summer months at this house. The dining-room was lofty but smaller than I had anticipated. Although I knew the gardens and the outside of the house, I had never been inside it. The walls of the dining-room were red ; the most important piece of furniture was a large cupboard with glass doors, containing some fine pieces of silver. Mme Wilkonska sat at one end of the table, Paderewski at the other, facing the large window. In the middle of the table was a large silver bowl filled with the magnificent peaches and grapes which I easily recognized as the famous products of Riond Bosson's gardens and hothouses. The cooking was French, but the cream sauces and the mushroom flavouring of several dishes suggested Poland. The meal was served by a young Swiss butler and a parlourmaid. Paderewski, who was on a diet, ate little. When he noticed that I did not drink any wine, he said : " I am sorry that you don't do honour to my cellar. You must know that I am rather proud of it."

All the kindness of my host could not prevent the conversation being somewhat strained during the early part of the meal. Suddenly I became conscious that my position was rather hypocritical. There was I, sitting with the air of meaningless superficiality which one assumes with people whom one has only just met. In reality I was most familiar with the intimate life-history of my hosts, with their childhood, their virtues and their faults, while they had merely a superficial knowledge of me. There was also something uncomfortable in the knowledge that they were fully aware of the fact that their words, their looks and their movements would be described later in a book. Their manners were almost inevitably too perfect to be really natural, their politeness emphasized to a degree that would have made any guest suspicious. The only person who was quite free from self-consciousness was Paderewski himself. After the first few minutes he was practically the only one who spoke ; the other members of the party contributed a remark but rarely. Although I was still conscious of the unfair advantage which I had over the rest of the luncheon party, I was not sorry for it, as I would be spared the horrors of that meaningless social chatter which (especially in England) so often spoils the pleasure of a meal among cultured people. The absence of it would enable me to hear Paderewski's opinions rather than those of people who at the moment naturally interested me less. Nevertheless I looked forward to the end of the meal when it would be possible to talk to my host alone and not in the presence of the people who quite unconsciously might rob his words of some of their directness and sincerity.

After the coffee, everyone waited for Paderewski to get up. He crossed the room, kissed his sister on both cheeks and put his lips to her hand ; he then proceeded to kiss the hand of all the ladies present, while his secretary and myself shook hands with him ; the ladies kissed each other on both cheeks and shook hands with me. Paderewski turned to me : " Do you still remember the old Polish custom of thanking one another after a meal ? *Après avoir bien mangé, les Polonais s'embrassent et se disent bonjour.* We, in this house, still stick to that custom." He then made one of his typical gestures of the hand and asked me to come out with him on to the terrace.

III

It was a beautiful day, and though autumn was approaching the sun was still hot ; the light clouds merely decorated the blue sky, and the trees in the park had not yet begun to turn colour.

Paderewski asked me about my " Life " of him, remarking what an arduous task it must be to write about a living man whose life had as yet produced little documentary evidence. He seemed surprised when I told him that there were many books in which reference was made to him, and that the " *Paderewsciana* " in my own library filled a whole shelf. Nevertheless I admitted that it was not an easy task. " On the other hand," I said, " your life brought with it one continuous intoxication. I have ' lived ' so intimately with you for more than a year that my life will be rather empty once my work is finished. There are moments when I imagine that I actually think your thoughts and share your emotions. Having all your life recreated the thoughts and emotions of others, you probably know that state of mind perfectly."

Paderewski's answer surprised me : " Your intoxication

was much deeper and much more lasting." He became thoughtful and said after a while : " An author's intoxication is more real than that of a virtuoso ; its result too is more lasting. Your work is more lasting than mine. It will live for generations," he added after a while, in a voice touched with melancholy.

But I was not deceived. It was not the artist resigned to his fate who spoke, but the master of conversation who, by paying me a compliment, at the same time forced me to contradict him and so to put him back on that pedestal whence, with his last words, he had deliberately descended. Of course I contradicted. " Is the impression I got from the great virtuoso not more lasting than that which one gets from a book, pushed back on a shelf and never taken out again ? "

Paderewski did not answer ; all the while he had been looking out over the lake, and after a moment's silence he lighted another of the fat Egyptian cigarettes that he always smoked. He then asked me : " How long did it take you to write my Life ? "

" I have been collecting material since the days when I was preparing my Life of Pilsudski, which was almost five years ago. For the last twelve months I have been doing nothing but work on your book. I have seen almost two hundred of your friends, your relatives, your pupils, colleagues and servants ; I have travelled in numerous countries, in search of details ; I dare say I have read most of the things ever published about you, and yet I know that the book won't be without mistakes. It distresses me that it should be almost impossible to find out the truth about a living man."

Paderewski interrupted : " The truth about a living man does not exist. There can be only interpretations of it, or the impression that that man leaves on different people. Everyone will show you a different aspect of the same man or the same thing, and what you create yourself is only one individual picture of your model." Paderewski paused for a second, then he continued : " I shall be frank with you and tell you that you have not been always fair to me when you dealt with my political career in a former book."

" Which do you consider were my worst mistakes ? "

" You said that while I was Prime Minister in Warsaw I often let foreign diplomats wait because I would not get up in time. Although I often had only three or four hours' sleep, this is a mistake, and I never kept a foreign Minister waiting. I cannot tell you how tiring those days were : endless Cabinet meetings, committees, interviews, deputations, speeches. It was terrible."

" Was not Paris," I interupted, " equally exhausting during the Peace Conference ? "

" Yes, it was, though in a different way."

"Is it true that Clemenceau, whom the world will probably always remember as the faithless old cynic, could be charming, and that you had a deep affection for him ? "

" Indeed it is. His cynicism was only one side of him. In reality he was an extremely kind man, and he possessed a true goodness which people who did not know him hardly ever realized."

" Whom did you like best at the Peace Conference in Paris ? "

" I had many friends in Paris, and many of them I was extremely fond of. The man for whom I had a very special affection was Arthur Balfour, and I feel very proud that he should have honoured me with his friendship. He was one of the purest characters I have ever known ; one of the most cultured and the most exquisitely mannered men of his time. His knowledge was deep and filled you with real delight. It is very rare to find a mixture of such great refinement, such wonderful education and culture, and at the same time such real simplicity and kindness of heart. If ever there was a gentleman it was Balfour ; and if ever there was a true friend it was he."

Paderewski stopped, and I could see that he was deeply moved ; there were tears in his eyes, and he paused for half a minute. In the course of our further conversations I noticed that this happened more than once. Whenever we spoke of someone who was dead and of whom he had been very fond, the emotional reaction was invariably so strong that it brought the tears to his eyes. It was not dramatic or embarrassing : there was something rather impressive about this white-haired man with his youthful face, his elegant appearance and his perfect manners, suddenly becoming silent with deep emotion at the thought of former friendships.

The name of Arthur Balfour brought English politics and politicians to my mind. " Whom would you choose to-day," I asked, " for the post of the British Foreign Minister ? "

Paderewski did not hesitate with his answer : " Lord Reading. I consider him one of the greatest of living Englishmen. I think it is a great pity that he is not in office to-day ; and I daresay many things might be different in the world situation to-day if he were Foreign Secretary."

" Whom do you consider the most brilliant man of the day in English politics ? "

A broad grin lit up Paderewski's face, producing many little lines and wrinkles in it, and giving his narrowed eyes a boyish look. " Why, but of course Winston Churchill. He is the man with the most vivid intelligence, with brains, with imagination, with talent and ambition ; an excellent orator, a gifted writer. Unfortunately, Winston Churchill generally seems to bet on the wrong horse." The last words were spoken in English. " Take the Dardanelles, the Denikin adventure and the money spent on it ; his opposition to the official Conservative Party on the eve of a General Election and a National Government. He is constantly on the wrong horse."

Paderewski was so candid and seemed in such good humour that I ventured to put a question which in other circumstances he might have refused to answer : " And what do you think of Lloyd George ? "

" He is a brilliant man with exceptional talents. What charm ! There were not many men at the Peace Conference half so charming as Lloyd George. I know many people don't agree with me, but I am convinced that he is a man who really strove after the very best both in life and in politics. He is only interested in things that are good and fine ; but in my opinion his great misfortune is his lack of stability and his apparent lack of principle."

Paderewski got up saying : " Come, I will show you some photographs." We entered the drawing-room through a door leading directly from the terrace.

It was a music-room rather than a drawing-room, though it was filled with furniture, Chinese vases, cloisonné ash-trays and pictures. On the wall hung the lovely portrait-drawing by Burne-Jones, much bigger than I had imagined it, almost life-size. Opposite the window I noticed that portrait that Alma Tadema had painted of Paderewski in 1891. It was much finer than its reproductions would lead one to believe. There was also a study of Mme Helena, painted by Siemiradzki, one of the leading Polish painters of the nineteenth century. The real *pièces de resistance*, however, were the two Steinway grand pianos, or rather the galaxy of impressive-looking photographs that almost sub-merged them. There were photographs with long dedi-cations from President Wilson, Colonel House, Queen Elena of Italy, the Pope, the Queen of Belgium, and one of the King of Belgium to the *Libérateur de la Pologne* ; there were photographs of Theodore Roosevelt and a resplendent one of " Ranji." I was surprised at seeing the cricketing Maharajah in this serious company, but Paderewski said : " He was a very dear friend of mine, and once he came to stay at Riond Bosson with his daughters and his household. I believe it is a rare honour to be allowed to receive Indian ladies as well as men in a European house."

In the centre of the photographs on one piano, in a massive silver frame, was one of Queen Victoria. I turned to my host : " It might interest you to know that I have in my possession the original letter in which the Queen's secretary notified you of the sending of this photograph. Was this photograph the only gift you received from the Queen ? "

" No, after my first recital at Windsor the Queen sent me a tie-pin ; after the second one, besides the photograph, she also sent me a ring. She was very musical, and it was most interesting to talk to her about music."

" You also played for Queen Alexandra. Was she really so beautiful ? "

Paderewski became very enthusiastic. "Beautiful? She was a vision, simply a vision of a woman. And she was fascinating. You may pity yourself for being too young to have seen her in the early nineties."

Taking up the photograph of Foch, Paderewski said : " This is a man whom I really loved. He had a wonderful character, and he was full of goodness."

By now I realized that I should wait in vain to hear from my host anything but the highest praise of his friends or former colleagues.

When I discovered a photograph with an impressive dedication from Mussolini, I could not resist the obvious question : " What do you think of Mussolini ? "

" I think he is a very great statesman. I am a great admirer both of Mussolini and of Italian Fascism. I must admit, though, that last time I visited the Duce I was rather less impressed than on my earlier visits." There were many interesting questions to ask in that connection, but I felt that it would be indiscreet to force Paderewski's opinions on highly topical subjects and about a man who was still alive and whom he will probably meet again.

It was now getting rather late and we had been talking without ceasing for some hours. Paderewski had just returned from a strenuous cure in the South of France. As I got up to say good-bye, he said : " I am sorry you are going. But as a matter of fact, the doctor did order me to have a rest after luncheon at least during the first few weeks after my cure. But you will come to lunch to-morrow, won't you ? At half-past one, please, and not at two," he added smilingly. I thanked him, and he insisted upon coming with me to the front door and waiting in the doorway until I left the garden path, and turned to walk down the hill to Morges.

IV

When I arrived at Riond Bosson next day a few minutes before the appointed time Paderewski was already waiting in the hall. He immediately began a conversation on topical political subjects ; events in Germany interested him especially, and there was no need to-day for any artificial preliminaries. He was wearing the same clothes as on the preceding day, and the impression of neatness that he conveyed was even more marked. It was true, as people said, that there was something extraordinarily civilized about his appearance. The powerful head with the long hair brushed back from a very high forehead, with the vivid eyes and the sensitive nostrils, suggested a lion ; but it was a beautifully civilized lion, courteous, engaging, and both graceful and gracious. I could not remember having ever met another human being whose presence filled me with such delight and such a sensation of well-being. I had heard too many enthusiastic accounts, I had met too many people who went into ecstasies when Paderewski's name was mentioned, to be altogether free of suspicion. When I lunched with Paderewski three years earlier in New York I had at first felt the same resistance set up by suspicion and by a desire to find fault ; however, it had melted after the first ten minutes. I was annoyed with myself for coming under the same spell and reacting in the same way as a number of people whom I knew to be uncritical and prone to exaggeration. Throughout my many months of work I had been careful not to become a partisan, but to remain an objective student and observer of an interesting life ; I had noted the influence which he exercised on other people, but I had tried to preserve an independence which should prevent me from coming under that spell myself. It was important to remain impartial in dealing with the life of a man who was still alive, who had been in the forefront of political battles, who had millions of admirers but also some outspoken enemies.

As there were a number of subjects on which I was anxious to hear Paderewski's opinion, I decided to begin putting questions to him even during lunch. The meal had hardly begun when I started : " What is your attitude towards Wireless ? "

Paderewski answered emphatically : " It is killing music and musicians."

" But doesn't it help to make people more musical than they were before ? "

" I don't believe it does. It just robs them of any possible personal musical activity and of their musical keenness ; it casts a spell of laziness on them. Musical understanding is not produced by lazily lounging in an arm-chair, reading a novel and listening vaguely to the Wireless, but by active interest and work. Much more important to me, however, is the fact of the hundreds of thousands of professional musicians whom the wireless is depriving of their livelihood. All the possible achievements of the radio can't undo the fate of those miserable unemployed musicians all over the world. It is heart-breaking, simply heart-breaking."

(I knew that during this very year Paderewski had given a great number of concerts for the benefit of unemployed musicians of several countries, and that altogether about twenty thousand pounds had been collected in this way.)

I went on to ask : " But you admit, I suppose, that the wireless and the gramophone bring a perfect musical product into millions of houses that otherwise would be entirely deprived of music ? "

" No, I don't. People just bear the music, because once a Wireless is in their house they can't help listening to it. I agree that the Wireless gives as perfect a transmission of the music as is possible. In this it is superior to the gramophone, which still suffers the disadvantage of continuous interruption caused by the changing of the records, and from the hissing noise of the needle."

"Don't you think, since the advent of the Wireless and the gramophone, people who never would have gone to a concert, now go because they want to get a personal impression of the artist whom they know through their instrument at home?"

"Is that true? The people you are talking about go to hear a particular musician only once, and then not for musical reasons, but out of curiosity and snobbery," and, Paderewski added caustically, "because they want to be able to say that they have actually seen him."

"Do you think, then, that a modern audience is much worse than an audience of, say, forty or fifty years ago?"

"Not at all, in fact the opposite is true. But this is merely a question of manners and not of music. The concert manners of the people have improved, though in some countries less so than in others. In France people used to exclaim ' Charmant ' after a brilliant passage or an effective phrase, and you knew exactly at which moment of your playing that terrible hissing noise ' cha, cha, cha, cha ! ' of dozens of people exclaiming ' Charmant ' would spread through the hall. It was chiefly women who indulged in that form of musical appreciation, while men had their own way of expressing their admiration : they would just content themselves with exclaiming energetically and not too softly : ' Bravo, bravo ! ' But nowhere were the audiences quite so bad as in South America. There the people would walk about during the whole of the concert, visiting each other in their boxes and in the stalls, and they would carry on a conversation as though they were meeting each other in a café. This would go on through the soft as well as through the louder passages of the item. It was exasperating ! Yet the tickets were expensive and there used to be a considerable musical response to one's playing.

A concert was, however, a purely social event, and their attitude towards music was fundamentally different. It is much better now."

" What do you think of English audiences ? "

" You know how warm-hearted and grateful they are. English audiences must have been the great surprise in the career of every foreign musician who, before his first English tour, expected an unmusical and unresponsive audience. There is hardly a country in the world where you find such a big musical audience as in England ; but of course it is not easy to say whether their devotion to music springs from an enthusiasm for, or an understanding of, music. In music, as in everything else in life, there are producers and consumers, and England is musically the consuming country par excellence."

Luncheon was over by now, and the same ceremony of *Après avoir bien mangé, les Polonais s'embrassent*, etc. . . . was gone through with due solemnity.

v

After Paderewski had lighted his cigarette he turned to me : " I will show you the house now." We walked through the drawing-room with its pianos and its photographs to reach the next room, which was smaller, and which one might almost call the " Room of Honour and Glory." The walls were covered with diplomas from universities that had bestowed on Paderewski an honorary degree ; with diplomas from towns which prided themselves on having Paderewski as an honorary citizen ; busts of Paderewski in bronze and in marble stood about on pedestals ; pictures and statues which were the gifts of nations, of cities, of corporations and of individuals filled the room. It was a show more of glory than of beauty. The small tables were covered with Chinese works of art, various statuettes and ornaments, and except the furniture, everything in this room had been a gift. We sat down in the midst of the obvious

17

proofs that the noblest impulses of gratitude and fame know only rarely how to find an expression as beautiful as themselves. I felt that Paderewski was ready for a lengthy conversation. Accordingly I began : " When I lunched with you three years ago in New York you said something which struck me very much and which made me particularly keen to know more about your literary taste. . . ."

Paderewski interrupted me : " I remember, I told you that I disliked Tolstoy and that I thought that as a writer he was and still is greatly overrated."

" Yes, exactly. Do you still believe the same ? "

" Indeed I do. I think Tolstoy was a marvellous draughtsman, but he could not paint. Yet his canvases require the art of a painter, and his characters need to be painted and not merely to be drawn, no matter how good the drawing may be. There are other reasons as well that make me dislike Tolstoy."

As Paderewski did not disclose them I did not press the point, but went on : " What about Turgeniev ? "

" Ah, that is a different matter. I am a great admirer of Turgeniev, but it is hard to talk of him in connection with Russian literature. He is absolutely Western. Indeed, Turgeniev is a French writer who happens to use the Russian language."

" Are there any particular writers whom you consider greater than all others : and who are they ? "

" Shakespeare, Molière and Gogol. Of all the Russian writers Gogol is for me the greatest. His *Dead Souls* and his *Revisor* are masterpieces conceived by one of the great literary geniuses of the world."

" What about contemporary literature ? Do you admire Bernard Shaw as much as most Poles do ? "

" I like him and I enjoy his plays, which never fail to make me laugh ; but I value him little. He is an excellent entertainer, brilliant and amusing, but not deep. There is nothing really creative in Shaw, and there is much too much cynicism. I mistrust cynicism, and I value paradox only

PADEREWSKI'S HANDS ON THE KEYBOARD

up to a point. It must remain an ornament and shouldn't become the very thing. I much prefer Galsworthy ; I even prefer Wells."

" What do you think of Aldous Huxley ? "

" I don't know him ; neither do I know the other young writers in England. I don't seem to find time for them. There is such a lot to read and to learn in life ; there are innumerable scientific books that I am trying to get through and that somehow or other I missed in my earlier days. One must not forget that there are also endless novels that one ought to read again, Balzac for instance. In my opinion he is one of the most important novelists of all times."

" I believe you are a great admirer of Goethe, Lessing and Schiller."

" Yes, I am. When I was younger I could quote many of the longest passages of those writers."

The conversation ceased for a minute or so, and Paderewski looked down at his hands, as he often did when he was not actually speaking. They were touching each other, and he was playing a sort of game with them which consisted of raising the individual fingers, especially the fourth and the fifth, glancing at them and pulling them up with the fingers of the other hand. There was hardly a moment during our conversation when I was not conscious of my host's hands. Though they were not large, their delicate whiteness, their disciplined strength and their sensitive shape were constantly in my mind.

I went on : " The other day I was telling some friends in London about your wonderful memory and your unconventional technique in reading and remembering books. One of my friends remarked that Carlyle had a similar ability. . . ."

Paderewski almost jumped from his chair and interrupted me with a shuddering sound : " Awful Carlyle ! Don't drag him in. You can compare me with anyone you want, but not with Carlyle. I can't stand him. Do you know what I call his seven volumes on Frederick the Great ? The seven deadly sins of Carlyle." Paderewski laughed, his eyes disappearing almost entirely, and every muscle of the face moving with his laughter. When his face was once more in repose I again noticed how intensely blue his eyes were. In his pale face with its white forehead, its white moustache in which there was still a faint gleam of gold, the eyes were the only spots of colour, and that of a vivid sapphire blue. Paderewski went on : " I once read the whole of Carlyle and, like the rest of my generation, I used to admire him. We were talking about Balfour yesterday. I will tell you a little story about Balfour and Carlyle, or rather about Balfour and myself in connection with Carlyle. It might amuse you, and it will show you why my attitude towards Carlyle has changed. When Balfour arrived in New York in 1917 on a special mission I went to see him. He had written to me from London, asking me to look him up as soon as he got to New York. He was staying at a friend's flat and when I arrived there was a crowd of people waiting to be received by him. I felt very proud when Balfour gave me yet another proof of his kindness by admitting me immediately. In 1915, when I visited London, Balfour had told me that Poland would be recreated, and I now asked him whether he still stood by his words of 1915, to which he answered that he did. I then said : ' But do you realize that there are many powers behind the scenes that are working against us, especially the Jews, who have become anti-Polish through German propaganda ? ' Balfour waved his hand as though that meant nothing to him. But I went on : ' Even in your own country there are many people who are pro-German and anti-Polish when Poland's future independence is under discussion. Do you know who these people are ? Englishmen who have studied at German Universities, where for years they have been taught that German *Kultur* is superior to any other culture or civilization ; they and the older generation of Englishmen who in their youth read and worshipped Carlyle.' Balfour made a face as though I had shocked him by touching something that was very near to him. He did not say a word, and I thought it wise not to press the point any further. When after half an hour I got up to go, he came with me to the door, took me by the arm, and pushing me gently through the door exclaimed : ' Carlyle be hanged ! ' " Paderewski laughed and repeated : " Carlyle be hanged ! "

For no particular reason the name of Anatole France came into my mind. I could well imagine France and Paderewski chuckling together over some particularly witty remark. I asked : " Did you ever meet Anatole France ? "

" No, never."

" But you admire him, don't you ? "

Paderewski looked down at his hands once again, striking one with the other. Then he said : " I don't think there is any deep intellectual or spiritual meaning in Anatole France, and he is much too cynical for me. I told you that I don't care for cynicism, especially not if it becomes the philosophy of a great man whose work is known to countless numbers of people and who exercises a strong intellectual influence over them ; but of course I should be foolish if I did not admire France. What beautifully chiselled sentences, what prose, what expressions ! It is like a marvellous piece of jewellery made of the most exquisite gems. But love him, no, certainly not."

" Who are your favourite contemporary authors ? "

" Above all, the Spaniards. Modern Spain has got some wonderful authors. There are one or two things by Blasco Ibañez that I consider great; there is Unamuno, for whom I have the greatest admiration ; above all, there is Ortega y Gasset, whom I consider one of the finest and most profound thinkers of our time. Certainly I disagree with many of his views, particularly those about Germany ; but I always read him with enormous joy and admiration. There is also a beautiful novel by Perez D'Ayala, who, as you know, is the present Spanish Ambassador in London. If it hasn't been translated into English it ought to be ; the sooner the better."

Paderewski got up with the words : " You haven't seen my study. I will take you upstairs and show it to you."

We went out into the big hall. The rest of the household seemed to have retired or to have gone out ; not a sound was to be heard. The walls of the hall were covered with portraits of Paderewski, of Mme Helena, of Colonel House, and there were several symbolical pictures by Malczewski, and one or two canvases by Wyczolkowski, two of Poland's leading contemporary painters.

I asked my host : " When did you really give up playing the piano ? There are so many contradictory versions about it."

We halted at the bottom of the staircase. " I definitely gave up playing in 1918," was Paderewski's answer. " The last time I played was at the Metropolitan Opera House in New York at a concert given in honour of Marshal Joffre, who was on an official visit to America."

" Do you then consider that in the years 1914 till 1918 you still played the piano in the same way as you did before the war ? " I was anxious lest all my investigations about this very important fact and its deeper significance had been wrong.

Paderewski answered : " No, the piano of those years was a different thing altogether. It was no longer the pianist who played, but the propagandist. I stood on a different platform, and the piano was no longer a musical instrument but a patriotic instrument. And," he added, after a moment's hesitation as though looking for the right word and in a voice which was almost apologetic, " a financial investment. You see, I was doing propaganda work in the United States during the war. I assure you it was not a cheap occupation ; it swallowed up my entire fortune and much more. Much more. I simply had to earn more money to keep up a political office, to go on with my propaganda work, to do all sorts of things for Poland. There was no Poland at the time to pay me for my expenses, and I had to play the piano in order to keep the necessary political machinery going; and I also played in order to explain to American audiences certain things about Poland that otherwise they might not have understood. But my career as a pianist was finished at the beginning of the war, and it seems quite natural to me that it should have finished."

VI

We had reached the gallery on the first floor, where there were more pictures on the walls and a large case containing some of Paderewski's Chinese collection. We then entered the study, which looked exactly as I knew it from pictures and descriptions, although it was somewhat larger than I had imagined. When we reached the window, in front of which was a show-case with more Chinese *objets d'art*, Paderewski pointed to the yellow glass saying : " These pieces of *Jaune Impérial* are the most precious bits of my collection. They were made for one of the Emperors of the Ming Dynasty."

I was advancing towards the piano when my eye fell on the book *Mein Kampf*, by Adolf Hitler, which was lying half opened on a little table. " Do you think that a movement like German Nazi-ism can be confined to one country only ? " I asked.

Paderewski stopped, took out another cigarette as though he meant to settle down to the subject, and answered : " I very much doubt it. My own traditions, political methods, education, my personal respect for the freedom of the individual and for his beliefs, all show clearly what my own attitude is towards all extreme movements, no matter where and for what reasons they exist. But I would not be surprised if sooner or later we saw such movements spreading even into such civilized countries as England and France. Misery and unemployment rob the people of all faculties of judgment and vision. The most fantastic promises and the cheapest forms of oratory have a tempting flavour if you don't see any prospects of satisfying your hunger. They make the people follow the most incredible doctrines. If conditions in the world don't improve within the next few years I can imagine a tremendous growth of national and even racial feeling both in France and in England. It seems impossible to-day, but in the last few years we have seen that many apparently impossible things have become realities."

" Don't you think it is most exasperating to see that all the achievements of modern civilization, personal freedom of thought, belief in the superiority of the mind over the mailed fist, should be destroyed ? "

" Proper civilization, the inner feeling of freedom and, therefore of democracy, are found only if there are men first to create and then to go on shaping them. The masses, in a deep and dark urge, desire nothing but chaos, yes, chaos. It is not the masses, but solely and only the individuals who dictate order and, therefore, civilization. Some of the extreme movements of to-day are for me not movements led by great leaders, but purely movements of the fanatical and ignorant masses who run blindly after the shrill voices of some orators who light themselves with the misleading light of a mysticism which is understood neither by them nor by their followers. The concentrated will-power of those masses has been focused on one particular man who calls himself a leader ; yet in reality he is not a leader, but even more a fanatic than they, believing with greater strength in the mysticism of a vague message, lacking even more all sense of proportion than do the masses. You cannot have real civilization without a definite sense of proportion. Such destruction of cultural values as we have witnessed in various countries in the years since the war cannot be the work of great men. Great men don't need to destroy a former civilization in order to create a new one. The present destruction in several countries of a great part of the older civilizations is the work of dumb masses who have instinctively chosen certain men to lead them to such negations. In reality they are deprived of either the clear vision or the knowledge of a newer and better civilization. The masses desire chaos, nothing but chaos."

" Do you consider, then, that our Western civilization is really doomed to final failure and chaos, and that there is no hope of overcoming the difficulties and checking the dangers ? "

" No one can say. Only great statesmen, men of true greatness, vision, understanding and courage can save our civilization."

The tone in which these words were spoken left little doubt as to Paderewski's views whether he saw any such statesmen in the modern world. I went on : " Don't you think that Germany is doing herself harm to-day in denying so many of the marvellous achievements of her former culture ? "

" From the point of view of the world she is certainly doing herself great harm, though from her own point of view she does not seem to be conscious of it or does not seem to mind it. On the other hand, I think that Germany's only real contribution towards world culture, a contribution that could not be replaced by any other nation, is in the field of music. The literature, architecture and sculpture, certainly painting, and even the philosophy of the world, would remain great if the German contribution in those fields were entirely destroyed. But German music could not be replaced ; that is tremendous. Look at these composers : Handel, Bach, Haydn, Mozart, Beethoven, Schumann, Schubert, Mendelssohn, Wagner and a score of smaller ones."

I interrupted : " Some people like to make of Beethoven a Dutchman who was absorbed by the culture and civilization of Vienna."

Paderewski retorted quickly : " You cannot do that. It is an utterly artificial construction. Of course Beethoven is German, a pure German."

" Do you mean racially pure German ? "

Paderewski laughed. " That is nonsense. Who has ever heard such nonsense about racial purity ? Can you show me one case of a genius who is racially one hundred per cent. pure ? If we accepted as purely German only those among German composers who, according to certain modern teachings, were racially pure and Aryan, I don't know where Beethoven would be. And what about Mozart, whose name to many anthropologists sounds very much like a distortion of the Slav word ' *Mocarz*,' which means the man of power, the ruler ? And what about Wagner's distinctly non-Aryan nose, and what about Mendelssohn ? Didn't you know that before the war a group of very distinguished German scientists were preparing a most important scientific work showing the racial purity of the German nation ? They had been working on it for years, and a tremendous amount of data had been collected. But then the Kaiser stopped the publication. Why ? You can guess. Because he had been told that the results of the work had proved beyond any doubt that the over-whelming majority of the German nation were racially neither German nor Aryan ; they were the results of the most ancient and most varied racial mixture, their ancestors being Dutch and French, Italian, Polish, Lithuanian, Jewish and so on. It is enough to study German names scientifically in order to see their foreign origin. This applies both to names of people as well as to names of places. Only a few Germans would stand the test of pure ' Germanisms '."

VII

We sat down near the huge writing table with its many books, letters and papers. It was fascinating to listen to Paderewski when he lost himself in his subject. I decided to approach a matter which we had not yet discussed and which, although I knew him to be reluctant to talk about,

I considered important enough to be mentioned : namely, his own attitude towards contemporary music and musicians. I began rather carefully : " Do you consider that the Germans are still leading in the world of music ? "

" No, certainly not. For me Richard Strauss is the last great German composer. You may like or you may dislike him, but you must admit that he is a composer of true greatness. Otherwise the creative musical genius seems to have shifted to France."

" What about Pfitzner, about Schönberg, Webern, Hindemith, Alban Berg, Weill ? "

" Don't ask me about them. Most of them belong to another generation that I don't understand, and there is little in common between them and myself."

I thought I might venture my final attack, and so I asked: " Mr. President, it is quite impossible to find out from other people your opinion about the younger generation of pianists. Nobody seems to know it. Have you ever heard Vladimir Horowitz ? "

Without a second's hesitation Paderewski replied : " I heard him a few years ago in Chicago. I must admit that I liked him very much ; I liked both his playing and his appearance and his general bearing." (I remembered how important Paderewski considered the latter point in a pianist.)

" What did you like best about him ? "

" He was self-disciplined, and, above all, he has rhythm and tone. I only heard him play the D Minor Concerto by Rachmaninoff, but it was very fine indeed. Of course I cannot tell how he tackles the great classical composers, what he does with Bach, Beethoven, Chopin or Schumann. If he does not get spoiled, and if he can keep up his present power, he ought to go very far."

" Did his technique impress you ? "

" I think it was good enough to carry him over any difficulties, and it was not obvious. Without any doubt he is the most convincing among the younger pianists."

" Whom else have you heard ? "

" Not many of them, I am afraid. When I am travelling I either play in the evenings or else I have to prepare for my own concert. There is not much opportunity for going to the concerts of other pianists. Nevertheless I have heard some other representatives of the younger generation. I have heard Iturbi, who was very effective and whom I liked, though much less than Horowitz. I also very much appreciated the playing of the German, Gieseking, in whom there is taste, musical refinement and a subtlety which is quite un-German. Both his Bach and his Debussy were very beautiful ; his Chopin disappointed me ; nevertheless I consider him a most cultured pianist. Backhaus convinced me much less, though I admit that his technical powers are considerable."

" Do you think there are any great pianists among the younger generation in Poland ? "

" I have confidence in several of my own pupils. More than that I cannot say, as I hardly ever visit Poland."

" Do you think Poland is musical as a whole ? "

" The people, the peasants, the mountain folk are extremely musical. Don't forget that Poland had given the world some of its most important musical rhythms, at any rate dance rhythms : the polonaise, the mazurka, the cracovienne, the oberek. This alone, and there is much more, would be sufficient to show Poland's natural genius for music. But if you ask me whether our middle classes and our upper classes, whether our bourgeoisie is musical then I must emphatically deny it. This is particularly obvious at the present moment. It is enough to look at the Polish philologists."

" Philologists ? "

" Yes, look at them. Look at the reforms they are introducing into the Polish language. Have you ever seen anything less musical, more unmusical ? They are trying to simplify Polish spelling, presumably in the hope that children will be able to spend fewer hours over their studies of their mother-tongue, and they don't see that with their reforms they are destroying the very roots of Polish phonetics. They are depriving poets and writers of many of their opportunities, and thus they are creating things that are fundamentally contrary to the musical spirit of the Polish language."

"Don't you agree that phonetical expressions are symbols of a more significant reality which is rooted in the character of a nation that has been using them for centuries?"

"Of course I do. That is exactly the reason why I deplore all those ridiculous linguistic reforms. They might even change the spirit and the character of a nation. I personally have been brought up on the Polish classics, and language means a great deal to me. When I see the mutilated corpses of words that I once used to know as beautiful expressions of the musical genius of my nation, I begin to lose contact with my own language."

"Are there any great Polish composers living at present?"

"Szymanowski is undoubtedly a man of great talent. Some of his songs are quite lovely, and they can well be compared with the songs of any composer you may care to mention. His instrumental, and more particularly his piano compositions, however, do not mean a great deal to me; I cannot find contact with them, and I must confess that although I tried to play one or two of them, I simply could not get into their spirit, and I was unable to find an interpretation for them. Once I used to play an early Etude by Szymanowski, but I am sure he would not care to be reminded of that early work; he might even repudiate it. His more recent compositions are too cold for me, too ' cérébrale.' "

"Is this the case with other modern composers too?"

"With most of them so far as I know them. Their music does not come from the heart; it is not felt, it is just written. Real music must be like a running stream of fresh water that satisfies your thirst. Most modern composers are like soda-water—sparkling at first, but leaving you quite unsatisfied after one or two sips."

" Is that the reason why you, a well-known gourmet, never play modern composers ? "

Paderewski laughed. " Yes, it is one of the reasons ; the other being that at my age it is difficult to readjust oneself. The modern composers demand a definite inner readjustment which means a tremendous amount of work. Such readjustment may interfere with my preoccupation with the classical composers, and that I am not prepared to allow. I don't play for myself, but for the masses of people who come to listen to me and whom it has always been my greatest wish to please. They respond to the older composers whom they have heard before, and I give them what I feel they expect to receive from me. Even piano playing is a form of service."

The absent look came into Paderewski's face, a look which I had noticed before when a subject seemed to have a special significance for him. I waited for him to " come back " ; this generally happened after a few seconds. When I saw that the intense blue of his eyes was once again focused on me, I said : " However, you do play Debussy and you have made a tremendous success of it."

" Yes, but I consider that Debussy expressed the spirit of his particular epoch better than any other composer of that period. What is more, in Debussy I feel a natural warmth, I feel a heart in him which I miss in most modern composers. In them I feel only a brain."

VIII

I realized by now that it mattered but little whether, from an ordinary point of view, Paderewski's opinions were particularly striking and original or not. He undoubtedly looked at the world from a standpoint which was attainable only by few very exceptional characters. Many things that

he said and which might have struck the modern listener
as old-fashioned or even as wrong were probably true and
right when viewed from his particular level. Who knows
whether they will not prove right in the future, when our
own nervously conceived modern opinions have long been
forgotten ? Irrespective of what Paderewski said, his words
never sounded like a topical pronouncement soon to be
forgotten ; rather did they create an intellectual atmosphere
in which the time factor became insignificant. One might
have disagreed with many things he said ; but always
something more than a purely intellectual understanding
forced one to accept them without argument. Now I
realized that it no longer mattered whether his piano
playing was still good, or whether his politics were successful. The achievements in themselves seemed of little
consequence. It no longer mattered what he did, but
what he was.

The background for our conversation could not have
been more perfect. Mont Blanc seemed suspended in the
early evening mist like a deity in a Japanese woodcut ;
the last rays of a setting sun caught it, bathing its peak in
rose and gold. The trees in the park below the window
showed a Poussin-like elegance of outline in that transparent
light ; the lake, motionless and blue, framed in loveliness
a few sailing-boats with their graceful sails. The picture
was almost too perfect.

" It is late, I ought to go," I said, getting up and re-
proaching myself for having forgotten the doctor's orders
and having kept Paderewski for so long. I tried to induce
him to remain in his study or to go straight to his bedroom
to lie down, but he insisted upon coming down with me.
He was as courteous as though he were escorting a guest of
rare distinction. Yet there was nothing embarrassing in
that courteousness ; it did not make his guest feel helpless,
but gave him a feeling of self-respect, of inner satisfaction,
and of a sureness which other people but seldom inspire
in us. A wonderful sense of harmony and strength eman-

ated from Paderewski. He opened the front door for me, and we shook hands. I passed down between the flaming geraniums and the paler hydrangeas towards the road. Before leaving the garden I turned and looked back. Paderewski was still standing in the doorway. He waved his hand and bowed with a gesture of incomparable grace.

THE END

BIBLIOGRAPHY

A BIOGRAPHY combining Paderewski's personal, musical and political life did not exist before the present volume was written. There are several small books dealing with Paderewski's musical career and books, dedicated to more general subjects in which, however, reference is made to Paderewski's varied activities. But the main bulk of the material is still contained in the personal knowledge and experience of his friends, pupils, collaborators and relatives, and in the memory of Paderewski himself. They are the proper source of information. As a great number of documents containing various aspects of Paderewski's political activities have not been, and will not be, published for a good many years to come, several important details could only be obtained from friends and collaborators or from Paderewski himself. Though all the books written till now naturally cannot give more than only an incomplete picture of the subject, there are a number among them which are very helpful to any serious student of Paderewski's life.

The Bibliography below contains 42 publications of this kind. Long periods of Paderewski's life—his childhood, certain parts of his political career, the years since the war—have till now remained more or less untouched by historic or literary curiosity, and will not be found in the books quoted below. The Bibliography follows the chronological continuity of Paderewski's life ; in a few cases, however, it was not possible to keep that order. A few of the Polish books quoted below are given under French titles, although in some cases a French (or other) translation does not exist.

18   273

1. Henryk Opienski, *I. J. Paderewski* (Warsaw, 1928).

This book was published first in Polish, and a few years later in French, with a new preface by the pianist Cortot. The author, a distinguished Polish musical writer, has been an intimate friend of Paderewski's for a great number of years, and lives at Morges only a mile or so from Riond Bosson. His little volume deals practically only with Paderewski's musical career, the political one being mentioned only briefly in a few pages. The book is very reliable ; its value is somewhat limited by its spirit of hero worship. Nevertheless it is the most trustworthy source of information of the musical part of Paderewski's life. It contains a list of Paderewski's compositions and a number of interesting illustrations not found in any other publication.

2. Alfred Nossig, *I. J. Paderewski* (Leipzig).

Dr. Nossig, the author of the libretto of Paderewski's opera " Manru," is a Pole who lived in Germany and wrote in German. His pamphlet on Paderewski came out before " Manru " was finished. It is an essay of a dozen or so pages, concerned with Paderewski as a pianist and mainly as a composer, and with the author's relationship with Paderewski. Dr. Nossig is a devout admirer of his subject and uncritical, but he writes with great sincerity, and he includes in his pamphlet one or two personal anecdotes otherwise unknown. There are a few reproductions of portraits and busts of Paderewski, one bust being the work of Dr. Nossig himself.

3. Henry T. Finck, *Paderewski and his Art* (New York).

This little book by the American critic and friend of Paderewski deals mainly with Paderewski's musical interpretation of the various composers.

4. E. A. Baughan, *Paderewski* (London, 1925).

This is one of the biographical sketches in the series " Living Masters of Music." It gives a short history of

Paderewski's musical career before the war ; it contains a number of anecdotes and a musical analysis. The author is impartial and well informed, but the slightly larger book by Opienski, quoted above, is more thorough and is provided with more precise data.

5. Cuthbert Hadden, *Modern Musicians* (London, 1914).

This book consists of a collection of short biographical essays. In the chapter on Paderewski nothing new is to be found, but there are one or two anecdotes which, though known to me from personal sources, had apparently never been published before.

6. William Mason, *Memories of a Musical Life* (New York, 1901).

The author, a pupil of Liszt, was a distinguished American pianist and pedagogue. The book is a survey of the musical history of the second half of the last century. The information contained in it is mostly first-hand and interesting.

7. Amy Fay, *Music Study in Germany* (New York).

Some fifty years ago this was an extremely popular book in America. Its author, a pupil of Liszt, paints a vivid picture of musical life in Germany between 1869 and 1875, and, incidentally, of Liszt. It is a useful source of information regarding the musical situation in the years preceding Paderewski's appearance in the concert halls of Europe.

8. Annete Hullah, *Theodore Leschetizky*.

One of Leschetizky's pupils paints a vivid picture of the Russian teacher's personality and work.

9. Malvine Brée, *The Groundwork of the Leschetizky Method*, and

10. Marie Unschuld, *The Hand of the Pianist*

are two books dealing with the methods of Leschetizky, written by two of his pupils and approved by him. The problem of Leschetizky's influence on Paderewski's technique

18*

will probably be dealt with in purely musical books of the near future. There exists some difference of opinion on the subject of Paderewski's dependence on Leschetizky's method, and it will be interesting to see to what conclusions musical experts will arrive. It could not be the scope of this book to deal with the controversial and mostly technical matter of how far Leschetizky's method was responsible for Paderewski's musical style and success.

11. Henry T. Finck, *Success in Music* (London, 1910).

H. T. Finck was one of the most popular American musical critics in the first twenty-five years of this century. He knew most of the musicians of the time and was a friend of Paderewski. The book is particularly important because it contains Paderewski's famous essay on *Tempo Rubato*, to my knowledge the only published writing of Paderewski on musical theory. Finck prided himself very much on having persuaded Paderewski to put his ideas to paper. The actual essay consists of about 2,500 words. Finck's book is also filled with entertaining facts about musical life at the time when Paderewski appeared among the virtuosi of the world. Finck describes the technique both of Paderewski and his teacher Leschetizky, and of a score of other composers, teachers and virtuosi. Most students of music probably know this vividly written book.

12. Franz Liszt, *The Gypsies and their Music*.

The book, though written long before Paderewski's début, explains certain aspects of his rendering of Liszt and of the gyspy-like and orchestral qualities which are the outstanding features of his interpretation of that composer's music. To understand Paderewski's style, especially in connection with Liszt, it is essential to have some knowledge of Liszt's temperament and of his teaching.

Valuable information of such a kind is to be found in one of his many German Lives, especially the one by :

13. Lina Ramann, *Franz Liszt* (1880–94).

14. Franz Liszt, *Life of Chopin*.

Liszt's book is particularly interesting when studied in connection with Paderewski's musical method. It shows clearly that Chopin used consciously to employ all the liberties and " tricks " of *Tempo Rubato* in which Paderewski excelled as few pianists did before or after him.

15. Frederick Niecks, *F. Chopin as a Man and a Musician*, 2 vols. (1890).

This is a most reliable book on Chopin. Many " Lives " and books on Chopin have appeared since : some of them are more literary, some more amusing, others more " psychological " than the book by Niecks. But few of them contain more trustworthy information about Chopin's style, and not many can be considered as important as this one.

Equally useful is the shorter book by :

16. James Huneker, *Chopin, the Man and his Music* (New York, 1900).

Many years ago Paderewski himself admired this book very much and referred to it in his essay on *Tempo Rubato*, saying : " Most striking and really beautiful things bearing upon the interpretation of Chopin's works are to be found in Mr. J. Huneker's book."

17. *Letters of Queen Victoria*, third series, Vol. III, page 48.

The nine volumes of Queen Victoria's letters and diaries need no special introduction. The passage written on July 2nd, 1891, and quoted in this book in the chapter "London," is to my knowledge the only reference to Paderewski to be found in the Queen's journals.

The Dowager Duchess of Rutland showed me a letter which she received in the summer of 1933 from H.R.H. Princess Beatrice and in which the writer refers to Paderewski's playing for the Queen : " . . . I was present on the occasion when Paderewsky played, and I know how much she "—the Queen—" admired his great talent."

18. Comtesse de Noailles, *Le Livre de ma vie* (Paris, 1932).

The slender volume is an autobiographical account of the early life of the late Anna de Noailles, one of the most remarkable French poets of our time and perhaps the greatest " foreign " writer of French. The book takes the reader straight into the heart of that world of art and luxury which was so typical of a certain section of Paris society in the last quarter of the nineteenth century. The Greek, Turkish and Rumanian origins of Countess de Noaille's family add an Oriental colour to the book which, however, lives mainly on the beauty of its style. Though the author's emotions are of a very exalted kind and the language is almost too romantic, the book never ceases to be a work of art, exuberant with literary merits.

I made no attempt to translate into English the few quoted passages, feeling that most of Anna de Noailles' irresistible style would get lost in a translation. *Le Livre de ma vie* is practically the only book in which Paderewski's earliest days on the shores of the Lake of Geneva are described.

19. I. J. Paderewski, *Chopin* (translated from the Polish by Laurence Alma Tadema). (London, 1911.)

Paderewski's speech about his great compatriot was delivered in 1910, in Lwow (Lemberg), Galicia, the Austrian part of Poland before the war. It was one of the first speeches through which Paderewski disclosed himself as one of the finest orators of his time. The translation by one of his oldest friends, Miss Laurence Alma Tadema, is very beautiful. The rich and extremely individual style of Paderewski must have rendered the work of the translator extremely difficult.

20. Colonel House, *Paderewski: the Paradox of Europe* (*Harper's Magazine*, December, 1925).

Colonel House tries to explain in a short article the duality of Paderewski's political and musical career. The author is full of admiration for his subject, and discloses the very intimate character of the relationship between himself and Paderewski.   I found this article very helpful, as its author gave up for once his usual reserve, and " let himself go." Though there is less actual material in this article than in other post-war publications connected with Colonel House, the personal character of the *Harper* article makes it in a way a more valuable contribution than the more " official " publications by Colonel House.

21. H. H. Fisher, *America and the New Poland* (New York, 1928).

This is a scholarly book, reliable and excellently documented, but of little interest to the general public.   It gives a fairly complete picture of the part the Poles in America played during the war, and of Paderewski's political leadership among them.   It also shows how wonderful the work was which the American Relief did in Poland during and especially after the war.

22. Count Bernstorff, *My Three Years in America* (1920).

The German war-time Ambassador in the United States speaks, among other things, of the great prestige which Paderewski enjoyed in America during the war, and of the importance which both the political and general world in the States attached to any of Paderewski's political pronouncements.

23. Duff Cooper, *Talleyrand* (London, 1932).

This brilliant biography of the French statesman quotes one or two surprising prophecies of Talleyrand's about the future of Poland.   In view of the country's restoration they are of special interest.   Duff Cooper's book also explains certain important facts in connection with Napoleon's " Polish policy," probably unknown to the English reader who is not particularly familiar with Polish history.

24. Maryan Seyda, *La Pologne au carrefour de l'histoire* (1931) (in Polish).

The author was one of the leading Polish politicians during and soon after the war, and played an important part in the preparatory work of Polish independence. He is scholarly, reliable and exact, but he thinks that accuracy postulates dryness. This makes his book a document for students who do not consider their research work an entertainment, but merely an arduous task.

25. Roman Dmowski, *La Politique Polonaise et la Restauration de l'État* (Varsovie, 1925) (in Polish).

An important political document written by one of the leading statesmen of modern Poland and President of the National Committee during the war. It will appeal more to the student of Polish politics than to the ordinary reader.

26. Robert Machray, *Poland* 1914–31 (London, 1932).

A dispassionately and objectively written book full of valuable information, but not so much for the serious student as rather for the general public that desires to learn more about the political history of modern Poland.

27. Casimir Smogorzewski, *La Poméranie Polonaise* (Paris, 1932).

The standard work on the subject. Its author is a Polish publicist in Paris and one of the most important writers on Polish politics since the war. He is internationally acknowledged one of the leading experts on Polish-German affairs. This volume of almost 200,000 words deals mainly with problems connected with Polish Pomerania and the so-called "Polish Corridor," but it also contains some interesting material about Paderewski's conversations with President Wilson and Colonel House and about the Polish problem at the Peace Conference in Paris. It is undoubtedly the most trustworthy and best documented book on the subject. Its many illustrations, maps, quoted documents and letters,

its official statistics from many sources, charts and bibliography, add considerably to its value.

28. Casimir Smogorzewski, *La Pologne restaurée* (Paris, 1927).

This is a political history of modern Poland, well documented and full of inside knowledge.

29. Francesco Tommasini, *La Risurrezione della Polonia*
    (Milano, 1925).

Tommasini was Italian Ambassador in Poland soon after
the war.   He was a keen and intelligent observer of the
political happenings around him, and possessed a great
knowledge of Poland and Polish affairs before starting his
book, which is written with temperament and conviction.
Tommasini knew many " secrets behind the scenes," and
he obviously revels in disclosing them.   He also writes
interestingly about the inner working of the new Polish State
machinery and of the fights between the various sections of
Polish politics and of the frictions between the foreign
representatives in Poland.   Like most professional diplomats
who describe history in which they acted as protagonists,
Tommasini defends himself by attacking others.   Such an
attitude robs the book of its impartiality, but it adds
character and life to it.

30. Rom Landau, *Pilsudski and Poland* (New York, 1929) and
    Pilsudski, Hero of Poland (London, 1930).

This is the first and, so far, only English biography of
one of the two makers of modern Poland.   It is based both
on documentary evidence and on personal investigation
among Pilsudski's past and present friends, collaborators
and colleagues. Several English authors dealing with
Polish problems, for example, Lord D'Abernon (in his
Portraits and Appreciations, and Sir Philip Gibbs (in his *Since
Then*), have based their books partly on this biography.   It
contains in a special chapter a short biography of
Paderewski, the musician and the statesman.   Paderewski
expressed on two different occasions his approval of this
biographical sketch, but he also pointed out to me two

errors contained in it. One of them is mentioned in the present volume, Postscript " Conversations at Riond Bosson." The other consisted in my stating that during the Peace Conference Paderewski used to submit the drafts of his speeches to Dmowski. I am glad to be able to correct this inaccuracy. Paderewski assured me that he never prepared any of his speeches in Paris with Dmowski, and that they were entirely his own independent pronouncements.

Extracts of the Pilsudski biography appeared during 1930 in German in the *Frankfurter Zeitung*.

31. J. de Carency, *Joseph Pilsudski* (Paris, 1929).

This short French biography was written by an expert on Polish politics : the publicist Casimir Smogorzewski, who occasionally uses a *nom de plume* for his French writings.

32. Josef Pilsudski, *Mes premiers combats* (Paris, 1930).

One of the many military and political books or pamphlets written by Pilsudski himself. It contains the story of Pilsudski's campaign at the beginning of the world war. It is a defence of Pilsudski's military methods, but at the same time provides a vivid narrative of the early activities of the Polish Legions that were the amateurish but heroic nucleus of the present Polish army.

33. Casimir Sosnkowski, *From the Legions to Magdeburg* (only in Polish).

General Sosnkowski's exciting account appeared in a Polish omnibus book called *Behind Prison Bars*. A number of former members of the Polish Legions who spent parts of the war in Russian, German or Austrian prisons or concentration camps, speak of their experiences. The account of Pilsudski's former friend, the then Colonel Sosnkowski, contains an extremely personal picture of Pilsudski's imprisonment by the Germans in the fortress of Magdeburg during the last two years of the war. It is based on daily experience, very candid and honest and of the greatest value.

36. H. W. Temperley, *A History of the Peace Conference of Paris* (London, 1924).

The standard work on the subject, which contains many important details about the negotiations in Paris in connection with Poland. The six volumes have been edited by Professor H. W. V. Temperley, of Cambridge. Different authors write about the many subjects that were dealt with by the Peace Conference. The interesting facts about Poland are given in a chapter published anonymously under the title " The Resurrection of Poland " (Vol. VI).

35. David Hunter Miller, *My Diary at the Conference of Peace* (New York, 1924).

Here is the book that compels the biographer to spend many a morning at the Library of the British Museum. It consists of 19 large volumes, one of which is entirely dedicated to indexes and plans of this mammoth work. Its author was the legal adviser to the American Delegation at the Peace Conference, and his diaries consist not only of very detailed daily diaries, but also of letters, minutes of meetings, conversations, negotiations, of documents, memoranda and telegrams.

36. Charles Seymour, *The Intimate Papers of Colonel House* (New York, 1926).

This book about the various incidents of President Wilson's policy is too well known to need any reference.

37. Harold Nicolson, *Peace Making* (London, 1933).

I am very indebted to this book, which paints a more vivid picture of the inner working of that complicated machinery known as the Peace Conference, 1919, than any other work on the subject. There are one or two sketches on Paderewski as brilliant as anything that Mr. Nicolson has produced. The author describes in one short sentence Mme Paderewska more strikingly than many writers have done in many pages. I also owe a debt of gratitude to Mr. Nicolson for summing up for me in a personal letter his own impression

of Paderewski's appearance in Paris with the words : " . . .
He spoke with extreme dignity and eloquence and made a
very marked impression. . . . I was struck by his extraordinary vision and power of expression."

38. *What really happened in Paris ?*   Edited by Colonel House
    and Charles Seymour (London, 1921).

   This is a composium of a series of most important lectures
held in Philadelphia in the winter 1920–21. Each lecture
dealt with one particular problem or country that occupied
the Peace Conference. The speakers were delegates
attached to the American Delegation in Paris ; each one
described the inner story of the problem for which he was
the special expert. The lecture on Poland was delivered
by the Harvard Professor, Robert Howard Lord, Chief of the
Polish Division attached to the American Peace Commission.
It is an impartial, matter-of-fact account of the various
stages of the negotiations in connection with the drafting
of the new frontiers of Poland. After each lecture a discussion used to take place. When asked by a member of the
audience what the services of Paderewski were, Professor
Lord answered :
   " M. Paderewski accomplished a wonderful service at the
start by ending a serious internal crisis, a dispute between
the Polish parties as to the control of the government. He
founded the first government of the new state that was
accepted by everyone at home and recognized by all the
powers. . . . He held the country successfully together
during the first and most trying year of its existence. . . . He
has many times spoken most effectively before the Paris
Conference and at the League of Nations meetings. . . .
He was able to win even the friendship of Mr. Lloyd
George, who was not on very friendly terms with the other
Poles. . . . He gained a great many things for Poland that a
statesman who was less trusted could never have secured . . . .
He did what no other Pole could have done."
   Among the speakers were Colonel House and Herbert

Hoover. The quotation in the chapter " Rebirth of the Piano " (page 194) is taken from the same volume, chapter " Constantinople and the Balkans," by Isaiah Bowman.

39. Joseph Tumulty, *On Wilson in Paris*.

The author was for many years President Wilson's chief private secretary. He had an inside knowledge of Wilson's method of work, and of the growing difficulties which Wilson encounted in Paris during the Conference. Devoted and loyal to his master, he thinks that loyalty must necessarily mean lack of impartiality and that nothing that Wilson ever did was not perfect. Though this curtails the value of his book, it makes it also more human and personal. There are some intimate details about Wilson's fight for the Treaty.

40. Robert Lansing, *The Big Four* (London, 1922).

This is the well-known book by the American Secretary of State who accompanied Wilson to Paris and who, after having been most antagonistic to Paderewski's political activities, became the greatest admirer of Paderewski the statesman. Anyone interested in Paderewski should not miss reading Lansing's chapter on Paderewski, most enlightening both historically and psychologically.

41. Leon Bilinski, *Souvenirs et documents* (1924) (only in Polish).

Leon Bilinski, a Polish economist, university professor and politician, was on intimate terms with the late Austrian Emperor, Francis Joseph, who made him twice his Minister of Finance. In his two volumes Bilinski draws a very exact picture of Austria's policy towards Poland and of the late Emperor's own attitude towards his Galician province. In July, 1919, Bilinski became Finance Minister in Paderewski's Cabinet, but the collaboration between the two men was never a success. In his second volume Bilinski makes some biting remarks both about Paderewski's premiership and about Mme Paderewska's political activities. The author goes so far as to say that it was Paderewski's wife who " ruled

in Poland." The value of Bilinski's opinion about Paderewski is somewhat diminished by the author's antagonistic
attitude towards his former chief. Nevertheless his account
of the last weeks of Paderewski's premiership are of great
interest. The book is rather typical of the self-importance
and egotism of pre-war diplomacy ; but even so it is amusing
and it discloses a man who, apart from taking himself very
seriously, must have possessed some charm.

42. Henry T. Finck, *My Adventures in the Golden Age of Music*
(New York, 1926).

This very personal, rather slight and superficial but
amusing and useful book was the last work that Finck did
before his death. There is a chapter on Paderewski, or rather
on Finck's friendship with Paderewski. Certain figures
and one or two details about Paderewski's first post-war
tour in America are taken from this chapter.

INDEX

INDEX

Adamowski, 238
Adlington, William, 98, 99
Albert, King of Belgium, 201, 252
Alexander II, Emperor of Russia, 15
Alexandra, Queen of England (*see also* Princess of Wales), 50, 253
Alma Tadema, Anna, 46
Alma Tadema, Lady, 46
Alma Tadema, Miss Laurence, 46, 106, 156–158, 278
Alma Tadema, Sir Laurence, 44–47, 50, 156, 252
Anthes, 67
Argyll, Duchess of, 45–47, 49
Asnyk, 67
Asquith, H. H., Prime Minister, 106, 149
Auchincloss, Gordon, 145
Ayala, Perez D', 261

Bach, Johann Sebastian, 28, 54, 61, 80, 133, 265, 267, 268
Backhaus, Wilhelm, 268
Balfour, Arthur, 106, 108, 119, 120, 145, 151, 164, 200, 201, 250, 251, 260
Balzac, Honoré, 259
Barrington, Lady, 50
Barry, C. A., 70
Battenberg, Prince, 49
Bauer, Harold, 221
Baughan, Edward A., 61, 64, 274
Beatrice, Princess, 48, 277
Beddington, Mrs. S. H., 51
Beethoven, Ludwig van, 28, 54, 55, 57–62, 76, 104, 133, 214, 222, 265, 267
Belgium, Queen of, 201, 252
Bell, Dr., 163
Benesh, Dr. Edward, 146, 159, 160
Bennett, Joseph, 40
Berg, Alban, 267
Bergson, Henri, 208
Berlioz, 55

Bernstorff, Count, 112, 279
Beseler, General von, 134
Bethmann-Hollweg, 112
Bibesco, Princess, 32, 34
Bilinski, Leo, 179, 285, 286
Bizet, Georges, 68
Blondel, A., 98, 213
Bowman, Isaiah, 194, 285
Brachocki, 224
Brahms, Johann, 54
Brancovan, Alexandre, 246
Brancovan, Prince, 86
Brancovan, Princess Bessaraba, 32, 34, 85–89, 246
Brée, Malvine, 275
Briand, Aristide, 106, 200
Brockdorff-Rantzau, Count, 163
Bülow, Hans von, 11, 22, 72
Burne-Jones, Sir Edward, 38, 39, 43, 44, 193, 223, 252
Busoni, Ferruccio, 11, 64

Cambon, Jules, 145, 146, 150, 153
Campanini, Italo, 73
Carency, J. de, 282
Carlyle, Thomas, 259, 260, 261
Carrasco, Señor E., 209
Carreño, Teresa, 51
Castle, Egerton, 50
Charles of Austria, 86
Chopin, Frederic, 11, 21, 28, 33, 35, 37, 46, 49, 54, 55, 57, 61–66, 70, 76, 85, 105, 110, 113, 133, 189, 214, 219, 223, 225, 240, 243, 267, 268, 277, 278
Choussou, Dr., 213
Christian, Princess, 49
Churchill, Lady Randolph, 50
Churchill, Winston, 251
Cielewicz, Ignace, 20
Clemenceau, Georges, 108, 144–148, 151–153, 159–165
Clementi, Muzio, 21
Colonne, Edouard, 32, 34
Combarieu, Jules, 70

288

Conrad, Joseph, 236
Coolidge, Calvin, 204
Cooper, Duff, 279
Corneille, Pierre, 86
Cory, Lady Annie, 50
Couperin, François, 74
Czerny, Charles, 21

D'Abernon, Lord, 281
D'Albert, Eugene, 11
Damrosch, Leopold, 73
Damrosch, Walter, 75
Davies, James, 204
Davies, Norman, 200, 204
Dawes, General, 204
Debussy, Claude, 80, 95, 268, 270
Denikin, General, 251
Devonshire, Duchess of, 39
Dmowski, Roman, 107, 108, 119, 134, 135, 139, 143–145, 168, 280, 282
Dolezal, 192, 193, 240
Dolmetsch, Albert, 98, 195
Dorszprung, Prince, 129
Dostoievsky, Feodor, 18
Dygat, Zygmunt, 225

Eames, Emma, 73
Eichendorff, 104
Elena, Queen of Italy, 252
Elgar, Sir Edward, 70
Erard, 31, 72, 97–99, 199, 200
Erzberger, Matthias, 163
Essipoff, Annette, 23, 31, 87
Estournelles, Count d', 89

Fay, Amy, 275
Finck, Henry T., 53, 56, 60, 64, 82, 274, 276, 286
Fischer, Edwin, 218
Fischer, H. H., 279
Foch, Marshal, 151, 173, 200
Fouché, widow of, 89
France, Anatole, 261
Francis Joseph, Emperor, 15, 179, 285
Frederick the Great, 23, 260

Gabrilowitsch, Ossip, 217
Galsworthy, John, 259
George V, King of England, 201
Gibbs, Sir Philip, 281
Gibson, Hugh, 203
Gieseking, Walter, 218, 268
Gilbert, Sir Alfred, 43
Giniatowicz, 129
Godowski, Leopold, 64

Goethe, Johann Wolfgang, 104, 259
Gogol, Nicolas, 258
Gorski, 88–90, 93
Gortschakoff, Prince, 15, 32
Gortschakoff, Princess, 32
Gounod, Charles, 34
Gouraud, General, 163
Grey, Lady de, 39
Grieg, Edward, 54, 61
Guicciardi, Countess, 29

Habsburg, Charles of, 86
Hadden, Cuthbert, 81, 275
Handel, G. F., 54, 265
Haller, General Joseph, 155, 156
Haydn, Joseph, 28, 54, 265
Hindemith, Paul, 267
Hitler, Adolf, 263
Hofmann, Josef, 106
Hohenzollern, 104
Hoover, Herbert, 141, 200, 201, 204, 284
Horner, Lady, 43
Horowitz, Vladimir, 218, 267, 268
House, E. M., Colonel, 111, 114, 117, 118, 145, 151, 154, 155, 158, 164, 200, 252, 262, 278, 279, 280, 283, 284
Hughes, Charles Evans, 117, 204
Hullah, Annette, 26, 275
Huneker, Adolf, 277
Huxley, Aldous, 259

Ibañez, Blasco, 261
Ingres, Dominique, 33, 43
Isaye, Eugéne, 52
Italy, King of, 200
Iturbi, 218, 268
Iwanowski, Major, 121

Janotha, 20
Jodko, 229
Joffre, Marshal, 262

Kakowski, Archbishop of Warsaw, 134
Kellogg, Frank B., 204
Kerntopf, Edward, 20
Kiel, Friedrich, 22, 23
Korfanty, Adalbert, 126
Korsak, Antonina (Paderewska), 21
Kosciuszko Tadeusz, 106, 132
Krasinski, Zygmunt, 66
Kraszewski, Josef Ignacy, 68
Krehbiehl, H. E., 72
Krull, Anna, 67

Lahee, Henry, 26
Lamoureux, 32, 34
Landau, Rom, 281, 282
Langtry, Lily, 42
Lansing, Robert, 154, 204, 285
Lehmann, Lilli, 73
Leschetizky, Theodore, 23–27, 29, 31, 51, 56, 70, 87, 122, 275, 276
Lessing, Efraim, 104, 259
Lewis, Lady George, 50
Lippmann, Walter, 118
Liszt, Franz, 11, 29, 33, 37, 54–56, 60–63, 76, 80, 214, 217, 218, 222, 223, 275, 276, 277
Lind, Jenny, 12
Levitzky, Mischa, 218
Lloyd George, David, 144–146, 149, 152–155, 164, 165, 251, 252, 284
Lobkowitz, Prince, 28, 59
Londonderry, Lady, 39
Lord, Robert, 118, 284
Louise, Princess (see Duchess of Argyll)
Lubomirski, Prince Zdzislaw, 134
Lucca, Pauline, 12, 31

MacArthur, Alexander, 63
Machray, Robert, 280
Malczewski, Jacek, 262
Malibran, Maria, 12
Manet, Edouard, 38
Mangin, General, 163
Manning, Bishop of New York, 204
Mantua, Duchess of, 87
Marcel, 192, 195, 198, 212, 213, 239, 242
Marois, Count de, 89
Masaryk, T. G., President, 160, 200
Mason, William, 60, 61, 62, 64, 275
Masson, Dr., 211
Materna, Amalie, 73
Mayer, Daniel, 41
Melba, Nellie, 39, 106
Mendelssohn, Franz, 49, 51, 61, 265, 266
Messager, André, 70
Mickiewicz, Adam, 66, 67, 106
Miller, David Hunter, 145, 283
Modjeska (Modrzejewska) Helena, 24
Molière, Jean-Baptiste, 86, 258
Moniuszko, Stanislaw, 66
Montesquiou, Marquise, 34
Moraczewski, André, 134
Möricke, 104

Morris, William, 38
Moschelés, Ignace, 56, 61
Moscicki, President of Poland, 107
Mozart, Wolfgang Amadeus, 28, 61, 133, 222, 265, 266
Mottl Felix, 22
Muck, 22
Müller, Hermann, 163
Murray, Butler Nicholas, 204
Mussolini, Benito, 200, 253

Napoléon, Jérôme, Prince, 86
Napoléon the Third, 86
Narutowicz, Gabriel, 107
Newman, Robert, 78
Nicolini, 73
Nicolson, Harold, 283
Niecks, Frederick, 277
Nietzsche, Friedrich, 22
Nikisch, Arthur, 106
Noailles, Anna de, Countess, 87, 88, 246, 278
Noske, 163
Noskowski, 66
Nossig, Alfred, 68, 274
Noulens, Joseph, 144
Nowicki, Prof., 16

Obrochta, Bartek, 69
Opienski, Henryk, 70, 274
Orlando, V. E., 153
Ortega y Gasset, 261
Ossowiecki, 171
Ostrowski, 134
Otranto, Duchess of, 89
Oxford, Lady Margot, 202

Pachmann, Wladimir, 11, 64
Paderewska, Antonina (Korsak), 21
Paderewska, Antonina (Wilkonska), 17, 18
Paderewska, Helena, 88–94, 96, 121, 127, 128, 138, 163, 171–181, 187, 189, 205–210, 224, 232, 237, 240, 252, 262, 283, 285
Paderewski, Alfred, 21, 85, 88, 89, 192
Paderewski, Jan, 17, 18, 19
Parratt, Sir Walter, 48
Paton, Captain, 121, 125
Patti, Adelina, 12
Pershing, General, 204
Pétain, General, 163
Pfitzner, Hans, 267
Pfohl, Ferdinand, 35

Pichon, Stephen, 106, 146, 147, 149, 164, 236, 237
Pilsudski, Joseph, 125, 128–141, 159, 167–171, 179–182, 281, 282
Pilsudski, Joseph, father, 129
Piltz, Erazm, 107
Pius XI, Pope, 200, 252
Poniatowski, Prince, 243
Poniatowski, Stanislaus August, King of Poland, 135
Potocka, Countess, 32
Poulenc, François, 218
Poussin, Nicolas, 271

Rachmaninoff, Serge, 267
Racine, Jean, 86
Ramann, Lina, 276
Ranji (Maharaja Nawanagar), 252
Ratti, Achille, 200
Reading, Lord, 111, 251
Reisenauer, 82
Reszke, de, brothers, 12
Reszke, Jean de, 39
Richter, Hans, 22
Ripon, Marchioness of, 39
Rockefeller, John D., jr., 204
Roguski, 20
Roosevelt, Franklin, President, 200, 201, 204
Roosevelt, Theodore, 106, 252
Root, Elihu, 204
Rosen, Helena de (Paderewska), 88
Rosen, Jan Henryk, 189, 190
Rosenthal, Moritz, 11
Rossetti, Dante Gabriel, 38
Rothschild, Alfred de, 39
Rothschild, Baroness de, 86
Roux, César, 211
Roux, Jacques, Dr., 211, 212
Rubens, Peter Paul, 87
Rubinstein, Anton, 11, 29, 33, 41, 49, 52, 60, 61, 63, 72, 76, 217, 218
Runowski, 17, 18
Ruskin, John, 38
Rutland, Violet, Duchess of, 43, 50, 277

Saint Martin, Marquise, 34
St. Paul, Marquise de, 32, 34
Saint-Saëns, Camille, 3, 34
Salaman, Charles, 51
Salisbury, Lord, 50
Sapieha, Prince, 137
Sazonoff, Serge, 108
Say, Monsieur, 86

Scheidemann, Philip, 163
Scheidemantel, 67
Schelling, Ernest, 95, 221
Schiller, Friedrich von, 104, 259
Schönberg, Arnold, 267
Schubert, Franz, 54, 265
Schuch, 67
Schumann, Robert, 49, 54, 55, 57, 61, 74, 214, 265, 267
Schuster, Frank Leo, 40, 51
Seidl, Anton, 22, 73
Sembrich-Kochanska, Marcella, 12, 68, 73, 106
Seyda, Maryan, 280
Seymour, Charles, 283, 284
Shakespeare, William, 258
Shaw, George Bernard, 41, 54, 258
Siemiradzki, Henryk, 252
Sienkiewicz, Henryk, 107
Skirmunt, Konstanty, 107
Skrzynski, Ladislas, 179
Sliwinski, 20
Slowacki, Juliusz, 66, 106
Smogorzewski, Casimir, 280, 281, 282
Sobanski, Count, 107
Sosnkowski, Casimir, Colonel, 132, 282
Sowinski, Piotr, 18
Steed, Wickham, 200
Steinway's, 72, 199, 200
Stojowski, 95, 221
Strakacz, Sylwin, 137, 138, 239, 244, 246
Strauss, Richard, 267
Stravinsky, Ivor, 202, 218
Strobl, Rudolf, 20
Stuart-Wortley, Lady, 50
Swinburne, Charles, 43
Szeptycki, Stanislaus, General, 137, 138
Szopen, Fryderyk, 11
Szpinalski, Stanislaus, 228
Sztompka, 228
Szymanowski, Waclaw, 269

Tadlewski, Albert, 227
Taft, President, 204
Talleyrand, Charles Maurice de, Prince, 109, 279
Temperley, H. W. V., 283
Teodorowicz, Archbishop, 182
Ternina, M., 39
Thalberg, Sigmund, 11, 41
Thomas, Theodore, 73
Tolstoy, Leo, Count, 233, 258
Tommasini, Francesco, 281

Trelat, Madame, 32
Tumulty, Joseph, 285
Turgeniev, Ivan, 233, 258
Twain, Mark, 217

Unamuno, Miguel de, 261
Unschuld, Marie, 275
Urban, Heinrich, 23

Valdemaras, Prof., 188
Van Gogh, Vincent, 29
Venizelos, Eleutherios, 146, 150, 164
Verlaine, Paul, 29
Victoria, Queen of England, 38, 45,
   48–50, 86, 252, 253, 277

Wade, Colonel, 125, 126
Wagner, Richard, 22, 23, 38, 68, 265,
   266
Wales, Prince of, 50

Wales, Princess, of, 39, 49
Weber, 61
Webern, 267
Weingartner, Felix, 106
Wells, H. G., 259
Wilhelm I of Prussia, 15
Wilkonska, Antonina (Paderewska),
   17, 18, 189, 207, 229, 246
Wilson, Woodrow, 113–118, 144, 145,
   147, 148, 151–155, 162–165, 189,
   252, 280, 285
Wiwulski, Antoni, 104
Wojciechowski, Stanislaw, 179
Wooley, Robert, 114
Wyczolkowski, Leon, 262
Wyspianski, Stanislaw, 66

Zarzycki, A., 66
Zelenski, W., 66
Zita, Empress of Austria, 86